הַסִּדּוּר שֶׁל:

כִּתָּה:

The Magerman Edition

The Koren Youth Siddur

Nusaḥ Sepharadim

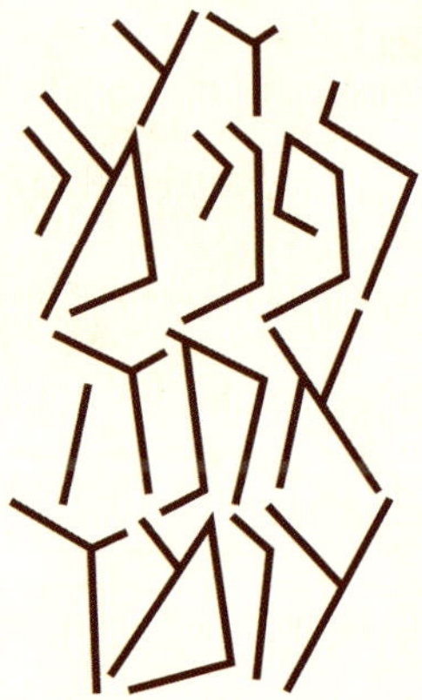

Developed by Rabbi Dr. Daniel Rose
with Dr. Scott Goldberg

Design by Tani Bayer

Illustrations by Rinat Gilboa

Koren Publishers Jerusalem

The Koren Youth Siddur, Nusaḥ Sepharadim
First Edition 2015

Koren Publishers Jerusalem Ltd.
POB 4044, Jerusalem 91040, Israel
POB 8531, New Milford, CT 06776, USA
www.korenpub.com

The creation of this Siddur was made possible through the generous support of Torah Education in Israel.

Standard size, hardcover, ISBN 978 965 301 671 2
CSAEM2
Printed in PRC

וְשִׁנַּנְתָּם לְבָנֶיךָ

Dedicated to my wife,

Debra צביה אהובה

and our children,

Elijah Matthew מנחם מנדל
Zachary Noah יצחק אבנר
Sydney Rachel אלקה שיינה
Lexie Belle רחל לאה

in celebration of our joint and individual journeys toward a better understanding of Torah and our relationship to Hashem.

David Magerman

WEEKDAY SHAḤARIT — **שַׁחֲרִית לְחֹל**

Preparation for Prayer	9	הֲכָנָה לִתְפִלָּה
Morning Blessings	15	בִּרְכוֹת הַשַּׁחַר
Pesukei DeZimra	37	פְּסוּקֵי דְזִמְרָה
The Shema and Its Blessings	65	קְרִיאַת שְׁמַע וּבִרְכוֹתֶיהָ
The Amida	91	עֲמִידָה
Avinu Malkenu	135	אָבִינוּ מַלְכֵּנוּ
Reading of the Torah	137	קְרִיאַת הַתּוֹרָה
Ashrei	138	אַשְׁרֵי
The Daily Psalm	141	שִׁיר שֶׁל יוֹם
Aleinu	143	עָלֵינוּ

SHABBAT — **שַׁבָּת**

Shabbat Evening	148	לֵיל שַׁבָּת
Shabbat Morning	180	יוֹם שַׁבָּת

HOLIDAYS — **חַגִּים**

Hallel	239	הַלֵּל
Musaf for Rosh Ḥodesh	248	מוּסַף לְרֹאשׁ חֹדֶשׁ
Sefirat HaOmer	258	סְפִירַת הָעֹמֶר
Ḥanukka	260	חֲנֻכָּה
Sukkot	263	סֻכּוֹת

GIVING THANKS — **בְּרָכוֹת**

Birkat HaMazon	266	בִּרְכַּת הַמָּזוֹן
Shema before Sleep at Night	274	קְרִיאַת שְׁמַע עַל הַמִּטָּה

Dear Parents and Teachers,

It is with great excitement that we present to you the Koren Youth Siddur, what we believe is a new approach to Tefilla education in the school and home. This Siddur, the second in a series of appropriately designed Siddurim for each developmental stage of the day-school journey, provides the teacher and parent with an educational resource as much as a conventional Siddur. Each page is replete with teaching opportunities to bring the tefillot contained in the Siddur alive cognitively and emotionally for our children, advancing the overall goal of developing a spiritual connection to prayer and to God.

It is always a privilege to collaborate on a project with those who share our commitment and enthusiasm for bringing out the beauty of Tefilla. We are grateful to Debra and David Magerman for their support and are proud to have their name grace this edition. On behalf of the scholars, editors and designers of this volume, we thank you; on behalf of the users of this Siddur, we are forever in your debt.

We are fortunate to benefit from a world-class Educational Editorial Board assisting us in the creation of this program. We would like to thank the Board's Chairman, Dr. Scott Goldberg of Yeshiva University; Rabbi Adam Englander of the Hillel Day School of Boca Raton; Rabbi Dr. Jay Goldmintz of the Azrieli Graduate School; Rabbi Benji Levy of Moriah College of Australia; and Rabbi Boruch Sufrin of the Harkham Hillel Hebrew Academy of Beverly Hills. Their broad knowledge and experience provided the framework to structure the program.

The small but highly professional team at Koren was led by Rabbi Dr. Daniel Rose, Director of Educational Projects. Rabbi Dr. Rose also prepared the Educator's Companion that accompanies the Siddur. For the beauty of this Siddur we owe thanks to Koren's Art Director, Tani Bayer, and to the very talented illustrator, Rinat Gilboa.

It is our sincere hope and prayer that this Siddur will provide a platform for the educational and spiritual growth of the next generation of committed Jewish children.

Matthew Miller, Publisher
Jerusalem, 5775 (2015)

שַׁחֲרִית לְחֹל
Weekday Shaḥarit

הֲכָנָה לַתְּפִלָּה	Preparation for Prayer
בִּרְכוֹת הַשַּׁחַר	Morning Blessings
פְּסוּקֵי דְזִמְרָה	Pesukei DeZimra
קְרִיאַת שְׁמַע	The Shema
עֲמִידָה	The Amida
קְרִיאַת הַתּוֹרָה	Reading of the Torah
אַשְׁרֵי	Ashrei
שִׁיר שֶׁל יוֹם	The Daily Psalm
עָלֵינוּ	Aleinu

I thank You, Hashem, You are our King forever,
You give me back my neshama with kindness.

Why is saying "thank you" important?

"Rabbi Akiva was forty years old and had never studied Torah before. He was once standing by a well and wondered to himself, 'Who made this hole in this rock?' The people there said to him, 'It was the water which drips on it every day.' Rabbi Akiva suddenly realized that if something as soft as water can cut through something as hard as the rock, then surely the words of Torah, which are as hard as iron, can enter his heart, which is just flesh and blood! From then on he decided to dedicate his life to studying Torah."

While you wash your hands, as you feel the water wash over your hands, think about the power of water.

What kind of things do you think can "enter your heart"? What will you allow to enter your heart today?

When we wake up, we thank Hashem with our first thoughts and words.

Boys say: / *Girls say:*

מוֹדֶה | מוֹדָה

אֲנִי לְפָנֶיךָ מֶלֶךְ חַי וְקַיָּם
שֶׁהֶחֱזַרְתָּ בִּי נִשְׁמָתִי בְּחֶמְלָה
רַבָּה אֱמוּנָתֶךָ.

When we wake up, we wash our hands in a special way. With a cup, pour water over your whole right hand, and then over your whole left hand. Do that again two more times, and then say this בְּרָכָה.

בָּרוּךְ אַתָּה יְהֹוָה, אֱלֹהֵינוּ מֶלֶךְ הָעוֹלָם
אֲשֶׁר קִדְּשָׁנוּ בְּמִצְוֹתָיו וְצִוָּנוּ עַל נְטִילַת יָדָיִם.

Hashem made the human body with many wonderful and important parts. If even one of them was slightly different and didn't work properly, then without extra help it would be impossible to live in this world.

Just a few hours after Aharon married Tzvia, Israel went to war in Gaza; Aharon, a commander in the paratroopers, was called to join his unit. He didn't have to go, he could have used the wedding as an excuse, but he wanted to join his men and fight to defend his country. Ten days later Aharon entered a booby-trapped house which detonated and he was crushed under the building. The first medic to reach him thought he had died. But as his body was evacuated a faint pulse was detected, and he was airlifted to safety in a helicopter. The medic aboard saw he was struggling to breathe and made a brave decision that would save his life. He inserted a tube into his throat so he could breathe, the first time such a procedure had been carried out in-flight. But still with serious head injuries it seemed unlikely that he would survive. Miraculously, within a week Aharon was sitting up, awake and alert, and after several surgeries and much treatment he was able to resume a normal life. Four years later Aharon ran the NYC marathon and raised money for a charity that supports victims of terror. Aharon's surgeon said that it was an honor to help such a hero of Israel!

This בְּרָכָה is said every morning and also each time you leave the restroom, to thank Hashem for our healthy working bodies.

1 בָּרוּךְ אַתָּה יְהֹוָה, אֱלֹהֵינוּ מֶלֶךְ הָעוֹלָם

2 אֲשֶׁר יָצַר אֶת הָאָדָם בְּחָכְמָה

3 וּבָרָא בוֹ נְקָבִים נְקָבִים, חֲלוּלִים חֲלוּלִים.

4 גָּלוּי וְיָדוּעַ לִפְנֵי כִסֵּא כְבוֹדֶךָ

5 שֶׁאִם יִסָּתֵם אֶחָד מֵהֶם אוֹ יִפָּתֵחַ אֶחָד מֵהֶם

6 אִי אֶפְשָׁר לְהִתְקַיֵּם אֲפִלּוּ שָׁעָה אֶחָת.

7 בָּרוּךְ אַתָּה יְהֹוָה

8 רוֹפֵא כָל בָּשָׂר וּמַפְלִיא לַעֲשׂוֹת.

"חָכְמָה is the truth we discover.
תּוֹרָה is the truth we inherit."

In which of your classes at school will you discover truth and in which will you inherit it?

Where do you see Hashem the most in school?

Hashem, You created my soul and breathed it into me. And You look after it while it is in me.

"Whoever destroys a single soul, it is as if he destroyed an entire world. And whoever saves a single soul, it is as if he has saved an entire world." (Mishna Sanhedrin, 4:5)

Why do you think the Mishna uses the word "soul" to describe a life?
Why do you think a single soul is equal to an entire world?

"Man creates a hundred coins from one press and each coin is exactly the same. But Hashem, the King of kings, creates all mankind from one man (Adam), and each person is totally unique!" (Mishna Sanhedrin, 4:5)

Look around at all your friends right now.
What is unique about you?

אֱלֹהַי

נְשָׁמָה שֶׁנָּתַתָּ בִּי טְהוֹרָה.
אַתָּה בְרָאתָהּ, אַתָּה יְצַרְתָּהּ, אַתָּה נְפַחְתָּהּ בִּי
וְאַתָּה מְשַׁמְּרָהּ בְּקִרְבִּי, וְאַתָּה עָתִיד לִטְּלָהּ מִמֶּנִּי
וּלְהַחֲזִירָהּ בִּי לֶעָתִיד לָבוֹא.
כָּל זְמַן שֶׁהַנְּשָׁמָה בְקִרְבִּי

מוֹדֶה | מוֹדָה

אֲנִי לְפָנֶיךָ
יְהֹוָה אֱלֹהַי וֵאלֹהֵי אֲבוֹתַי
רִבּוֹן כָּל הַמַּעֲשִׂים
אֲדוֹן כָּל הַנְּשָׁמוֹת.
בָּרוּךְ אַתָּה יְהֹוָה
הַמַּחֲזִיר נְשָׁמוֹת לִפְגָרִים מֵתִים.

"The eyes are the window to your soul."

What can you use your eyes for?

What do you plan to use your sight for today?

The people of Chelm were not a bright bunch. Once, when a rabbi and his student from Chelm were staying at an inn, the student asked the innkeeper to wake him up early to catch a train. When he awoke he didn't want to disturb the rabbi, so he dressed himself in the dark. But by mistake he put on the rabbi's long black coat instead of his own clothes. When he arrived at the train station he caught a glimpse of his reflection in a window. When he saw the rabbi's long black coat he shouted aloud "Oh no... The inn keeper woke the Rabbi up instead of me!"

The following בְּרָכוֹת help you to think about and thank Hashem for all the things we are and have. They were originally said at home after each stage of waking up and getting ready for the day, as we realize how much we have to be thankful to Hashem for. Now we say them as part of our תְּפִלָּה.

בָּרוּךְ אַתָּה יְהוָה, אֱלֹהֵינוּ מֶלֶךְ הָעוֹלָם
אֲשֶׁר נָתַן לַשֶּׂכְוִי בִינָה
לְהַבְחִין בֵּין יוֹם וּבֵין לָיְלָה.

בָּרוּךְ אַתָּה יְהוָה, אֱלֹהֵינוּ מֶלֶךְ הָעוֹלָם
פּוֹקֵחַ עִוְרִים.

בָּרוּךְ אַתָּה יְהוָה, אֱלֹהֵינוּ מֶלֶךְ הָעוֹלָם
מַתִּיר אֲסוּרִים.

בָּרוּךְ אַתָּה יְהוָה, אֱלֹהֵינוּ מֶלֶךְ הָעוֹלָם
זוֹקֵף כְּפוּפִים.

בָּרוּךְ אַתָּה יְהוָה, אֱלֹהֵינוּ מֶלֶךְ הָעוֹלָם
מַלְבִּישׁ עֲרֻמִּים.

The Beren Academy Stars were having their most successful basketball season ever. In fact, they were the first Jewish day school to ever reach the Texas state semi-final. But they couldn't play in it. The game was scheduled for the evening of Shabbat, and the state tournament refused to move it. It wasn't even a question for the team. The decision was made. To give up their dream and to stand up for what they believed in. But as their story spread reaching the national and international news across the globe, the tournament relented and allowed the game to be moved. The Stars' prayers were answered, and they got their chance to achieve their dreams. And they took it, convincingly beating their semi-final opponents 58–46 and making history, reaching the championship game. Unfortunately they narrowly lost in the final (46–42), but won hearts and inspired people across the world with their commitment to their values and to Shabbat.

בָּרוּךְ אַתָּה יְהוָה, אֱלֹהֵינוּ מֶלֶךְ הָעוֹלָם
הַנּוֹתֵן לַיָּעֵף כֹּחַ.

בָּרוּךְ אַתָּה יְהוָה, אֱלֹהֵינוּ מֶלֶךְ הָעוֹלָם
רוֹקַע הָאָרֶץ עַל הַמָּיִם.

בָּרוּךְ אַתָּה יְהוָה, אֱלֹהֵינוּ מֶלֶךְ הָעוֹלָם
הַמֵּכִין מִצְעֲדֵי גָבֶר.

בָּרוּךְ אַתָּה יְהוָה, אֱלֹהֵינוּ מֶלֶךְ הָעוֹלָם
שֶׁעָשָׂה לִי כָּל צְרָכָי.

בָּרוּךְ אַתָּה יְהוָה, אֱלֹהֵינוּ מֶלֶךְ הָעוֹלָם
אוֹזֵר יִשְׂרָאֵל בִּגְבוּרָה.

בָּרוּךְ אַתָּה יְהוָה, אֱלֹהֵינוּ מֶלֶךְ הָעוֹלָם
עוֹטֵר יִשְׂרָאֵל בְּתִפְאָרָה.

**When you look in the mirror what do you see?
Who are you? Who would you like to be?**

The great Hasidic leader Reb Zusia once began crying in front of his followers, pale faced and with red eyes. "What's the matter Rebbe?" his Hasidim inquired. "I had a dream," he explained, "and the question the angels will ask me when I pass on to the World to Come was revealed to me," he said, trembling. His followers were puzzled. "But Rebbe, you are pious and holy and scholarly and humble. What question could they possibly ask of you that you should fear so much?" Zusia turned to heaven and replied with his eyes closed tightly, "I have learned that the angels will not ask me why I wasn't more like Avraham our father or Moses our teacher. But they will ask me why I wasn't more like Zusia!"

1 בָּרוּךְ אַתָּה יְהֹוָה, אֱלֹהֵינוּ מֶלֶךְ הָעוֹלָם

2 שֶׁלֹּא עָשַׂנִי גּוֹי | שֶׁלֹּא עָשַׂנִי גּוֹיָה

3 בָּרוּךְ אַתָּה יְהֹוָה, אֱלֹהֵינוּ מֶלֶךְ הָעוֹלָם

4 שֶׁלֹּא עָשַׂנִי עָבֶד | שֶׁלֹּא עָשַׂנִי שִׁפְחָה.

5 בָּרוּךְ אַתָּה יְהֹוָה | בָּרוּךְ שֶׁעָשַׂנִי כִּרְצוֹנוֹ.

6 אֱלֹהֵינוּ מֶלֶךְ הָעוֹלָם

7 שֶׁלֹּא עָשַׂנִי אִשָּׁה

"Who is a strong person? Someone who controls their bad wishes." (Pirkei Avot 4:1)

What does it mean to be strong and where does strength come from?

Who do you know that is really strong?

How will you be strong today?

Please, Hashem, keep us away from bad influences and bring us close to good influences, so we can do good things and do everything You ask of us. Give us kindness, love and care, today, and every day.

Close your eyes. Relax your body. Think about what has happened to you today so far. Or yesterday, or the day before. Can you think of something you have done recently that you are very proud of? Watch yourself achieve this. How did you feel at the time? How do you feel about it now? Now think of something you did recently that you are not proud of. Something you wish you had done differently. Something you wouldn't do again. In both cases, try to think what you were thinking at the time, and what led you to behave the way that you did. Did you take a moment to think through your actions? Did you have thoughts that told you to act differently at that time? Did you have to make a decision between two things? Did you make the right choice? Would you choose differently now? How can you make sure to make the right decision each time?

1 בָּרוּךְ אַתָּה יְהֹוָה, אֱלֹהֵינוּ מֶלֶךְ הָעוֹלָם

2 הַמַּעֲבִיר חֶבְלֵי שֵׁנָה מֵעֵינַי וּתְנוּמָה מֵעַפְעַפָּי.

3 וִיהִי רָצוֹן מִלְּפָנֶיךָ

4 יְהֹוָה אֱלֹהַי וֵאלֹהֵי אֲבוֹתַי

5 שֶׁתַּרְגִּילֵנִי בְּתוֹרָתֶךָ

6 וְתַדְבִּיקֵנִי בְּמִצְוֹתֶיךָ

7 וְאַל תְּבִיאֵנִי לִידֵי חֵטְא

8 וְלֹא לִידֵי עֲבֵרָה

9 וְלֹא לִידֵי נִסָּיוֹן וְלֹא לִידֵי בִזָּיוֹן

10 וְתַרְחִיקֵנִי מִיֵּצֶר הָרָע וְתַדְבִּיקֵנִי בְּיֵצֶר הַטּוֹב

11 וְכֹף אֶת יִצְרִי לְהִשְׁתַּעְבֶּד לָךְ

12 וּתְנֵנִי הַיּוֹם וּבְכָל יוֹם

13 לְחֵן וּלְחֶסֶד וּלְרַחֲמִים בְּעֵינֶיךָ וּבְעֵינֵי כָל רוֹאַי

14 וְגָמְלֵנִי חֲסָדִים טוֹבִים.

15 בָּרוּךְ אַתָּה יְהֹוָה

16 גּוֹמֵל חֲסָדִים טוֹבִים לְעַמּוֹ יִשְׂרָאֵל.

Please, Hashem, make it enjoyable for us to learn Your Torah. And help us and our future generations to learn more about You and Your Torah.

"When the Romans had forbidden Jews from learning Torah in Eretz Yisrael, Rabbi Akiva continued to teach Torah to his students. 'Aren't you scared that the Romans will catch you?' he was once asked. He replied with this story: 'Once a fox was walking along a riverbank when he noticed fish darting from place to place in the river. He asked them, "What are you swimming away from?" They replied, "We are fleeing from the nets that humans use to try and catch us." The wily fox asked, "Why don't you come and live with me on dry land?" The fish replied to him, "Oh, Fox, they say the fox is one of the cleverest animals, but you are not clever at all. If we are afraid when we are in the water, a place that gives us life, then how will it be for us if we live on dry land, a place of death for us?"' Rabbi Akiva said, 'So too with us. If we are scared while we learn Torah, our life-source, then imagine how our lives would be if we stop learning Torah?'"

How is Torah like oxygen for us?

The following בְּרָכוֹת are said for the mitzva of learning Torah. Even though we will do this mitzva throughout the day, we only say them once in the morning. We then immediately do the mitzva by saying some words of Torah following the בְּרָכוֹת.

1 בָּרוּךְ אַתָּה יְהֹוָה, אֱלֹהֵינוּ מֶלֶךְ הָעוֹלָם
2 אֲשֶׁר קִדְּשָׁנוּ בְּמִצְוֹתָיו
3 וְצִוָּנוּ עַל דִּבְרֵי תוֹרָה.

4 וְהַעֲרֶב נָא יְהֹוָה אֱלֹהֵינוּ אֶת דִּבְרֵי תוֹרָתְךָ
5 בְּפִינוּ וּבְפִיפִיּוֹת עַמְּךָ בֵּית יִשְׂרָאֵל
6 וְנִהְיֶה אֲנַחְנוּ וְצֶאֱצָאֵינוּ
7 וְצֶאֱצָאֵי צֶאֱצָאֵינוּ
8 וְצֶאֱצָאֵי עַמְּךָ בֵּית יִשְׂרָאֵל
9 כֻּלָּנוּ יוֹדְעֵי שְׁמֶךָ וְלוֹמְדֵי תוֹרָתְךָ לִשְׁמָהּ.
10 בָּרוּךְ אַתָּה יְהֹוָה
11 הַמְלַמֵּד תּוֹרָה לְעַמּוֹ יִשְׂרָאֵל.

אֲנִי יְהֹוָה קְרָאתִיךָ בְצֶדֶק וְאַחְזֵק בְּיָדֶךָ וְאֶצׇּרְךָ וְאֶתֶּנְךָ לִבְרִית עָם לְאוֹר גּוֹיִם.

(Yeshayahu 42:6)

The Jewish People are a "Chosen People."

Who chose us and for what purpose? How does that affect you?

The saintly Rebbe of Sanz was famous for his warmth and love. He survived the Shoah but lost his wife and eleven children. On Erev Yom Kippur in 1947 he was still living in a refugee camp in Germany. As the holy day approached the rebbe heard a gentle knock on his door. As he opened the door he saw a young girl with tears in her eyes. She explained that every year on Erev Yom Kippur her father would bless her with the Priestly Blessing, but this year there was no one to bless her. "My child, I will be your father this year," he said to her as he placed his hands on her head and recited the ancient blessing with concentration and emotion. The girl left smiling and comforted. A short while later a group of young girls came to his door, asking for the same from him, and he blessed them with tears in his eyes. As the news spread, the rebbe spent the rest of Erev Yom Kippur blessing all 87 orphaned girls of the refugee camp. Each one was touched by his love and warmth forever.

1 בָּרוּךְ אַתָּה יְהֹוָה, אֱלֹהֵינוּ מֶלֶךְ הָעוֹלָם

2 אֲשֶׁר בָּחַר בָּנוּ מִכָּל הָעַמִּים

3 וְנָתַן לָנוּ אֶת תּוֹרָתוֹ.

4 בָּרוּךְ אַתָּה יְהֹוָה, נוֹתֵן הַתּוֹרָה.

5 וַיְדַבֵּר יְהֹוָה אֶל־מֹשֶׁה לֵּאמֹר:

6 דַּבֵּר אֶל־אַהֲרֹן וְאֶל־בָּנָיו לֵאמֹר

7 כֹּה תְבָרֲכוּ אֶת־בְּנֵי יִשְׂרָאֵל, אָמוֹר לָהֶם:

8 יְבָרֶכְךָ יְהֹוָה וְיִשְׁמְרֶךָ:

9 יָאֵר יְהֹוָה פָּנָיו אֵלֶיךָ וִיחֻנֶּךָּ:

10 יִשָּׂא יְהֹוָה פָּנָיו אֵלֶיךָ וְיָשֵׂם לְךָ שָׁלוֹם:

11 וְשָׂמוּ אֶת־שְׁמִי עַל־בְּנֵי יִשְׂרָאֵל, וַאֲנִי אֲבָרֲכֵם:

"A person who didn't believe in God once came to Rabbi Akiva and asked him to prove that Hashem created the world. Rabbi Akiva replied to him by asking his own question: 'Who created the clothes you are wearing?' The man answered, 'A weaver.' Rabbi Akiva said to him, 'I don't believe you. Prove it!' The man said, 'I can't. But everyone knows a weaver weaved them.' Rabbi Akiva said, 'Exactly! Everyone knows that Hashem created the world.' When Rabbi Akiva's students asked him how that was proof, he told them, 'Just as a house tells us that it was built by a builder, and clothes that they were weaved by a weaver, so the world tells us that Hashem created it!'"

Look around at your world.

Where is it obvious to you that Hashem created the world?

The following two תְּפִלּוֹת *are poems that contain the most important Jewish beliefs for you to think about before you start talking to Hashem.*

אֲדוֹן עוֹלָם

אֲשֶׁר מָלַךְ בְּטֶרֶם כָּל־יְצִיר נִבְרָא.
לְעֵת נַעֲשָׂה בְחֶפְצוֹ כֹּל אֲזַי מֶלֶךְ שְׁמוֹ נִקְרָא.
וְאַחֲרֵי כִּכְלוֹת הַכֹּל לְבַדּוֹ יִמְלֹךְ נוֹרָא.
וְהוּא הָיָה וְהוּא הֹוֶה וְהוּא יִהְיֶה בְּתִפְאָרָה.
וְהוּא אֶחָד וְאֵין שֵׁנִי לְהַמְשִׁיל לוֹ לְהַחְבִּירָה.
בְּלִי רֵאשִׁית בְּלִי תַכְלִית וְלוֹ הָעֹז וְהַמִּשְׂרָה.
בְּלִי עֵרֶךְ, בְּלִי דִמְיוֹן, בְּלִי שִׁנּוּי וּתְמוּרָה.
בְּלִי חִבּוּר, בְּלִי פֵרוּד, גְּדָל כֹּחַ וּגְבוּרָה.
וְהוּא אֵלִי וְחַי גּוֹאֲלִי וְצוּר חֶבְלִי בְּעֵת צָרָה.
וְהוּא נִסִּי וּמָנוּסִי, מְנָת כּוֹסִי בְּיוֹם אֶקְרָא.
בְּיָדוֹ אַפְקִיד רוּחִי בְּעֵת אִישַׁן וְאָעִירָה.
וְעִם רוּחִי גְּוִיָּתִי, יְהֹוָה לִי וְלֹא אִירָא.

Rambam was a famous Jewish thinker and doctor, and was the personal physician to the Sultan of Egypt. This caused much jealousy among the local doctors who believed that a Jew should not have this prestigious honor. They would often devise plans to discredit Rambam in the hope that the sultan would replace him with one of them instead. Once, they informed the sultan that Rambam's words contradicted Islam. Rambam believed that an animal can never change its nature. They disproved this in front of the sultan by training a cat to serve him like a waiter. But Rambam had a plan! He opened a small box that contained a mouse and let the mouse free. The cat instantly dropped the drinks it was carrying and chased the mouse. Rambam said to the sultan, "You see! Every one of God's creatures has its own nature. Only man can change his nature and become better."

"Moshe received the Torah at Sinai and gave it to Yehoshua. Yehoshua gave it to the elders, and the elders gave it to the prophets, and the prophets gave it to the men of the Great Assembly." (Pirkei Avot 1:1)

Who gives you the Torah?
Who will you give it to?

יִגְדַּל

אֱלֹהִים חַי וְיִשְׁתַּבַּח, נִמְצָא וְאֵין עֵת אֶל מְצִיאוּתוֹ.
אֶחָד וְאֵין יָחִיד כְּיִחוּדוֹ, נֶעְלָם וְגַם אֵין סוֹף לְאַחְדוּתוֹ.
אֵין לוֹ דְּמוּת הַגּוּף וְאֵינוֹ גוּף, לֹא נַעֲרֹךְ אֵלָיו קְדֻשָּׁתוֹ.
קַדְמוֹן לְכָל דָּבָר אֲשֶׁר נִבְרָא, רִאשׁוֹן וְאֵין רֵאשִׁית לְרֵאשִׁיתוֹ.
הִנּוֹ אֲדוֹן עוֹלָם, וְכָל נוֹצָר יוֹרֶה גְדֻלָּתוֹ וּמַלְכוּתוֹ.
שֶׁפַע נְבוּאָתוֹ נְתָנוֹ אֶל־אַנְשֵׁי סְגֻלָּתוֹ וְתִפְאַרְתּוֹ.
לֹא קָם בְּיִשְׂרָאֵל כְּמֹשֶׁה עוֹד נָבִיא וּמַבִּיט אֶת תְּמוּנָתוֹ.
תּוֹרַת אֱמֶת נָתַן לְעַמּוֹ אֵל עַל יַד נְבִיאוֹ נֶאֱמַן בֵּיתוֹ.
לֹא יַחֲלִיף הָאֵל וְלֹא יָמִיר דָּתוֹ לְעוֹלָמִים לְזוּלָתוֹ.
צוֹפֶה וְיוֹדֵעַ סְתָרֵינוּ, מַבִּיט לְסוֹף דָּבָר בְּקַדְמָתוֹ.
גּוֹמֵל לְאִישׁ חֶסֶד כְּמִפְעָלוֹ, נוֹתֵן לְרָשָׁע רָע כְּרִשְׁעָתוֹ.
יִשְׁלַח לְקֵץ יָמִין מְשִׁיחֵנוּ לִפְדּוֹת מְחַכֵּי קֵץ יְשׁוּעָתוֹ.
מֵתִים יְחַיֶּה אֵל בְּרֹב חַסְדּוֹ, בָּרוּךְ עֲדֵי עַד שֵׁם תְּהִלָּתוֹ.
אֵלֶּה שְׁלֹשׁ עֶשְׂרֵה לְעִקָּרִים, הֵן הֵם יְסוֹד דַּת אֵל וְתוֹרָתוֹ.
תּוֹרַת מֹשֶׁה אֱמֶת וּנְבוּאָתוֹ, בָּרוּךְ עֲדֵי עַד שֵׁם תְּהִלָּתוֹ.

Rabbi Ḥaim ibn Attar was a goldsmith and a famous Torah scholar. He would only work enough to live so he could learn Torah undisturbed. The goldsmith for who Rabbi Ḥaim worked offered him more work for more money, but he wasn't tempted. One day, the Sultan made a large order with the goldsmith for his daughter's wedding, but he couldn't make all the jewelry in time, and blamed this on Rabbi Ḥaim. The furious Sultan ordered that Rabbi Ḥaim be thrown to the lions and eaten alive. When the guards came to take him away he pleaded with them to allow him to take his tallit and tefillin. They laughed at him, replying "you won't need them where you are going" but nevertheless allowed him. After the guards had thrown him in to the lion's den, they thought it strange there was no roaring and screaming. When they returned later that day they were surprised to see him wrapped in his tallit and tefillin sitting next to the lions who were peacefully listening to the melodious voice of his tefilla. When the Sultan heard the story, he asked Rabbi Ḥaim to become his advisor and friend.

Some people wear a טַלִּית for תְּפִלָּה and some only wear a טַלִּית קָטָן. If you are only going to wear a טַלִּית קָטָן today say the first בְּרָכָה below. If you are going to wear a טַלִּית, then only say the second בְּרָכָה below before putting it on.

This בְּרָכָה is said before putting on the טַלִּית קָטָן. Some people hold the front two צִיצִיּוֹת while they say the בְּרָכָה and then kiss them.

1 בָּרוּךְ אַתָּה יהוה אֱלֹהֵינוּ מֶלֶךְ הָעוֹלָם

2 אֲשֶׁר קִדְּשָׁנוּ בְּמִצְוֹתָיו וְצִוָּנוּ עַל מִצְוַת צִיצִית.

This בְּרָכָה is said before putting on a טַלִּית.

3 בָּרוּךְ אַתָּה יְהוָה, אֱלֹהֵינוּ מֶלֶךְ הָעוֹלָם

4 אֲשֶׁר קִדְּשָׁנוּ בְּמִצְוֹתָיו וְצִוָּנוּ לְהִתְעַטֵּף בְּצִיצִית.

לְמַעַן תִּזְכְּרוּ, וַעֲשִׂיתֶם אֶת-כָּל-מִצְוֹתָי (Bamidbar 15:40)

"A man slipped and fell overboard from the boat he was sailing in. The captain of the boat threw him a rope and called, 'As long as you hold on to this rope you will be fine. Don't forget to keep holding on tight. If you let go you won't survive!'"

How can *tzitzit* be a lifeline for you?

When the great Hasidic rebbe Menaḥem Mendel of Kotzk was a small boy of just five years old, he asked his father, "Where is God?" His father replied, "God is everywhere, my son." Young Menaḥem Mendel said to him, "I think God is only where you let Him in!"

How can you let Hashem in today?

Why do you think a synagogue is called a בֵּית כְּנֶסֶת and not a בֵּית תְּפִלָּה?

Many people say this תְּפִלָּה when they first enter the בֵּית כְּנֶסֶת in the morning.

1 וַאֲנִי בְּרֹב חַסְדְּךָ אָבוֹא בֵיתֶךָ
2 אֶשְׁתַּחֲוֶה אֶל־הֵיכַל־קָדְשְׁךָ בְּיִרְאָתֶךָ:

1 מַה־טֹּבוּ

2 אֹהָלֶיךָ יַעֲקֹב, מִשְׁכְּנֹתֶיךָ יִשְׂרָאֵל:
3 בְּבֵית אֱלֹהִים נְהַלֵּךְ בְּרָגֶשׁ:

4 יְהֹוָה צְבָאוֹת עִמָּנוּ
5 מִשְׂגָּב לָנוּ אֱלֹהֵי יַעֲקֹב סֶלָה:
6 יְהֹוָה צְבָאוֹת, אַשְׁרֵי אָדָם בֹּטֵחַ בָּךְ:
7 יְהֹוָה הוֹשִׁיעָה, הַמֶּלֶךְ יַעֲנֵנוּ בְיוֹם־קָרְאֵנוּ:

Ariella was five when her one-year-old cousin was diagnosed with cancer. He was a brave little boy, and fought the disease, and beat it, and was an inspiration to all the family. When Ariella was a little older she decided she wanted to help other children who had cancer like her cousin. She raised money for the hospital that had treated her cousin by running in a race that was a mile long. But she wanted to do even more for children with cancer. So she grew her beautiful hair long enough so that she could donate it to a charity that made wigs for children who had lost their hair because of the cancer treatment. She loved her long blond hair, but didn't think twice about donating it to this very important cause. When Ariella turned ten she also became ill with cancer, and became a patient in the very same hospital as her cousin. She also beat the disease and became an inspiration to everyone that met her. This only made her want to give more and more to the children she saw fighting alongside her, and she continues to do so to this day.

Since the בֵּית הַמִּקְדָּשׁ was destroyed it has not been possible to offer sacrifices to Hashem. The rabbis decided that instead we should learn the laws of the sacrifices every day as the next best thing. The following passage contains the laws of the Daily Sacrifice, the קָרְבַּן תָּמִיד, as found in the Torah (Bemidbar 28).

וַיְדַבֵּר יְהֹוָה אֶל־מֹשֶׁה לֵּאמֹר: צַו אֶת־בְּנֵי יִשְׂרָאֵל וְאָמַרְתָּ אֲלֵהֶם אֶת־קָרְבָּנִי לַחְמִי לְאִשַּׁי רֵיחַ נִיחֹחִי תִּשְׁמְרוּ לְהַקְרִיב לִי בְּמוֹעֲדוֹ: וְאָמַרְתָּ לָהֶם זֶה הָאִשֶּׁה אֲשֶׁר תַּקְרִיבוּ לַיהֹוָה כְּבָשִׂים בְּנֵי־שָׁנָה תְמִימִם שְׁנַיִם לַיּוֹם עֹלָה תָמִיד: אֶת־הַכֶּבֶשׂ אֶחָד תַּעֲשֶׂה בַבֹּקֶר וְאֵת הַכֶּבֶשׂ הַשֵּׁנִי תַּעֲשֶׂה בֵּין הָעַרְבָּיִם: וַעֲשִׂירִית הָאֵיפָה סֹלֶת לְמִנְחָה בְּלוּלָה בְּשֶׁמֶן כָּתִית רְבִיעִת הַהִין: עֹלַת תָּמִיד הָעֲשֻׂיָה בְּהַר סִינַי לְרֵיחַ נִיחֹחַ אִשֶּׁה לַיהֹוָה: וְנִסְכּוֹ רְבִיעִת הַהִין לַכֶּבֶשׂ הָאֶחָד בַּקֹּדֶשׁ הַסֵּךְ נֶסֶךְ שֵׁכָר לַיהֹוָה: וְאֵת הַכֶּבֶשׂ הַשֵּׁנִי תַּעֲשֶׂה בֵּין הָעַרְבָּיִם כְּמִנְחַת הַבֹּקֶר וּכְנִסְכּוֹ תַּעֲשֶׂה אִשֵּׁה רֵיחַ נִיחֹחַ לַיהֹוָה:

I recognize that God created the world, and I recognize that God is still involved in the world and in our lives today. He is involved with the world and with all His creations for their benefit.

There once was an old man who loved to gossip. He would often be found shuffling around town whispering gossip to his friends. One day, he just couldn't resist telling the rabbi the latest news he had just heard. The rabbi ran into his house and brought out a feather pillow. He told the old man to rip open the pillow. Puzzled, he did as the rabbi asked. As the wind picked up the feathers and blew them all over the village, a smile crossed the man's face as he began to enjoy the spectacle. "Right. Now go and collect all the feathers from my pillow!" said the rabbi. "But Rabbi, that is impossible! I can't get them all back. They are spread all across the village and beyond!" the man exclaimed. The rabbi looked him in the eye and with a satisfied look said, "That is exactly the same with your words of gossip. Once it has crossed your lips it cannot be controlled or taken back. It is gone forever and spread across the world. Think carefully about that the next time you are tempted to gossip about a neighbor!"

The next section of שַׁחֲרִית is called פְּסוּקֵי דְזִמְרָה and consists mainly of verses from Tanakh describing the beauty of the universe that Hashem has created. This section of our תְּפִלָּה is designed to inspire you to be ready to stand before Hashem and pray the עֲמִידָה. You should not speak to others from this point until the end of the עֲמִידָה. Stand for בָּרוּךְ שֶׁאָמַר and if you are wearing צִיצִיּוֹת hold the front two and kiss them at the end.

בָּרוּךְ 1

שֶׁאָמַר 2

וְהָיָה הָעוֹלָם, בָּרוּךְ הוּא. 3

בָּרוּךְ אוֹמֵר וְעוֹשֶׂה 4

בָּרוּךְ גּוֹזֵר וּמְקַיֵּם 5

בָּרוּךְ עוֹשֶׂה בְרֵאשִׁית 6

בָּרוּךְ מְרַחֵם עַל הָאָרֶץ 7

בָּרוּךְ מְרַחֵם עַל הַבְּרִיּוֹת 8

בָּרוּךְ מְשַׁלֵּם שָׂכָר טוֹב לִירֵאָיו 9

בָּרוּךְ חַי לָעַד וְקַיָּם לָנֶצַח 10

בָּרוּךְ פּוֹדֶה וּמַצִּיל 11

בָּרוּךְ שְׁמוֹ 12

Hashem, You are our God and our Father, You are kind, and we Your people compliment You, and sing praises to You with the songs of King David.

A well-known Jerusalem educator was once in a bakery waiting in line, when she noticed she was standing behind Natan Sharansky, the famous Jewish leader and author who spent many years in prison in Soviet Russia because he wanted to make aliya to Israel. She couldn't resist turning to him and telling him that she had quoted him only the day before in a class she was teaching. He asked her why, and she replied that she told her students the inspiring story of how he had kept a tiny book of Tehillim with him at all times, even at risk to his safety, because it inspired him and protected him. Sharansky reached into his shirt pocket and pulled out that very book of Tehillim. "You mean this?" he said with a smile. She was amazed, and asked him, "Do you carry that wherever you go?" Sharansky smiled with an even bigger grin and replied, "No. It carries me!"

בָּרוּךְ אַתָּה יְהֹוָה, אֱלֹהֵינוּ מֶלֶךְ הָעוֹלָם
הָאֵל הָאָב הָרַחֲמָן הַמְהֻלָּל בְּפֶה עַמּוֹ
מְשֻׁבָּח וּמְפֹאָר בִּלְשׁוֹן חֲסִידָיו וַעֲבָדָיו
וּבְשִׁירֵי דָוִד עַבְדֶּךָ, נְהַלֶּלְךָ יְהֹוָה אֱלֹהֵינוּ.
בִּשְׁבָחוֹת וּבִזְמִירוֹת
וּנְגַדֶּלְךָ וּנְשַׁבֵּחֲךָ וּנְפָאֶרְךָ וְנַמְלִיכְךָ
וְנַזְכִּיר שִׁמְךָ מַלְכֵּנוּ אֱלֹהֵינוּ, יָחִיד חֵי הָעוֹלָמִים
מֶלֶךְ מְשֻׁבָּח וּמְפֹאָר עֲדֵי עַד שְׁמוֹ הַגָּדוֹל.
בָּרוּךְ אַתָּה יְהֹוָה
מֶלֶךְ מְהֻלָּל בַּתִּשְׁבָּחוֹת.

Why do you think music is an important part of our *tefilla*?

Those people who are connected to You, Hashem, and pray to You, are happy that they know You are their God!

"מִצְוָה גְּדוֹלָה לִהְיוֹת בְּשִׂמְחָה"

What makes you happy? How can having Hashem in your life make you happy?

"It once happened that Ḥoni the Circle Drawer was walking along the way and he saw an old man planting a young fruit tree. Ḥoni asked the man how long it would take until the tree would produce fruit. 'Seventy years,' the old man answered him. 'Do you really think you will be alive for another seventy years so you can enjoy the fruit from this tree?' Ḥoni asked the man with wonder. The man replied, 'Just as I was born into a world with fully grown fruit trees that were planted by my ancestors, so I plant a tree for my children.'"

1 אַשְׁרֵי יוֹשְׁבֵי בֵיתֶךָ, עוֹד יְהַלְלוּךָ סֶּלָה:
2 אַשְׁרֵי הָעָם שֶׁכָּכָה לּוֹ, אַשְׁרֵי הָעָם שֶׁיְהֹוָה אֱלֹהָיו:
3 תְּהִלָּה לְדָוִד

4 אֲרוֹמִמְךָ אֱלוֹהַי הַמֶּלֶךְ, וַאֲבָרְכָה שִׁמְךָ לְעוֹלָם וָעֶד:

5 בְּכָל־יוֹם אֲבָרְכֶךָּ, וַאֲהַלְלָה שִׁמְךָ לְעוֹלָם וָעֶד:

6 גָּדוֹל יְהֹוָה וּמְהֻלָּל מְאֹד, וְלִגְדֻלָּתוֹ אֵין חֵקֶר:

7 דּוֹר לְדוֹר יְשַׁבַּח מַעֲשֶׂיךָ, וּגְבוּרֹתֶיךָ יַגִּידוּ:

8 הֲדַר כְּבוֹד הוֹדֶךָ, וְדִבְרֵי נִפְלְאֹתֶיךָ אָשִׂיחָה:

9 וֶעֱזוּז נוֹרְאֹתֶיךָ יֹאמֵרוּ, וּגְדוּלָּתְךָ אֲסַפְּרֶנָּה:

10 זֵכֶר רַב־טוּבְךָ יַבִּיעוּ, וְצִדְקָתְךָ יְרַנֵּנוּ:

11 חַנּוּן וְרַחוּם יְהֹוָה, אֶרֶךְ אַפַּיִם וּגְדָל־חָסֶד:

12 טוֹב־יְהֹוָה לַכֹּל, וְרַחֲמָיו עַל־כָּל־מַעֲשָׂיו:

You want Hashem to be close to you? Call on Him and He will be!

One night I dreamed I was walking on the beach with God. I saw memories from my life flash across the sky. In each scene I noticed footprints in the sand. Sometimes there were two sets of footprints and sometimes there was only one.

This bothered me because I noticed that during the difficult times in my life, I could see only one set of footprints. So I said to God, "You promised me that if I followed You, You would walk with me always. But I have noticed that during the most difficult periods of my life there has been only one set of footprints in the sand. Why, when I needed You most, were You not there for me?"

God replied, "The times when there was only one set of footprints, My child, is when I carried you."

Can you think of a time when you know Hashem was with you in your life?

13 יוֹדוּךָ יְהוָה כָּל־מַעֲשֶׂיךָ, וַחֲסִידֶיךָ יְבָרְכוּכָה:

14 כְּבוֹד מַלְכוּתְךָ יֹאמֵרוּ, וּגְבוּרָתְךָ יְדַבֵּרוּ:

15 לְהוֹדִיעַ לִבְנֵי הָאָדָם גְּבוּרֹתָיו, וּכְבוֹד הֲדַר מַלְכוּתוֹ:

16 מַלְכוּתְךָ מַלְכוּת כָּל־עֹלָמִים, וּמֶמְשַׁלְתְּךָ בְּכָל־דּוֹר וָדֹר:

17 סוֹמֵךְ יְהוָה לְכָל־הַנֹּפְלִים, וְזוֹקֵף לְכָל־הַכְּפוּפִים:

18 עֵינֵי־כֹל אֵלֶיךָ יְשַׂבֵּרוּ וְאַתָּה נוֹתֵן־לָהֶם אֶת־אָכְלָם בְּעִתּוֹ:

19 פּוֹתֵחַ אֶת־יָדֶךָ, וּמַשְׂבִּיעַ לְכָל־חַי רָצוֹן:

20 צַדִּיק יְהוָה בְּכָל־דְּרָכָיו, וְחָסִיד בְּכָל־מַעֲשָׂיו:

21 קָרוֹב יְהוָה לְכָל־קֹרְאָיו, לְכֹל אֲשֶׁר יִקְרָאֻהוּ בֶאֱמֶת:

22 רְצוֹן־יְרֵאָיו יַעֲשֶׂה, וְאֶת־שַׁוְעָתָם יִשְׁמַע, וְיוֹשִׁיעֵם:

23 שׁוֹמֵר יְהוָה אֶת־כָּל־אֹהֲבָיו, וְאֵת כָּל־הָרְשָׁעִים יַשְׁמִיד:

24 תְּהִלַּת יְהוָה יְדַבֶּר פִּי וִיבָרֵךְ כָּל־בָּשָׂר שֵׁם קָדְשׁוֹ לְעוֹלָם וָעֶד:

25 וַאֲנַחְנוּ נְבָרֵךְ יָהּ מֵעַתָּה וְעַד־עוֹלָם, הַלְלוּיָהּ:

"Rabbi Akiva was once on a journey when he came to a town where there was no room for him to stay. He said to himself, 'Everything God does He does for the best,' and he slept in a field on the outskirts of the town. He had with him a candle, a rooster, and a donkey. During the night the wind blew out the candle, a cat came and ate the rooster, and a lion came and ate the donkey. Each time he once again said to himself, 'Everything God does He does for the best.' When he awoke in the morning he realized that an army had come and taken the town captive. If he had had a candle, a noisy rooster and a donkey with him, his location would have been discovered, but instead he was saved."

"Naḥum Ish Gamzu used to say 'גַּם זוֹ לְטוֹבָה'."

Think of the last thing that you felt wasn't good that happened to you? Can you think of a positive outcome that came from it?

הַלְלוּיָהּ, הַלְלִי נַפְשִׁי אֶת־יְהֹוָה: אֲהַלְלָה יְהֹוָה בְּחַיָּי, אֲזַמְּרָה לֵאלֹהַי בְּעוֹדִי: אַל־תִּבְטְחוּ בִנְדִיבִים, בְּבֶן־אָדָם שֶׁאֵין לוֹ תְשׁוּעָה: תֵּצֵא רוּחוֹ, יָשֻׁב לְאַדְמָתוֹ, בַּיּוֹם הַהוּא אָבְדוּ עֶשְׁתֹּנֹתָיו: אַשְׁרֵי שֶׁאֵל יַעֲקֹב בְּעֶזְרוֹ, שִׂבְרוֹ עַל־יְהֹוָה אֱלֹהָיו: עֹשֶׂה שָׁמַיִם וָאָרֶץ, אֶת־הַיָּם וְאֶת־כָּל־אֲשֶׁר־בָּם, הַשֹּׁמֵר אֱמֶת לְעוֹלָם: עֹשֶׂה מִשְׁפָּט לַעֲשׁוּקִים, נֹתֵן לֶחֶם לָרְעֵבִים, יְהֹוָה מַתִּיר אֲסוּרִים: יְהֹוָה פֹּקֵחַ עִוְרִים, יְהֹוָה זֹקֵף כְּפוּפִים, יְהֹוָה אֹהֵב צַדִּיקִים: יְהֹוָה שֹׁמֵר אֶת־גֵּרִים, יָתוֹם וְאַלְמָנָה יְעוֹדֵד, וְדֶרֶךְ רְשָׁעִים יְעַוֵּת: יִמְלֹךְ יְהֹוָה לְעוֹלָם, אֱלֹהַיִךְ צִיּוֹן לְדֹר וָדֹר, הַלְלוּיָהּ:

The brave Jewish soldiers fighting to conquer the holy city of Tzefat during Israel's War of Independence in 1948 found themselves greatly outnumbered and severely lacking in supplies to fight the Arab army they faced. The Jews had a secret weapon though. The Davidka! Named after its inventor, David Leibowitch, it was a homemade cannon that fired homemade bombs that were inaccurate and largely ineffective. However they made a tremendous noise when they exploded. There were rumors that because many of the inventors of the atomic bomb used by America in World War II were Jewish, the Jews fighting in Israel also had the atomic bomb, which made a very loud noise as well. It was also believed that it would "rain" after an atomic explosion. Miraculously it rained as soon as the Davidka was fired in Tzefat. Fearing for their lives, the Arabs retreated, allowing the Jews to take full control of the city of Tzefat!

"Each blade of grass has an angel pushing it and telling it to grow."

Hashem cares for everything in creation, including you.

How is Hashem caring for you today? Where in your life do you feel it?

1 הַלְלוּיָהּ, כִּי־טוֹב זַמְּרָה אֱלֹהֵינוּ, כִּי־נָעִים נָאוָה תְהִלָּה: בּוֹנֵה
2 יְרוּשָׁלַםִ יְהוָֹה, נִדְחֵי יִשְׂרָאֵל יְכַנֵּס: הָרוֹפֵא לִשְׁבוּרֵי לֵב,
3 וּמְחַבֵּשׁ לְעַצְּבוֹתָם: מוֹנֶה מִסְפָּר לַכּוֹכָבִים, לְכֻלָּם שֵׁמוֹת
4 יִקְרָא: גָּדוֹל אֲדוֹנֵינוּ וְרַב־כֹּחַ, לִתְבוּנָתוֹ אֵין מִסְפָּר: מְעוֹדֵד
5 עֲנָוִים יְהוָֹה, מַשְׁפִּיל רְשָׁעִים עֲדֵי־אָרֶץ: עֱנוּ לַיהוָֹה בְּתוֹדָה,
6 זַמְּרוּ לֵאלֹהֵינוּ בְכִנּוֹר: הַמְכַסֶּה שָׁמַיִם בְּעָבִים, הַמֵּכִין לָאָרֶץ
7 מָטָר, הַמַּצְמִיחַ הָרִים חָצִיר: נוֹתֵן לִבְהֵמָה לַחְמָהּ, לִבְנֵי עֹרֵב
8 אֲשֶׁר יִקְרָאוּ: לֹא בִגְבוּרַת הַסּוּס יֶחְפָּץ, לֹא־בְשׁוֹקֵי הָאִישׁ
9 יִרְצֶה: רוֹצֶה יְהוָֹה אֶת־יְרֵאָיו, אֶת־הַמְיַחֲלִים לְחַסְדּוֹ: שַׁבְּחִי
10 יְרוּשָׁלַםִ אֶת־יְהוָֹה, הַלְלִי אֱלֹהַיִךְ צִיּוֹן: כִּי־חִזַּק בְּרִיחֵי
11 שְׁעָרָיִךְ, בֵּרַךְ בָּנַיִךְ בְּקִרְבֵּךְ: הַשָּׂם־גְּבוּלֵךְ שָׁלוֹם, חֵלֶב
12 חִטִּים יַשְׂבִּיעֵךְ: הַשֹּׁלֵחַ אִמְרָתוֹ אָרֶץ, עַד־מְהֵרָה יָרוּץ
13 דְּבָרוֹ: הַנֹּתֵן שֶׁלֶג כַּצָּמֶר, כְּפוֹר כָּאֵפֶר יְפַזֵּר: מַשְׁלִיךְ קַרְחוֹ
14 כְפִתִּים, לִפְנֵי קָרָתוֹ מִי יַעֲמֹד: יִשְׁלַח דְּבָרוֹ וְיַמְסֵם, יַשֵּׁב
15 רוּחוֹ יִזְּלוּ־מָיִם: מַגִּיד דְּבָרָו לְיַעֲקֹב, חֻקָּיו וּמִשְׁפָּטָיו
16 לְיִשְׂרָאֵל: לֹא עָשָׂה כֵן לְכָל־גּוֹי, וּמִשְׁפָּטִים בַּל־יְדָעוּם, הַלְלוּיָהּ:

God, when you thought of a pine tree, how did you think of a star?
How did you dream of the Milky Way, to guide us from afar.
How did you think of a clean brown pool, where flecks of shadows are?
[...]
God, when you chiseled a raindrop, how did you think of a stem,
Bearing a lovely satin leaf, to hold the tiny gem?
How did you know a million drops, would deck the morning's hem?

Why did you mate the moonlit night, with the honeysuckle vines?
How did you know Madeira bloom, distilled ecstatic wines?

How did you weave the velvet disk, where tangled perfumes are?
God, when you thought of a pine tree, how did you think of a star?

Where do you see Hashem in your world?

הַלְלוּיָהּ, הַלְלוּ אֶת־יְהוָה מִן־הַשָּׁמַיִם, הַלְלוּהוּ בַּמְּרוֹמִים: הַלְלוּהוּ כָל־מַלְאָכָיו, הַלְלוּהוּ כָּל־צְבָאָו: הַלְלוּהוּ שֶׁמֶשׁ וְיָרֵחַ, הַלְלוּהוּ כָּל־כּוֹכְבֵי אוֹר: הַלְלוּהוּ שְׁמֵי הַשָּׁמָיִם, וְהַמַּיִם אֲשֶׁר מֵעַל הַשָּׁמָיִם: יְהַלְלוּ אֶת־שֵׁם יְהוָה, כִּי הוּא צִוָּה וְנִבְרָאוּ: וַיַּעֲמִידֵם לָעַד לְעוֹלָם, חָק־נָתַן וְלֹא יַעֲבוֹר: הַלְלוּ אֶת־יְהוָה מִן־הָאָרֶץ, תַּנִּינִים וְכָל־תְּהֹמוֹת: אֵשׁ וּבָרָד שֶׁלֶג וְקִיטוֹר, רוּחַ סְעָרָה עֹשָׂה דְבָרוֹ: הֶהָרִים וְכָל־גְּבָעוֹת, עֵץ פְּרִי וְכָל־אֲרָזִים: הַחַיָּה וְכָל־בְּהֵמָה, רֶמֶשׂ וְצִפּוֹר כָּנָף: מַלְכֵי־אֶרֶץ וְכָל־לְאֻמִּים, שָׂרִים וְכָל־שֹׁפְטֵי אָרֶץ: בַּחוּרִים וְגַם־בְּתוּלוֹת, זְקֵנִים עִם־נְעָרִים: יְהַלְלוּ אֶת־שֵׁם יְהוָה, כִּי־נִשְׂגָּב שְׁמוֹ לְבַדּוֹ, הוֹדוֹ עַל־אֶרֶץ וְשָׁמָיִם: וַיָּרֶם קֶרֶן לְעַמּוֹ, תְּהִלָּה לְכָל־חֲסִידָיו, לִבְנֵי יִשְׂרָאֵל עַם קְרֹבוֹ, הַלְלוּיָהּ:

"Song is more precious than words."

"One fragment of melody can contain all the joy in the world."

How do you feel when you sing? Why do you think we sing so many of our *tefillot*?

Rebbe Leib the grandfather of Shpole was well known for making people happy, playing with children, and telling stories. He was the first Hasidic Rebbe to declare dancing a mitzva. When the Maggid of Mezeritch saw him dancing he commented, "Your dancing counts for more than my prayers!"

1 הַלְלוּיָהּ, שִׁירוּ לַיהוָה שִׁיר חָדָשׁ, תְּהִלָּתוֹ בִּקְהַל חֲסִידִים:
2 יִשְׂמַח יִשְׂרָאֵל בְּעֹשָׂיו, בְּנֵי־צִיּוֹן יָגִילוּ בְמַלְכָּם: יְהַלְלוּ שְׁמוֹ
3 בְמָחוֹל, בְּתֹף וְכִנּוֹר יְזַמְּרוּ־לוֹ: כִּי־רוֹצֶה יְהֹוָה בְּעַמּוֹ,
4 יְפָאֵר עֲנָוִים בִּישׁוּעָה: יַעְלְזוּ חֲסִידִים בְּכָבוֹד, יְרַנְּנוּ עַל־
5 מִשְׁכְּבוֹתָם: רוֹמְמוֹת אֵל בִּגְרוֹנָם, וְחֶרֶב פִּיפִיּוֹת בְּיָדָם:
6 לַעֲשׂוֹת נְקָמָה בַּגּוֹיִם, תּוֹכֵחוֹת בַּלְאֻמִּים: לֶאְסֹר
7 מַלְכֵיהֶם בְּזִקִּים, וְנִכְבְּדֵיהֶם בְּכַבְלֵי בַרְזֶל: לַעֲשׂוֹת
8 בָּהֶם מִשְׁפָּט כָּתוּב, הָדָר הוּא לְכָל־חֲסִידָיו, הַלְלוּיָהּ:

Haile Gebrselassie was an Ethiopian long-distance runner who over the course of his career broke 27 world records. Any time Haile trains in the gym he likes to listen to fast loud music. In 1995 he smashed the 5,000-meters world record by playing his favorite song over and over in his head. The song has more than 130 beats per minute, and motivated him to keep the pace he needed and helped him to focus on what he had to do to win the race. This gave him an idea. For his next world-record attempt, the 10,000 meters, he requested the song be played over the loudspeakers in the stadium. With the help of the music, focusing his heart and mind, almost lifting him out of the stadium and on to greatness, he smashed that record too!

What music do you like to listen to? How does it make you feel?

הַלְלוּיָהּ, הַלְלוּ־אֵל בְּקָדְשׁוֹ 1

הַלְלוּהוּ בִּרְקִיעַ עֻזּוֹ: 2

הַלְלוּהוּ בִגְבוּרֹתָיו 3

הַלְלוּהוּ כְּרֹב גֻּדְלוֹ: 4

הַלְלוּהוּ בְּתֵקַע שׁוֹפָר 5

הַלְלוּהוּ בְּנֵבֶל וְכִנּוֹר: 6

הַלְלוּהוּ בְתֹף וּמָחוֹל 7

הַלְלוּהוּ בְּמִנִּים וְעֻגָב: 8

הַלְלוּהוּ בְצִלְצְלֵי־שָׁמַע 9

הַלְלוּהוּ בְּצִלְצְלֵי תְרוּעָה: 10

כֹּל הַנְּשָׁמָה תְּהַלֵּל יָהּ, הַלְלוּיָהּ: 11

כֹּל הַנְּשָׁמָה תְּהַלֵּל יָהּ, הַלְלוּיָהּ: 12

One day a young girl went in to the forest to pray to Hashem. When she returned her parents asked her where she had been. "I went to the forest to pray," she told them. The next day the same thing happened, and again her parents asked her where she had gone. "I went to the forest to pray," again she replied. When this happened on the third day they became disturbed and confronted her. "My daughter," her mother said, "why do you go to the forest to pray to Hashem? There is no need to search for Hashem in the forest, Hashem is everywhere. Even in our house. Hashem is no different in the forest. Why do you insist on going there to pray?" The girl looked into her parents' eyes and said, "I know that Hashem is no different in the forest. But out in the forest, I know that I am different."

1 בָּרוּךְ יְהֹוָה לְעוֹלָם

2 אָמֵן וְאָמֵן:

3 בָּרוּךְ יְהֹוָה מִצִּיּוֹן, שֹׁכֵן יְרוּשָׁלָםִ, הַלְלוּיָהּ:

4 בָּרוּךְ יְהֹוָה אֱלֹהִים אֱלֹהֵי יִשְׂרָאֵל

5 עֹשֵׂה נִפְלָאוֹת לְבַדּוֹ:

6 וּבָרוּךְ שֵׁם כְּבוֹדוֹ לְעוֹלָם

7 וְיִמָּלֵא כְבוֹדוֹ אֶת־כֹּל־הָאָרֶץ

8 אָמֵן וְאָמֵן:

Some people connect to Hashem more in Yerushalayim, or in a *Beit Kenesset,* or in a forest.

Where do you connect best to Hashem? Why?

"When the Benei Yisrael reached the shores of the Yam Suf, none of the tribes wanted to be the first to enter the sea before it had split. Naḥshon ben Aminadav from the tribe of Yehuda ran forward into the sea, and because of that the tribe of Yehuda were given the honor of having Yerushalayim in their territory."

"You should imagine that you are actually crossing through the Yam Suf when you sing the *shira*!"

Take a moment to imagine how scared the Benei Yisrael must have been the moment before the sea split. The Egyptian army was behind them and the sea in front of them, with no way to escape. Now imagine when the waters split and they were led through on dry land.

How do you think they felt then? Now sing the *shira*.

The following verses are the song that the Jews sang after the miracle of the splitting of the Yam Suf. Notice how it is arranged in columns, exactly how it is written in the סֵפֶר תּוֹרָה*. This represents the journey through the sea. The middle column represents the people walking between the walls of water (the two outer columns).*

אָז יָשִׁיר־מֹשֶׁה וּבְנֵי יִשְׂרָאֵל אֶת־הַשִּׁירָה הַזֹּאת לַיהוָה, וַיֹּאמְרוּ
לֵאמֹר,   אָשִׁירָה לַיהוָה כִּי־גָאֹה גָּאָה,   סוּס
וְרֹכְבוֹ רָמָה בַיָּם: עָזִּי וְזִמְרָת יָהּ וַיְהִי־לִי
לִישׁוּעָה,   זֶה אֵלִי וְאַנְוֵהוּ,   אֱלֹהֵי
אָבִי וַאֲרֹמְמֶנְהוּ:   יְהוָה אִישׁ מִלְחָמָה, יְהוָה
שְׁמוֹ:   מַרְכְּבֹת פַּרְעֹה וְחֵילוֹ יָרָה בַיָּם,   וּמִבְחַר
שָׁלִשָׁיו טֻבְּעוּ בְיַם־סוּף: תְּהֹמֹת יְכַסְיֻמוּ, יָרְדוּ בִמְצוֹלֹת כְּמוֹ־
אָבֶן: יְמִינְךָ יְהוָה נֶאְדָּרִי בַּכֹּחַ,   יְמִינְךָ
יְהוָה תִּרְעַץ אוֹיֵב: וּבְרֹב גְּאוֹנְךָ תַּהֲרֹס
קָמֶיךָ,   תְּשַׁלַּח חֲרֹנְךָ יֹאכְלֵמוֹ כַּקַּשׁ:   וּבְרוּחַ
אַפֶּיךָ נֶעֶרְמוּ מַיִם,   נִצְּבוּ כְמוֹ־נֵד
נֹזְלִים,   קָפְאוּ תְהֹמֹת בְּלֶב־יָם: אָמַר
אוֹיֵב אֶרְדֹּף, אַשִּׂיג,   אֲחַלֵּק שָׁלָל, תִּמְלָאֵמוֹ
נַפְשִׁי,   אָרִיק חַרְבִּי תּוֹרִישֵׁמוֹ יָדִי: נָשַׁפְתָּ

Close your eyes. Imagine traveling back in time in a time machine to 500 years ago. Look around you and find a person passing. Show them the cell phone in your pocket. Show them what you can do with it. Show them how you can write messages to a friend on the other side of the world in an instant. Show them how you can take a selfie of the two of you and share it instantly with thousands of people all over the world. Show them how you can have a live visual conversation with someone on the other side of the world. And show them how you could use your phone to find out a piece of information on almost anything that has happened in history with the swipe of your finger.

What do you think they would say to you? Do you think they would use the world "miracle"? Would you?

If you could relive any event in Jewish history which would it be? Why? Shut your eyes and imagine you are there.

בְּר֤וּחֲךָ֙ כִּסָּ֣מוֹ יָ֔ם צָֽלְלוּ֙ כַּֽעוֹפֶ֔רֶת בְּמַ֖יִם
אַדִּירִֽים׃ מִֽי־כָמֹ֤כָה בָּֽאֵלִם֙ יְהוָ֔ה מִ֥י
כָּמֹ֖כָה נֶאְדָּ֣ר בַּקֹּ֑דֶשׁ נוֹרָ֥א תְהִלֹּ֖ת עֹ֥שֵׂה
פֶֽלֶא׃ נָטִ֙יתָ֙ יְמִ֣ינְךָ֔ תִּבְלָעֵ֖מוֹ אָֽרֶץ׃ נָחִ֥יתָ
בְחַסְדְּךָ֖ עַם־ז֣וּ גָּאָ֑לְתָּ נֵהַ֥לְתָּ בְעָזְּךָ֖ אֶל־נְוֵ֥ה
קָדְשֶֽׁךָ׃ שָֽׁמְע֥וּ עַמִּ֖ים יִרְגָּז֑וּן חִ֣יל
אָחַ֔ז יֹשְׁבֵ֖י פְּלָֽשֶׁת׃ אָ֤ז נִבְהֲלוּ֙ אַלּוּפֵ֣י
אֱד֔וֹם אֵילֵ֣י מוֹאָ֔ב יֹֽאחֲזֵ֖מוֹ רָ֑עַד נָמֹ֕גוּ
כֹּ֖ל יֹשְׁבֵ֥י כְנָֽעַן׃ תִּפֹּ֨ל עֲלֵיהֶ֤ם אֵימָ֙תָה֙
וָפַ֔חַד בִּגְדֹ֥ל זְרוֹעֲךָ֖ יִדְּמ֣וּ כָּאָ֑בֶן עַֽד־
יַעֲבֹ֤ר עַמְּךָ֙ יְהוָ֔ה עַֽד־יַעֲבֹ֖ר עַם־ז֥וּ
קָנִֽיתָ׃ תְּבִאֵ֗מוֹ וְתִטָּעֵ֙מוֹ֙ בְּהַ֣ר נַחֲלָֽתְךָ֔ מָכ֥וֹן
לְשִׁבְתְּךָ֛ פָּעַ֖לְתָּ יְהוָ֑ה מִקְּדָ֕שׁ אֲדֹנָ֖י כּוֹנְנ֥וּ
יָדֶֽיךָ׃ יְהוָ֥ה ׀ יִמְלֹ֖ךְ לְעֹלָ֥ם וָעֶֽד׃
יְהוָ֥ה ׀ יִמְלֹ֖ךְ לְעֹלָ֥ם וָעֶֽד׃
יְהוָה מַלְכוּתֵהּ קָאֵם לְעָלַם וּלְעָלְמֵי עָלְמַיָּא.

David Ben-Gurion, Israel's first Prime Minister once said that to be a realistic person in Israel, you have to believe in miracles! And this little country has produced miracle after miracle in its short history. In 1948, this young country with its tiny, inexperienced, ill-equipped and under-trained army managed to fend off five Arab armies bent on its destruction. And that was just the first of many other wars over the years, each equally miraculous. Once the fighting was over in 1949, this brand-new country of just 600,000 people took in more than a million Jewish refugees from around the world, finding them places to live, food to eat, and jobs to do. Two-thirds of this tiny country is arid uninhabitable desert. Yet Israel managed to settle thousands of people there, and "green the desert," growing crops and vegetation, using ingenious computerized irrigation systems. Israel became one of the most educated populations in the world, with one of the fastest growing economies of the world, inventing many of the products that we all take for granted, such as the computer chip, the technology behind the cell phone, the disk-on-key, and the cherry-tomato! And all of this while continuously having to fight for its very existence. Israel truly is a place of modern miracles!

כִּי

בָא סוּס פַּרְעֹה בְּרִכְבּוֹ וּבְפָרָשָׁיו בַּיָּם, וַיָּשֶׁב יְהֹוָה עֲלֵהֶם אֶת־מֵי

הַיָּם, וּבְנֵי יִשְׂרָאֵל הָלְכוּ בַיַּבָּשָׁה בְּתוֹךְ הַיָּם:

כִּי לַיהֹוָה הַמְּלוּכָה, וּמשֵׁל בַּגּוֹיִם:

וְעָלוּ מוֹשִׁעִים בְּהַר צִיּוֹן לִשְׁפֹּט אֶת־הַר עֵשָׂו

וְהָיְתָה לַיהֹוָה הַמְּלוּכָה:

וְהָיָה יְהֹוָה לְמֶלֶךְ עַל־כָּל־הָאָרֶץ

בַּיּוֹם הַהוּא יִהְיֶה יְהֹוָה אֶחָד וּשְׁמוֹ אֶחָד:

"In every generation, every person must see themselves as if they came out of Egypt."

Close your eyes and imagine you were there when Benei Yisrael left Egypt.

How does *Leil HaSeder* help us to do this?

Why do you think it is so important to do this at least once a year?

Your name, Hashem, will always remind us of how wonderful You are, our King. You are a great and holy God in heaven and on earth.

Which do you find easier, praising Hashem or talking with Hashem? Why?

Amazing. Astonishing. Astounding. Awe-inspiring. Awesome. Beautiful. Brilliant. Exceptional. Exquisite. Extraordinary. Fabulous. Fantastic. Faultless. Glorious. Great. Incredible. Magnificent. Majestic. Marvelous. Outstanding. Perfect. Phenomenal. Remarkable. Sensational. Spectacular. Splendid. Stunning. Sublime. Superb. Terrific. Tremendous. Unbelievable. Wonderful. Wondrous.

Can you think of any more words of praise? Which apply most to Hashem?

יִשְׁתַּבַּח

שִׁמְךָ לָעַד מַלְכֵּנוּ
הָאֵל הַמֶּלֶךְ הַגָּדוֹל וְהַקָּדוֹשׁ בַּשָּׁמַיִם וּבָאָרֶץ
כִּי לְךָ נָאֶה, יְהֹוָה אֱלֹהֵינוּ וֵאלֹהֵי אֲבוֹתֵינוּ
לְעוֹלָם וָעֶד
שִׁיר וּשְׁבָחָה, הַלֵּל וְזִמְרָה
עֹז וּמֶמְשָׁלָה, נֶצַח, גְּדֻלָּה וּגְבוּרָה
תְּהִלָּה וְתִפְאֶרֶת, קְדֻשָּׁה וּמַלְכוּת
בְּרָכוֹת וְהוֹדָאוֹת לְשִׁמְךָ הַגָּדוֹל וְהַקָּדוֹשׁ
וּמֵעוֹלָם עַד־עוֹלָם אַתָּה אֵל:
בָּרוּךְ אַתָּה יְהֹוָה
מֶלֶךְ גָּדוֹל וּמְהֻלָּל בַּתִּשְׁבָּחוֹת
אֵל הַהוֹדָאוֹת, אֲדוֹן הַנִּפְלָאוֹת
בּוֹרֵא כָּל הַנְּשָׁמוֹת, רִבּוֹן כָּל הַמַּעֲשִׂים
הַבּוֹחֵר בְּשִׁירֵי זִמְרָה
מֶלֶךְ, אֵל, חַי הָעוֹלָמִים. אָמֵן.

Hashem, You create light and darkness, and make peace in the world and You created absolutely everything. With kindness You give light to the earth and to all the people that live here.

וְזָרַח הַשֶּׁמֶשׁ וּבָא הַשָּׁמֶשׁ,
וְאֶל-מְקוֹמוֹ שׁוֹאֵף זוֹרֵחַ הוּא שָׁם.
(Kohelet 1:5)

Imagine yourself outside on a sunny day. Feel the rays of the sun on your face.

How does it feel?

Why is light so important to us? What would life be like without light?

A young boy who could not read came to the Beit Kenesset and wanted to pray. He said to Hashem: "I don't know the prayers. All I know is the letters of the Alef-Beit. Please take the letters and turn them into the right words to say what I feel in my heart," and he sang them over and over again. The Ba'al Shem Tov said that the boy's prayer not only broke through the gates of heaven, but helped everyone else's prayers to enter as well.

The next section of תְּפִלַּת שַׁחֲרִית is the שְׁמַע and its בְּרָכוֹת. There are two בְּרָכוֹת before and one after the שְׁמַע.

1 בָּרוּךְ אַתָּה יְהוָֹה אֱלֹהֵינוּ מֶלֶךְ הָעוֹלָם
2 יוֹצֵר אוֹר וּבוֹרֵא חֹשֶׁךְ, עֹשֶׂה שָׁלוֹם וּבוֹרֵא אֶת הַכֹּל.

3 הַמֵּאִיר לָאָרֶץ וְלַדָּרִים עָלֶיהָ בְּרַחֲמִים
4 וּבְטוּבוֹ מְחַדֵּשׁ בְּכָל יוֹם תָּמִיד מַעֲשֵׂה בְרֵאשִׁית.
5 מָה־רַבּוּ מַעֲשֶׂיךָ יְהוָֹה, כֻּלָּם בְּחָכְמָה עָשִׂיתָ
6 מָלְאָה הָאָרֶץ קִנְיָנֶךָ:
7 הַמֶּלֶךְ הַמְרוֹמָם לְבַדּוֹ מֵאָז
8 הַמְשֻׁבָּח וְהַמְפֹאָר וְהַמִּתְנַשֵּׂא מִימוֹת עוֹלָם.
9 אֱלֹהֵי עוֹלָם
10 בְּרַחֲמֶיךָ הָרַבִּים רַחֵם עָלֵינוּ
11 אֲדוֹן עֻזֵּנוּ, צוּר מִשְׂגַּבֵּנוּ
12 מָגֵן יִשְׁעֵנוּ, מִשְׂגָּב בַּעֲדֵנוּ.
13 אֵל בָּרוּךְ גְּדוֹל דֵּעָה, הֵכִין וּפָעַל זָהֳרֵי חַמָּה
14 טוֹב יָצַר כָּבוֹד לִשְׁמוֹ, מְאוֹרוֹת נָתַן סְבִיבוֹת עֻזּוֹ
15 פִּנּוֹת צְבָאוֹת קְדוֹשִׁים, רוֹמְמֵי שַׁדַּי
16 תָּמִיד מְסַפְּרִים כְּבוֹד אֵל וּקְדֻשָּׁתוֹ.

You are our Rock! Our King! Our Rescuer! You created all holy beings, including us and the angels.

"Don't be like a servant who serves his master because he wants to receive a reward, but be like a servant who wants to serve even if there is no reward." (Pirkei Avot 1:3)

Angels can't choose to be good or bad. They serve Hashem because that is what they were created to do.

How would your life be different if you were an angel?

"Sometimes Hashem creates angels sitting, and sometimes He creates them standing. Sometimes He creates them looking like men, and sometimes looking like women. Sometimes the angels He creates are like winds, and sometimes like fire."

תִּתְבָּרַךְ יְהוָֹה אֱלֹהֵינוּ
בַּשָּׁמַיִם מִמַּעַל וְעַל הָאָרֶץ מִתַּחַת
עַל כָּל שֶׁבַח מַעֲשֵׂה יָדֶיךָ, וְעַל מְאוֹרֵי אוֹר שֶׁיָּצַרְתָּ
הֵמָּה יְפָאֲרוּךָ סֶּלָה.

תִּתְבָּרַךְ לָנֶצַח צוּרֵנוּ
מַלְכֵּנוּ וְגוֹאֲלֵנוּ, בּוֹרֵא קְדוֹשִׁים
יִשְׁתַּבַּח שִׁמְךָ לָעַד מַלְכֵּנוּ, יוֹצֵר מְשָׁרְתִים
וַאֲשֶׁר מְשָׁרְתָיו כֻּלָּם, עוֹמְדִים בְּרוּם עוֹלָם
וּמַשְׁמִיעִים בְּיִרְאָה יַחַד בְּקוֹל
דִּבְרֵי אֱלֹהִים חַיִּים וּמֶלֶךְ עוֹלָם.
כֻּלָּם אֲהוּבִים כֻּלָּם בְּרוּרִים
כֻּלָּם גִּבּוֹרִים כֻּלָּם קְדוֹשִׁים
כֻּלָּם עוֹשִׂים בְּאֵימָה וּבְיִרְאָה רְצוֹן קוֹנֵיהֶם
וְכֻלָּם פּוֹתְחִים אֶת פִּיהֶם בִּקְדֻשָּׁה וּבְטָהֳרָה
בְּשִׁירָה וּבְזִמְרָה
וּמְבָרְכִין וּמְשַׁבְּחִין וּמְפָאֲרִין
וּמַקְדִּישִׁין וּמַעֲרִיצִין וּמַמְלִיכִין

The angels all tremble as they say: Hashem the Creator of all things is holy, holy, holy, and the whole world is full of His greatness.

"When Moshe climbed to the top of Har Sinai to receive the Torah from Hashem, he found the angels complaining to Hashem: 'Why would You give Your precious Torah to a lowly human being?' they challenged. Hashem turned to Moshe and asked him to reply to the angels. Moshe asked Hashem what was in the Torah, and He replied, "אָנֹכִי יְהֹוָה אֱלֹהֶיךָ, אֲשֶׁר הוֹצֵאתִיךָ מֵאֶרֶץ מִצְרַיִם מִבֵּית עֲבָדִים" (Shemot 20:2). *Moshe turned to the angels and said, 'Were you slaves in Egypt? Did Hashem take you out from there? Why should you get the Torah?' Moshe again asked Hashem what was in the Torah, and He replied, "זָכוֹר אֶת־יוֹם הַשַּׁבָּת לְקַדְּשׁוֹ"* (Shemot 20:7). *Once again, Moshe turned to the angels and asked them: 'Do you work hard for six days that you need to rest on the seventh?' And again Moshe asked Hashem what was in the Torah, and He replied "כַּבֵּד אֶת־אָבִיךָ וְאֶת־אִמֶּךָ"* (Shemot 20:12). *Moshe then turned to the angels again and asked: 'Do you have a father and a mother that you can respect?' and the angels had nothing to say."*

1 אֶת שֵׁם הָאֵל הַמֶּלֶךְ הַגָּדוֹל, הַגִּבּוֹר וְהַנּוֹרָא

2 קָדוֹשׁ הוּא.

3 וְכֻלָּם מְקַבְּלִים עֲלֵיהֶם עֹל מַלְכוּת שָׁמַיִם זֶה מִזֶּה

4 וְנוֹתְנִים רְשׁוּת זֶה לָזֶה

5 לְהַקְדִּישׁ לְיוֹצְרָם בְּנַחַת רוּחַ

6 בְּשָׂפָה בְרוּרָה וּבִנְעִימָה

7 קְדֻשָּׁה כֻּלָּם כְּאֶחָד

8 עוֹנִים בְּאֵימָה וְאוֹמְרִים בְּיִרְאָה

These words are said together aloud:

9 קָדוֹשׁ ׀ קָדוֹשׁ קָדוֹשׁ יְהוָה צְבָאוֹת

10 מְלֹא כָל־הָאָרֶץ כְּבוֹדוֹ:

11 וְהָאוֹפַנִּים וְחַיּוֹת הַקֹּדֶשׁ

12 בְּרַעַשׁ גָּדוֹל מִתְנַשְּׂאִים לְעֻמַּת הַשְּׂרָפִים

13 לְעֻמָּתָם מְשַׁבְּחִים וְאוֹמְרִים

These words are said together aloud:

14 בָּרוּךְ כְּבוֹד־יְהוָה מִמְּקוֹמוֹ:

Hashem re-creates the world from new, continually, each day.

"Look at the light of God's Presence in everything."

Where can you see God's light today?

"The glory of Hashem can be felt in the rays of sunshine from the morning sun."

How are the rays of the sun like feeling God Himself?

Close your eyes and feel Hashem in the rays of the morning sunshine on your face.

לָאֵל בָּרוּךְ, נְעִימוֹת יִתֵּנוּ
לַמֶּלֶךְ אֵל חַי וְקַיָּם, זְמִירוֹת יֹאמֵרוּ וְתִשְׁבָּחוֹת יַשְׁמִיעוּ
כִּי הוּא לְבַדּוֹ מָרוֹם וְקָדוֹשׁ
פּוֹעֵל גְּבוּרוֹת, עוֹשֶׂה חֲדָשׁוֹת
בַּעַל מִלְחָמוֹת, זוֹרֵעַ צְדָקוֹת
מַצְמִיחַ יְשׁוּעוֹת, בּוֹרֵא רְפוּאוֹת
נוֹרָא תְהִלּוֹת, אֲדוֹן הַנִּפְלָאוֹת
הַמְחַדֵּשׁ בְּטוּבוֹ בְּכָל יוֹם תָּמִיד מַעֲשֵׂה בְרֵאשִׁית
כָּאָמוּר
לְעֹשֵׂה אוֹרִים גְּדֹלִים, כִּי לְעוֹלָם חַסְדּוֹ:
בָּרוּךְ אַתָּה יְהוָֹה, יוֹצֵר הַמְּאוֹרוֹת.

Hashem, Your love for us is so great, and You are so kind to us. Our Father and King, our ancestors trusted in You and You taught them how to live. Teach us the same and care for us like You cared for them.

"One who learns so they can teach, will get the opportunity to learn and teach. One who learns so they can do, will get the opportunity to learn, teach, keep, and do."

(Pirkei Avot 4:6)

Which do you think is most important, learning, teaching, or doing?

"Love and giving always come together."

How has Hashem shown His love for you in your life? How has He shown it today?

How do you show Hashem you love Him? How will you show it today?

אַהֲבַת עוֹלָם אֲהַבְתָּנוּ, יְהֹוָה אֱלֹהֵינוּ
חֶמְלָה גְדוֹלָה וִיתֵרָה חָמַלְתָּ עָלֵינוּ.
אָבִינוּ מַלְכֵּנוּ
בַּעֲבוּר שִׁמְךָ הַגָּדוֹל
וּבַעֲבוּר אֲבוֹתֵינוּ שֶׁבָּטְחוּ בָךְ
וַתְּלַמְּדֵמוֹ חֻקֵּי חַיִּים
לַעֲשׂוֹת רְצוֹנְךָ בְּלֵבָב שָׁלֵם
כֵּן תְּחָנֵּנוּ אָבִינוּ, אָב הָרַחֲמָן
הַמְרַחֵם, רַחֵם נָא עָלֵינוּ
וְתֵן בְּלִבֵּנוּ בִּינָה לְהָבִין, לְהַשְׂכִּיל
לִשְׁמֹעַ, לִלְמֹד וּלְלַמֵּד
לִשְׁמֹר וְלַעֲשׂוֹת וּלְקַיֵּם
אֶת כָּל דִּבְרֵי תַלְמוּד תּוֹרָתֶךָ בְּאַהֲבָה.

Bring us from the four corners of the earth in peace, and lead us proudly to our land.

On January 12, 2010, a massive earthquake struck the poor nation of Haiti in the Caribbean. Over 320,000 people lost their lives and a million people were left homeless. Two days later two El Al 747 jets brought a 220-strong team of volunteers, doctors, and soldiers from Israel to help care for the people of Haiti. A week later an additional team from the IDF arrived in Haiti and set up a field hospital to treat the injured. During its stay in Haiti, the Israeli team treated well over a thousand patients, performed 319 successful surgeries, and delivered 16 healthy babies. The mother of the first of the babies to be born in the hospital was so grateful to Israel, that she decided to name her newborn son "Israel."

"לִבִּי בַמִּזְרָח
וְאָנֹכִי בְּסוֹף מַעֲרָב"

Why do you think we ask Hashem to bring us back to Eretz Yisrael in a *tefilla* about Hashem's love for us?

וְהָאֵר עֵינֵינוּ בְּתוֹרָתֶךָ וְדַבֵּק לִבֵּנוּ בְּמִצְוֹתֶיךָ
וְיַחֵד לְבָבֵנוּ לְאַהֲבָה וּלְיִרְאָה אֶת שְׁמֶךָ.
לֹא נֵבוֹשׁ וְלֹא נִכָּלֵם וְלֹא נִכָּשֵׁל לְעוֹלָם וָעֶד
כִּי בְשֵׁם קָדְשְׁךָ הַגָּדוֹל הַגִּבּוֹר וְהַנּוֹרָא בָּטָחְנוּ
נָגִילָה וְנִשְׂמְחָה בִּישׁוּעָתֶךָ.
וְרַחֲמֶיךָ יְהוָֹה אֱלֹהֵינוּ וַחֲסָדֶיךָ הָרַבִּים
אַל יַעַזְבוּנוּ נֶצַח סֶלָה וָעֶד.

At this point if you are wearing צִיצִית *or a* טַלִּית *you should gather the* צִיצִיּוֹת *together in preparation for the* שְׁמַע.

מַהֵר וְהָבֵא עָלֵינוּ בְּרָכָה וְשָׁלוֹם
מְהֵרָה מֵאַרְבַּע כַּנְפוֹת כָּל הָאָרֶץ
וּשְׁבוֹר עֹל הַגּוֹיִם מֵעַל צַוָּארֵנוּ
וְהוֹלִיכֵנוּ מְהֵרָה קוֹמְמִיּוּת לְאַרְצֵנוּ.
כִּי אֵל פּוֹעֵל יְשׁוּעוֹת אָתָּה
וּבָנוּ בָחַרְתָּ מִכָּל עַם וְלָשׁוֹן
וְקֵרַבְתָּנוּ מַלְכֵּנוּ לְשִׁמְךָ הַגָּדוֹל בְּאַהֲבָה
לְהוֹדוֹת לְךָ וּלְיַחֶדְךָ, לְיִרְאָה וּלְאַהֲבָה אֶת שְׁמֶךָ.
בָּרוּךְ אַתָּה יְהוָֹה, הַבּוֹחֵר בְּעַמּוֹ יִשְׂרָאֵל בְּאַהֲבָה.

Listen, Israel: Hashem is our God, Hashem is the only One. You should love Hashem with all your heart and soul and strength. The words that I, Hashem, am telling you today should be in your heart. You should teach them to your children, speak about them when you are at home and when you are out, when you go to sleep and when you wake up. You should place them into the tefillin on your arm and head, and in the mezuza on your door.

"The Persian ruler Arvadan sent a precious pearl to his friend Rav as a gift, and asked him to send something equally precious in return. Rav sent his friend a mezuza. Arvadan sent him a message back saying, 'I sent you something priceless and you sent me something that can be bought in the market for just a coin.' Rav replied to him, 'None of your possessions or mine is equal to its value. You sent me something I need to look after, but I sent you something that looks after you!'"

It is a special מִצְוָה to say the שְׁמַע every morning and evening.
Say the first verse aloud while covering your eyes
with your right hand. Say line 3 quietly to yourself.

שְׁמַע יִשְׂרָאֵל
יְהֹוָה אֱלֹהֵינוּ, יְהֹוָה ׀ אֶחָד:

בָּרוּךְ שֵׁם כְּבוֹד מַלְכוּתוֹ לְעוֹלָם וָעֶד.

וְאָהַבְתָּ אֵת יְהֹוָה אֱלֹהֶיךָ, בְּכָל־לְבָבְךָ וּבְכָל־נַפְשְׁךָ וּבְכָל־
מְאֹדֶךָ: וְהָיוּ הַדְּבָרִים הָאֵלֶּה, אֲשֶׁר אָנֹכִי מְצַוְּךָ הַיּוֹם,
עַל־לְבָבֶךָ: וְשִׁנַּנְתָּם לְבָנֶיךָ וְדִבַּרְתָּ בָּם, בְּשִׁבְתְּךָ בְּבֵיתֶךָ
וּבְלֶכְתְּךָ בַדֶּרֶךְ, וּבְשָׁכְבְּךָ וּבְקוּמֶךָ: וּקְשַׁרְתָּם לְאוֹת עַל־יָדֶךָ
וְהָיוּ לְטֹטָפֹת בֵּין עֵינֶיךָ: וּכְתַבְתָּם עַל־מְזֻזוֹת בֵּיתֶךָ וּבִשְׁעָרֶיךָ:

If you listen to My mitzvot, which I am commanding you today, to love Hashem and worship Me with all your heart and soul, then I will give you enough rain to farm the land and grow your crops, and feed your animals. And you will eat and be full.

"Every Friday afternoon Rabbi Yehoshua ben Levi would learn Torah with his grandson. One week, he forgot and went instead to the special healing hot pools of Teveria. When he suddenly remembered that he had not learned with his grandson that day he ran out of the pools to return to him. When Rabbi Ḥiyya questioned this he replied to him, 'Ḥiyya, learning with a child may seem unimportant to you, but listening to one's grandson reading Torah is like listening to the Torah on Mount Sinai!'"

"If you want to save the Jewish future, you have to build Jewish schools."

Why do you think the Torah values education so highly?

וְהָיָה אִם־שָׁמֹעַ תִּשְׁמְעוּ אֶל־מִצְוֹתַי אֲשֶׁר אָנֹכִי מְצַוֶּה
אֶתְכֶם הַיּוֹם, לְאַהֲבָה אֶת־יְהֹוָה אֱלֹהֵיכֶם וּלְעָבְדוֹ, בְּכָל
לְבַבְכֶם וּבְכָל־נַפְשְׁכֶם: וְנָתַתִּי מְטַר־אַרְצְכֶם בְּעִתּוֹ, יוֹרֶה
וּמַלְקוֹשׁ, וְאָסַפְתָּ דְגָנֶךָ וְתִירֹשְׁךָ וְיִצְהָרֶךָ: וְנָתַתִּי עֵשֶׂב בְּשָׂדְךָ
לִבְהֶמְתֶּךָ, וְאָכַלְתָּ וְשָׂבָעְתָּ: הִשָּׁמְרוּ לָכֶם פֶּן־יִפְתֶּה לְבַבְכֶם,
וְסַרְתֶּם וַעֲבַדְתֶּם אֱלֹהִים אֲחֵרִים וְהִשְׁתַּחֲוִיתֶם לָהֶם: וְחָרָה
אַף־יְהֹוָה בָּכֶם, וְעָצַר אֶת־הַשָּׁמַיִם וְלֹא־יִהְיֶה מָטָר, וְהָאֲדָמָה
לֹא תִתֵּן אֶת־יְבוּלָהּ, וַאֲבַדְתֶּם מְהֵרָה מֵעַל הָאָרֶץ הַטֹּבָה
אֲשֶׁר יְהֹוָה נֹתֵן לָכֶם: וְשַׂמְתֶּם אֶת־דְּבָרַי אֵלֶּה עַל־לְבַבְכֶם
10 וְעַל־נַפְשְׁכֶם, וּקְשַׁרְתֶּם אֹתָם לְאוֹת עַל־יֶדְכֶם, וְהָיוּ
11 לְטוֹטָפֹת בֵּין עֵינֵיכֶם: וְלִמַּדְתֶּם אֹתָם אֶת־בְּנֵיכֶם לְדַבֵּר
12 בָּם, בְּשִׁבְתְּךָ בְּבֵיתֶךָ וּבְלֶכְתְּךָ בַדֶּרֶךְ, וּבְשָׁכְבְּךָ וּבְקוּמֶךָ:
13 וּכְתַבְתָּם עַל מְזוּזוֹת בֵּיתֶךָ וּבִשְׁעָרֶיךָ: לְמַעַן יִרְבּוּ
14 יְמֵיכֶם וִימֵי בְנֵיכֶם עַל הָאֲדָמָה אֲשֶׁר נִשְׁבַּע יְהֹוָה לַאֲבֹתֵיכֶם
15 לָתֵת לָהֶם, כִּימֵי הַשָּׁמַיִם עַל־הָאָרֶץ:

I am Hashem your God who took you out of the land of Egypt, to be your God. I am Hashem your God.

When I was a little boy in Russia it was forbidden to practice mitzvot. My family observed as many as we could in secret. One day in school, the principal and the school nurse announced that we would have to receive immunization shots that day. I began to shake and sweat… when the nurse lifted my shirt to give me the shot she would see my tzitzit, and report this to the principal. This would most likely be terrible news for me and my family, and my father and I could even end up in jail in Siberia. When it was my turn I tried to hide my tzitzit the best I could but I was sure the nurse saw them even though she didn't say anything. The next day I was called into her office and I was sure that this was the end for me. She closed the door behind me and gently asked: "Are they tzitzit or tefillin?" I was speechless. She explained to me that she was Jewish and remembers her grandfather wearing a similar garment, and hearing about tzitzit and tefillin. She told me she was inspired by my courage and if I ever needed help to come to her.

Can your clothes send a message? Who is the message to? What message are they sending today?

If you are wearing צִיצִית pass them before your eyes and kiss them when you say the words וּרְאִיתֶם אֹתוֹ and kiss them and then pass them before your eyes when you say the word עֵינֵיכֶם.

וַיֹּאמֶר יְהֹוָה אֶל־מֹשֶׁה לֵּאמֹר: דַּבֵּר אֶל־בְּנֵי יִשְׂרָאֵל וְאָמַרְתָּ אֲלֵהֶם, וְעָשׂוּ לָהֶם צִיצִת עַל־כַּנְפֵי בִגְדֵיהֶם לְדֹרֹתָם, וְנָתְנוּ עַל־צִיצִת הַכָּנָף פְּתִיל תְּכֵלֶת: וְהָיָה לָכֶם לְצִיצִת, וּרְאִיתֶם אֹתוֹ וּזְכַרְתֶּם אֶת־כָּל־מִצְוֹת יְהֹוָה וַעֲשִׂיתֶם אֹתָם, וְלֹא תָתֻורוּ אַחֲרֵי לְבַבְכֶם וְאַחֲרֵי עֵינֵיכֶם, אֲשֶׁר־אַתֶּם זֹנִים אַחֲרֵיהֶם: לְמַעַן תִּזְכְּרוּ וַעֲשִׂיתֶם אֶת־כָּל־מִצְוֹתָי, וִהְיִיתֶם קְדֹשִׁים לֵאלֹהֵיכֶם: אֲנִי יְהֹוָה אֱלֹהֵיכֶם, אֲשֶׁר הוֹצֵאתִי אֶתְכֶם מֵאֶרֶץ מִצְרַיִם, לִהְיוֹת לָכֶם לֵאלֹהִים, אֲנִי יְהֹוָה אֱלֹהֵיכֶם:

אֱמֶת

יְהֹוָה אֱלֹהֵיכֶם אֱמֶת

There once was a simple man called Yankele, whose job it was to stand in the village train station and wave a lantern to direct approaching trains to the correct track. One night there was a terrible train crash, with many people injured. A court was established to investigate what had happened. The judge called Yankele to the stand and asked him to his face, under oath, "Yankele, did you wave the lantern to warn the train?" Yankele, looking scared, hesitated, and finally, trembling, answered, "Yes. Yes, I waved my lantern." Yankele and the train company were cleared of all wrongdoing. But Yankele left the courthouse pale and still trembling. The station manager asked him, "Why do you look so sad? This is a happy day, the company has been cleared of all wrongdoing." Yankele couldn't even speak. The manager looked into Yankele's eyes and asked him, "Yankele, did you lie to the judge? Did you fall asleep and fail to wave your lantern?" Yankele began to weep. "No. I didn't lie," he cried. "I waved my lantern… but the lantern… it wasn't lit."

Did Yankele tell the truth in court? Do you think there can be a difference between fact and truth?

What is true about Hashem?

Can you describe Hashem? Can anyone?

Try it – what can you say about Hashem?

וְיַצִּיב, וְנָכוֹן וְקַיָּם, וְיָשָׁר וְנֶאֱמָן
וְאָהוּב וְחָבִיב, וְנֶחְמָד וְנָעִים
וְנוֹרָא וְאַדִּיר, וּמְתֻקָּן וּמְקֻבָּל
וְטוֹב וְיָפֶה
הַדָּבָר הַזֶּה עָלֵינוּ לְעוֹלָם וָעֶד.

אֱמֶת אֱלֹהֵי עוֹלָם מַלְכֵּנוּ
צוּר יַעֲקֹב מָגֵן יִשְׁעֵנוּ
לְדוֹר וָדוֹר הוּא קַיָּם וּשְׁמוֹ קַיָּם
וְכִסְאוֹ נָכוֹן
וּמַלְכוּתוֹ וֶאֱמוּנָתוֹ לָעַד קַיֶּמֶת

If you are wearing צִיצִית *kiss them at the word* לָעַד.

וּדְבָרָיו חַיִּים וְקַיָּמִים
וְנֶאֱמָנִים וְנֶחֱמָדִים
לָעַד וּלְעוֹלְמֵי עוֹלָמִים
עַל אֲבוֹתֵינוּ, עָלֵינוּ
וְעַל בָּנֵינוּ וְעַל דּוֹרוֹתֵינוּ
וְעַל כָּל דּוֹרוֹת זֶרַע יִשְׂרָאֵל עֲבָדֶיךָ

זְכֹר לְאַבְרָהָם לְיִצְחָק וּלְיִשְׂרָאֵל עֲבָדֶיךָ, אֲשֶׁר נִשְׁבַּעְתָּ לָהֶם בָּךְ, וַתְּדַבֵּר אֲלֵהֶם, אַרְבֶּה אֶת־זַרְעֲכֶם כְּכוֹכְבֵי הַשָּׁמָיִם, וְכָל־הָאָרֶץ הַזֹּאת אֲשֶׁר אָמַרְתִּי, אֶתֵּן לְזַרְעֲכֶם, וְנָחֲלוּ לְעֹלָם. (Shemot 32:13)

Why do you think we remind Hashem of His relationship with our ancestors? How does this help us?

Why is it important for us to know about who our ancestors were?

כַּבֵּד אֶת־אָבִיךָ וְאֶת־אִמֶּךָ. (Shemot 20:12)

Why do you think there is a special commandment to honor and love your parents?

עַל הָרִאשׁוֹנִים וְעַל הָאַחֲרוֹנִים
דָּבָר טוֹב וְקַיָּם
בֶּאֱמֶת וּבֶאֱמוּנָה, חֹק וְלֹא יַעֲבֹר.
אֱמֶת שָׁאַתָּה הוּא יְהֹוָה
אֱלֹהֵינוּ וֵאלֹהֵי אֲבוֹתֵינוּ
מַלְכֵּנוּ מֶלֶךְ אֲבוֹתֵינוּ
גּוֹאֲלֵנוּ גּוֹאֵל אֲבוֹתֵינוּ
יוֹצְרֵנוּ צוּר יְשׁוּעָתֵנוּ
פּוֹדֵנוּ וּמַצִּילֵנוּ מֵעוֹלָם הוּא שְׁמֶךָ
וְאֵין לָנוּ עוֹד אֱלֹהִים זוּלָתְךָ
סֶלָה.

עֶזְרַת אֲבוֹתֵינוּ אַתָּה הוּא מֵעוֹלָם
מָגֵן וּמוֹשִׁיעַ לָהֶם וְלִבְנֵיהֶם אַחֲרֵיהֶם
בְּכָל דּוֹר וָדוֹר.
בְּרוּם עוֹלָם מוֹשָׁבֶךָ
וּמִשְׁפָּטֶיךָ וְצִדְקָתְךָ עַד אַפְסֵי אָרֶץ.

אֱמֶת אַשְׁרֵי אִישׁ שֶׁיִּשְׁמַע לְמִצְוֹתֶיךָ
וְתוֹרָתְךָ וּדְבָרְךָ יָשִׂים עַל לִבּוֹ.

There once was a man that fell off the side of a ship into the ocean. The crew of the ship went into action mode, and devised a plan to rescue him. First they threw him a life saver. But the man shouted up at them, "Don't worry. I believe that God will save me," and he didn't take it. Then they sent a life boat to pick him up, but he refused to climb up onto the boat, telling them, "Don't worry. I believe that God will save me." Finally they called for a helicopter to come and rescue him, but he refused to climb on to the ladder dangling from it. "Don't worry," he said. "I believe that God will save me." Finally the man drowned, and went to heaven. When he got there, he was angry with God. "I had total faith in You that You would rescue me, but You abandoned me!" he said to God. God replied, "My son, I sent you a life saver, and then a life boat, and then a helicopter. But you refused to see My hand in them."

לֹא תַטֶּה מִשְׁפַּט גֵּר יָתוֹם וְלֹא תַחֲבֹל בֶּגֶד אַלְמָנָה. וְזָכַרְתָּ כִּי עֶבֶד הָיִיתָ בְּמִצְרַיִם וַיִּפְדְּךָ יְהוָֹה אֱלֹהֶיךָ מִשָּׁם עַל־כֵּן אָנֹכִי מְצַוְּךָ לַעֲשׂוֹת אֶת־הַדָּבָר הַזֶּה.

(Devarim 24:17–18)

Why do you think we take so much time talking about and remembering our experiences in Egypt?

35 אֱמֶת שָׁאַתָּה הוּא אָדוֹן לְעַמֶּךָ

36 וּמֶלֶךְ גִּבּוֹר לָרִיב רִיבָם לְאָבוֹת וּבָנִים.

37 אֱמֶת אַתָּה הוּא רִאשׁוֹן וְאַתָּה הוּא אַחֲרוֹן

38 וּמִבַּלְעָדֶיךָ אֵין לָנוּ מֶלֶךְ גּוֹאֵל וּמוֹשִׁיעַ.

39 אֱמֶת מִמִּצְרַיִם גְּאַלְתָּנוּ, יְהוָה אֱלֹהֵינוּ

40 מִבֵּית עֲבָדִים פְּדִיתָנוּ

41 כָּל בְּכוֹרֵיהֶם הָרַגְתָּ, וּבְכוֹרְךָ יִשְׂרָאֵל גָּאָלְתָּ

42 וְיַם סוּף לָהֶם בָּקַעְתָּ, וְזֵדִים טִבַּעְתָּ

43 וִידִידִים עָבְרוּ יָם

44 וַיְכַסּוּ־מַיִם צָרֵיהֶם, אֶחָד מֵהֶם לֹא נוֹתָר:

45 עַל זֹאת שִׁבְּחוּ אֲהוּבִים וְרוֹמְמוּ לָאֵל

46 וְנָתְנוּ יְדִידִים זְמִירוֹת, שִׁירוֹת וְתִשְׁבָּחוֹת

47 בְּרָכוֹת וְהוֹדָאוֹת לַמֶּלֶךְ אֵל חַי וְקַיָּם

48 רָם וְנִשָּׂא, גָּדוֹל וְנוֹרָא

49 מַשְׁפִּיל גֵּאִים עֲדֵי אָרֶץ, מַגְבִּיהַּ שְׁפָלִים עַד מָרוֹם

50 מוֹצִיא אֲסִירִים, פּוֹדֶה עֲנָוִים, עוֹזֵר דַּלִּים

51 הָעוֹנֶה לְעַמּוֹ יִשְׂרָאֵל בְּעֵת שַׁוְּעָם אֵלָיו.

Hashem You are our Rock! Please rise up and help Israel, Your people, as You promised and bring the Mashiaḥ!

Rabbi Dov Ber of Radoshitz was once traveling on a road when it became dark, so he stopped for the night at an inn. In the morning he looked for the inn keeper, to ask him about the wondrous clock that was found hanging on the wall of his room. "But that's just an ordinary clock like any other," replied the inn keeper. "No, no," said Reb Dov Ber. "This is a very special clock. Please find out from where you bought it." And so, out of curiosity, the inn keeper made some enquiries, and returned with some information. "This clock," the inn keeper announced, "once belonged to the famous Ḥozeh of Lublin, the famous Hasidic master." "Of course. I should have known. This clock could only have ever belonged to the Ḥozeh," Reb Dov Ber said. "Ordinary clocks strike a sad tone each hour, telling of another hour passed, another hour lost. But the Ḥozeh's clock has a sweet tone each hour, singing in celebration as we are another hour closer to the Mashiaḥ!"

Why is one of Hashem's names צוּר יִשְׂרָאֵל? What does God have in common with a rock?

How might this and the other ideas contained in these *tefillot* help us prepare to stand before Hashem and say the Amida?

At this point you should stand in preparation for the עֲמִידָה.

52 תְּהִלּוֹת לְאֵל עֶלְיוֹן גּוֹאֲלָם
53 בָּרוּךְ הוּא וּמְבֹרָךְ
54 מֹשֶׁה וּבְנֵי יִשְׂרָאֵל
55 לְךָ עָנוּ שִׁירָה בְּשִׂמְחָה רַבָּה
56 וְאָמְרוּ כֻלָּם
57 מִי־כָמֹכָה בָּאֵלִם, יְהֹוָה
58 מִי כָּמֹכָה נֶאְדָּר בַּקֹּדֶשׁ
59 נוֹרָא תְהִלֹּת, עֹשֵׂה פֶלֶא:
60 שִׁירָה חֲדָשָׁה שִׁבְּחוּ גְאוּלִים
61 לְשִׁמְךָ הַגָּדוֹל עַל שְׂפַת הַיָּם
62 יַחַד כֻּלָּם הוֹדוּ וְהִמְלִיכוּ
63 וְאָמְרוּ
64 יְהֹוָה יִמְלֹךְ לְעֹלָם וָעֶד:
65 צוּר יִשְׂרָאֵל, קוּמָה בְּעֶזְרַת יִשְׂרָאֵל
66 וּנְאֻם
67 גֹּאֲלֵנוּ יְהֹוָה צְבָאוֹת שְׁמוֹ, קְדוֹשׁ יִשְׂרָאֵל:
68 בָּרוּךְ אַתָּה יְהֹוָה, גָּאַל יִשְׂרָאֵל.

You are Avraham's, Yitzḥak's, and Yaakov's God, the great, powerful, and breathtaking God, the God of heaven, who acts with kindness, and You created everything. You remember the lives of our ancestors, and will lovingly bring Mashiaḥ to us their descendants. **Hashem, You are the Source of all blessing, who is the Protector of Avraham and his descendants.**

"Your house should be a place where the sages meet. Sit at their feet in the dust, and drink in their words with thirst." (Pirkei Avot 1:4)

Who are your role models?

How and why would you like to be like them?

"Avraham Avinu would bring people into his home and give them food and drink. He would be kind and loving to them and become friends with them, so that they would become interested in the Torah and in being close to Hashem. This is what the Torah means when it says that they, 'made souls in Ḥaran' (Bereshit 12:5), *teaching us that when a person brings another close to Hashem it is like he created them."*

The עֲמִידָה is the climax of our תְּפִלָּה, where we stand before Hashem and open our hearts in prayer. You should mouth the words of the עֲמִידָה but without a sound. We learn this from the prayer of Ḥanna when she prayed to have a child. Some take three steps forward now. Say the עֲמִידָה while standing with your feet together.

1 אֲדֹנָי, שְׂפָתַי תִּפְתָּח, וּפִי יַגִּיד תְּהִלָּתֶךָ:

2 בָּרוּךְ אַתָּה יְהֹוָה

3 אֱלֹהֵינוּ וֵאלֹהֵי אֲבוֹתֵינוּ

4 אֱלֹהֵי אַבְרָהָם, אֱלֹהֵי יִצְחָק, וֵאלֹהֵי יַעֲקֹב

5 הָאֵל הַגָּדוֹל הַגִּבּוֹר וְהַנּוֹרָא, אֵל עֶלְיוֹן

6 גּוֹמֵל חֲסָדִים טוֹבִים, קוֹנֵה הַכֹּל

7 וְזוֹכֵר חַסְדֵי אָבוֹת

8 וּמֵבִיא גוֹאֵל לִבְנֵי בְנֵיהֶם לְמַעַן שְׁמוֹ בְּאַהֲבָה.

Between Rosh HaShana and Yom Kippur add these words:

9 זָכְרֵנוּ לְחַיִּים, מֶלֶךְ חָפֵץ בַּחַיִּים כָּתְבֵנוּ בְּסֵפֶר חַיִּים, לְמַעַנְךָ אֱלֹהִים חַיִּים.

10 מֶלֶךְ עוֹזֵר וּמוֹשִׁיעַ וּמָגֵן.

11 בָּרוּךְ אַתָּה יְהֹוָה

12 מָגֵן אַבְרָהָם.

Hashem, You are forever powerful. You make the winds blow and the rains fall. You are kind to provide for all living things. You give life to those who are dying, You support those who are falling, You heal those that are sick, and You free those that are imprisoned.

Hashem, You are the Source of all blessing, who gives life to those who died.

"Once it happened that it didn't rain for almost the whole of winter in Eretz Yisrael. The people were desperate and so they sent for Ḥoni to whom they knew Hashem would listen. Ḥoni drew a circle with a stick in the dirt and cried out to Hashem: 'Hashem, have mercy on Your children and let it rain. I won't leave this circle until You do!' At once a few drops of rain began to fall but nothing more than a drizzle. Ḥoni cried out to Hashem again: 'I didn't pray to You for rain like this. Your children need real rain that will fill their wells and reservoirs.' Immediately torrents of rain began to pour, threatening to flood the towns and villages. Once again Ḥoni cried to Hashem, 'I didn't pray to You, Hashem, for rain like this. This rain will destroy the world! Your children need rain of love and kindness.' Finally the rains calmed to a normal level, and the people were saved."

To life, to life, לְחַיִּים!

How does Hashem bring life to the world every day?

1 אַתָּה גִּבּוֹר לְעוֹלָם, אֲדֹנָי

2 מְחַיֵּה מֵתִים אַתָּה, רַב לְהוֹשִׁיעַ

Between Simḥat Torah and Pesaḥ add these words:

3 מַשִּׁיב הָרְוּחַ וּמוֹרִיד הַגֶּשֶׁם

Between Pesaḥ and Shemini Atzeret add these words:

מוֹרִיד הַטָּל

4 מְכַלְכֵּל חַיִּים בְּחֶסֶד, מְחַיֵּה מֵתִים בְּרַחֲמִים רַבִּים

5 סוֹמֵךְ נוֹפְלִים, וְרוֹפֵא חוֹלִים, וּמַתִּיר אֲסוּרִים

6 וּמְקַיֵּם אֱמוּנָתוֹ לִישֵׁנֵי עָפָר.

7 מִי כָמְוֹךָ, בַּעַל גְּבוּרוֹת

8 וּמִי דְּוֹמֶה לָּךְ

9 מֶלֶךְ, מֵמִית וּמְחַיֶּה וּמַצְמְיחַ יְשׁוּעָה.

Between Rosh HaShana and Yom Kippur add these words:

10 מִי כָמְוֹךָ אָב הָרַחֲמָן, זוֹכֵר יְצוּרָיו בְּרַחֲמִים לְחַיִּים.

11 וְנֶאֱמָן אַתָּה לְהַחֲיוֹת מֵתִים.

12 בָּרוּךְ אַתָּה יְהֹוָה

13 **מְחַיֵּה הַמֵּתִים.**

You are so holy, and Your name is also holy, and holy people praise You every day!

Hashem, You are the Source of all blessing, the holy God.

וַיֹּאמֶר אֵלָיו, מַה שְּׁמֶךָ;
וַיֹּאמֶר, יַעֲקֹב.
וַיֹּאמֶר, לֹא יַעֲקֹב יֵאָמֵר עוֹד שִׁמְךָ
כִּי, אִם יִשְׂרָאֵל: כִּי שָׂרִיתָ עִם
אֱלֹהִים וְעִם אֲנָשִׁים, וַתּוּכָל.

(Bereshit 32:28–29)

What's in a name?
Just as our names represent who we are, Hashem's name helps us understand who He is.

What names do you have? What can others learn about you from these names?

What can we learn about Hashem from His names?

The Bobover Rebbe was famous for his ḥesed and love of all Jews. One year on Kol Nidrei night, a survivor of the Holocaust walked into his shul. He was weak and looked ill, and the rebbe soon found out that his voice box had been removed due to a serious illness. He couldn't even lift his voice in prayer. When the rebbe took the Sefer Torah out of the ark, and passed the silent man, the rebbe embraced him and the Sefer Torah at the same time, creating a circle of holiness. The rebbe, the Sefer Torah, and the man. They both began to weep, as the rebbe felt the man's pain, and gave it a voice.

1 אַתָּה קָדוֹשׁ וְשִׁמְךָ קָדוֹשׁ

2 וּקְדוֹשִׁים בְּכָל יוֹם יְהַלְלוּךָ סֶּלָה.

3 בָּרוּךְ אַתָּה יְהֹוָה

4 הָאֵל הַקָּדוֹשׁ.

Between Rosh HaShana and Yom Kippur change the ending of this בְּרָכָה *to these words:*

הַמֶּלֶךְ הַקָּדוֹשׁ.

You give people knowledge, and teach humanity understanding because You are kind. You are kind to share with us Your knowledge, understanding, and intelligence. **Hashem, You are the Source of all blessing, who kindly gives knowledge.**

"Who is a wise person? Someone who learns from everyone."
(Pirkei Avot 4:1)

Where does wisdom come from?

What will you do today to become wise?

"In a faraway land the king wanted to honor his most loyal minister with a gift. He asked the minister to choose whatever his heart desired. The minister thought to himself, 'If I ask for silver and gold then that will be all I will receive. If I ask for precious stones and pearls, then that will be all I receive. But if I ask to marry the king's daughter then eventually I will receive all of the king's riches when I become king!' Similarly, when Hashem promised Shlomo HaMelekh that he could have whatever he wished, he thought to himself, 'If I ask for riches then that will be all I receive. But if I ask for wisdom, then that will ultimately include everything else!'"

אַתָּה חוֹנֵן לְאָדָם דַּעַת
וּמְלַמֵּד לֶאֱנוֹשׁ בִּינָה.
וְחָנֵּנוּ מֵאִתְּךָ חָכְמָה בִּינָה וָדָעַת.
בָּרוּךְ אַתָּה יְהֹוָה

חוֹנֵן הַדָּעַת.

Our Father, bring us back to Your Torah, and close to Your service, our King. Lead us back to You in sincere teshuva. **Hashem, You are the Source of all blessing, who wants teshuva.**

"There once was a king who invited all of his servants to a magnificent banquet. But he forgot to write on the invitation the exact date and time. No one was brave enough to point this out to him and so no one knew when to prepare themselves for the feast. Those who were wise prepared themselves immediately for the banquet and remained close to the palace. But the foolish among the servants did not prepare themselves. Suddenly the king called for the banquet to begin, and all the clever servants were ready to enter in their finest clothes, while the foolish were in their everyday work clothes, and embarrassed to enter the palace. When the king saw that they had come dressed so disrespectfully he was disappointed and made them stand and watch while the wise servants sat and ate and enjoyed the wonderful feast. The Rabbis tell us this is why we must do teshuva every day, because we never know when Hashem will call us before Him to judge us."

אָבִינוּ מַלְכֵּנוּ, חָטָאנוּ לְפָנֶיךָ.

Why do you think we refer to Hashem as a Parent and a King in this *berakha*?

הֲשִׁיבֵנוּ אָבִינוּ לְתוֹרָתֶךָ
וְקָרְבֵנוּ מַלְכֵּנוּ לַעֲבוֹדָתֶךָ
וְהַחֲזִירֵנוּ בִּתְשׁוּבָה שְׁלֵמָה לְפָנֶיךָ.
בָּרוּךְ אַתָּה יְהֹוָה

הָרוֹצֶה בִּתְשׁוּבָה.

Forgive us, Hashem our Father, we have sinned.
Pardon us, our King.

Hashem, You are the Source of all blessing, who keeps forgiving.

What do you need to say sorry for today?

Who do you need to say sorry to today?

"At first, I wanted to change the world. I tried, but the world did not change. Then I tried to change my town, but the town did not change. Then I tried to change my family, but my family did not change. Then I realized: first, I must change myself."

Some people gently tap the left side of your chest with your right fist when you say the words חָטָאנוּ and פָּשָׁעְנוּ, two different words for sin. This helps us experience feeling sorry for our sins.

1 סְלַח לָנוּ אָבִינוּ כִּי חָטָאנוּ

2 מְחוֹל לָנוּ מַלְכֵּנוּ כִּי פָּשָׁעְנוּ

3 כִּי אֵל טוֹב וְסַלָּח אָתָּה.

4 בָּרוּךְ אַתָּה יְהֹוָה

5 חַנּוּן הַמַּרְבֶּה לִסְלֹחַ.

Please, Hashem, see the difficulties we have in our life, and stand up for us.

Hashem, You are the Source of all blessing, who saves Israel.

When the British controlled the Land of Israel, before the State of Israel was created, there were many Jewish fighters in British jails. Rabbi Aryeh Levine, the famous rabbi of Jerusalem, would visit the prisoners each Shabbat, to comfort them and send their messages to their families. One snowy Shabbat morning in the winter of 1937, Reb Aryeh stopped a stranger he met in the street on the way home from the prison and asked for his help. He explained to him that he had messages for the families of 25 Jewish prisoners. Normally he would deliver all the messages immediately, but this Shabbat, due to the heavy snow, he would not be able to. "Would you memorize the names and addresses of five families," asked Reb Aryeh, "and after Shabbat I will return for them." Of course the man agreed. A few years later this man too was arrested by the British and thrown into that very same jail and his wife and family had no idea where he was. On his next visit to the prison, Reb Aryeh recognized the man instantly, and immediately ran to inform his family. When the man was eventually freed, before even going home, he went directly to visit Reb Aryeh to thank him for his kindness and share his good news. When Reb Aryeh saw him, they hugged tightly, and Reb Aryeh made him promise that he could be the one to give his family the good news!

1 רְאֵה נָא בְעָנְיֵנוּ, וְרִיבָה רִיבֵנוּ
2 וּמַהֵר לְגָאֳלֵנוּ גְּאֻלָּה שְׁלֵמָה לְמַעַן שְׁמֶךָ
3 כִּי אֵל גּוֹאֵל חָזָק אָתָּה.
4 בָּרוּךְ אַתָּה יְהֹוָה
5 גּוֹאֵל יִשְׂרָאֵל.

Heal us Hashem, and help us to be healthy.

Hashem, You are the Source of all blessing, who heals sick people.

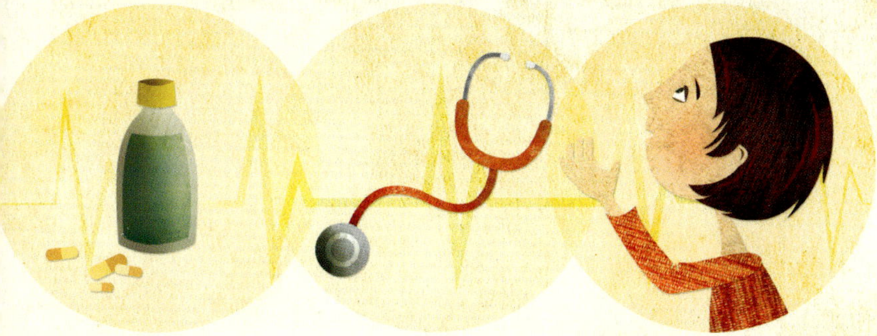

"Judaism sees the doctor as Hashem's messenger."

Who makes us healthy? What different roles do Hashem, doctors, and ourselves play?

A friend of Rabbi Aryeh Levine once came to visit him crying and upset because his son was dangerously ill and in the hospital. The father pleaded with Reb Aryeh to pray on behalf of his son. Reb Aryeh reassured him, "Of course I will, and do not despair, there is a Master Physician in heaven. I believe your son will fully recover." Sometime after this, when the boy's father arrived to visit his son who was on the road to recovery, the doctor asked him who was the old man that visits his son every morning at 5:00 AM. The father had no idea Reb Aryeh came every morning to visit and pray for his son.

1 רְפָאֵנוּ יְהֹוָה וְנֵרָפֵא

2 הוֹשִׁיעֵנוּ וְנִוָּשֵׁעָה, כִּי תְהִלָּתֵנוּ אָתָּה

3 וְהַעֲלֵה אֲרוּכָה וּמַרְפֵּא לְכָל תַּחֲלוּאֵינוּ

4 וּלְכָל מַכְאוֹבֵינוּ וּלְכָל מַכּוֹתֵינוּ

Add these words if there is a specific person you would like to pray for who is sick:

5 יְהִי רָצוֹן מִלְּפָנֶיךָ יְהֹוָה אֱלֹהַי וֵאלֹהֵי אֲבוֹתַי

6 שֶׁתִּשְׁלַח מְהֵרָה רְפוּאָה שְׁלֵמָה מִן הַשָּׁמַיִם

7 רְפוּאַת הַנֶּפֶשׁ וּרְפוּאַת הַגּוּף

8 לַחוֹלֶה/לַחוֹלָה (*name*)

9 בֶּן/בַּת (*name of their mother*)

10 בְּתוֹךְ שְׁאָר חוֹלֵי יִשְׂרָאֵל.

11 כִּי אֵל רוֹפֵא רַחֲמָן וְנֶאֱמָן אָתָּה.

12 בָּרוּךְ אַתָּה יְהֹוָה

13 **רוֹפֵא חוֹלֵי עַמּוֹ יִשְׂרָאֵל.**

Hashem, bless this year for us. Make it a very successful year and help the land provide the food we need.

Hashem, You are the Source of all blessing, who provides blessings.

There once was a drought, and the people of the town had no water to drink. The Rabbi called everyone together to pray for rain. The people came together and cried out with emotion and sincerity to ask Hashem to send the rains they so desperately needed. A small girl tugged on her father's hand and asked him, "Abba, if we have all come to pray to Hashem for rain, then how come nobody has brought an umbrella?"

The umbrella represents *Emuna*. When you pray to Hashem today, do you have your "umbrella"?

בָּרוּךְ אַתָּה ה'...
הַמּוֹצִיא לֶחֶם מִן הָאָרֶץ.

Look at the food you are going to eat for lunch today.

How did it get into your hand?

Trace its journey from your hand all the way back to where it came from.

What role did Hashem play in that journey?

During the summer say this בְּרָכָה:

1 בָּרְכֵנוּ יְהוָֹה אֱלֹהֵינוּ בְּכׇל מַעֲשֵׂי יָדֵינוּ

2 וּבָרֵךְ שְׁנָתֵנוּ בְּטַלְלֵי רָצוֹן בְּרָכָה וּנְדָבָה

3 וּתְהִי אַחֲרִיתָהּ חַיִּים וְשָׂבָע וְשָׁלוֹם כַּשָּׁנִים הַטּוֹבוֹת לִבְרָכָה

4 כִּי אֵל טוֹב וּמֵטִיב אַתָּה וּמְבָרֵךְ הַשָּׁנִים.

5 בָּרוּךְ אַתָּה יְהוָֹה

6 **מְבָרֵךְ הַשָּׁנִים.**

During the winter say this בְּרָכָה:

7 בָּרֵךְ עָלֵינוּ יְהוָֹה אֱלֹהֵינוּ אֶת הַשָּׁנָה הַזֹּאת

8 וְאֶת כׇּל מִינֵי תְבוּאָתָהּ לְטוֹבָה

9 וְתֵן טַל וּמָטָר לִבְרָכָה עַל כׇּל פְּנֵי הָאֲדָמָה

10 וְרַוֵּה פְּנֵי תֵבֵל, וְשַׂבַּע אֶת הָעוֹלָם כֻּלּוֹ מִטּוּבָךְ

11 וּמַלֵּא יָדֵינוּ מִבִּרְכוֹתֶיךָ, וּמֵעֹשֶׁר מַתְּנוֹת יָדֶיךָ

12 שָׁמְרָה וְהַצִּילָה שָׁנָה זוֹ מִכׇּל דָּבָר רָע

13 וּמִכׇּל מִינֵי מַשְׁחִית, וּמִכׇּל מִינֵי פֻרְעָנוּת

14 וַעֲשֵׂה לָהּ תִּקְוָה טוֹבָה וְאַחֲרִית שָׁלוֹם

15 חוּס וְרַחֵם עָלֶיהָ וְעַל כׇּל תְּבוּאָתָהּ וּפֵרוֹתֶיהָ

16 וּבָרְכָהּ בְּגִשְׁמֵי רָצוֹן בְּרָכָה וּנְדָבָה

17 וּתְהִי אַחֲרִיתָהּ חַיִּים וְשָׂבָע וְשָׁלוֹם כַּשָּׁנִים הַטּוֹבוֹת לִבְרָכָה

18 כִּי אֵל טוֹב וּמֵטִיב אַתָּה וּמְבָרֵךְ הַשָּׁנִים.

19 בָּרוּךְ אַתָּה יְהוָֹה

20 **מְבָרֵךְ הַשָּׁנִים.**

Blow the great shofar to announce the arrival of the Mashiaḥ, and show a sign to gather us together in Israel from the four corners of the earth.

Hashem, You are the Source of all blessing, who brings all Jews together in Israel.

In 1991 Ethiopia had a terrible civil war – people in the same country fought against each other. The State of Israel wanted to save the Jewish community in the country. During Operation Shlomo, 35 Israeli aircraft brought 14,000 Ethiopian Jews to safety over a period of 36 hours. This ancient Jewish community always dreamt of joining our people in our ancient homeland, despite the obvious dangers involved. The seats were ripped out of the planes to make as much room as possible and 1,200 people managed to cram aboard each plane. Many of the passengers only brought with them clothes and cooking utensils, and during the flights seven babies were born on the planes. Everyone felt that this was the fulfillment of the promise to gather all the Jewish people from the four corners of the earth.

וַיֹּאמֶר יְהוָה אֶל־אַבְרָם,
לֶךְ־לְךָ מֵאַרְצְךָ וּמִמּוֹלַדְתְּךָ
וּמִבֵּית אָבִיךָ אֶל־הָאָרֶץ אֲשֶׁר אַרְאֶךָּ.
(Bereshit 12:1)

What signs has Hashem already shown us that the process mentioned in this *berakha* has already begun?

תְּקַע בְּשׁוֹפָר גָּדוֹל לְחֵרוּתֵנוּ
וְשָׂא נֵס לְקַבֵּץ גָּלֻיּוֹתֵינוּ
וְקַבְּצֵנוּ יַחַד מֵאַרְבַּע כַּנְפוֹת הָאָרֶץ לְאַרְצֵנוּ.
בָּרוּךְ אַתָּה יְהֹוָה

מְקַבֵּץ נִדְחֵי עַמּוֹ יִשְׂרָאֵל.

Give us strong and just leaders, as we had in the past. **Hashem, You are the Source of all blessing, who loves justice and laws.**

In Israel…

Policemen wish you a Shabbat Shalom

The president quotes the Talmud in his swearing-in ceremony

Politicians debate about Shabbat in the Knesset

Teachers teach Tanakh in ALL schools

Judges use Jewish as well as non-Jewish sources to make their judgments

The Chief Rabbis are appointed by the government

Officers in the army teach their soldiers the ethics of war

1 הָשִׁיבָה שׁוֹפְטֵינוּ כְּבָרִאשׁוֹנָה וְיוֹעֲצֵינוּ כְּבַתְּחִלָּה

2 וְהָסֵר מִמֶּנּוּ יָגוֹן וַאֲנָחָה

3 וּמְלֹךְ עָלֵינוּ מְהֵרָה אַתָּה יְהֹוָה לְבַדְּךָ

4 בְּחֶסֶד וּבְרַחֲמִים בְּצֶדֶק וּבְמִשְׁפָּט.

5 בָּרוּךְ אַתָּה יְהֹוָה

6 מֶלֶךְ אוֹהֵב

7 צְדָקָה וּמִשְׁפָּט.

Between Rosh HaShana and Yom Kippur change the ending of this בְּרָכָה *to these words:*

הַמֶּלֶךְ הַמִּשְׁפָּט.

וִיהוֹשֻׁעַ בִּן־נוּן, מָלֵא רוּחַ חָכְמָה כִּי־סָמַךְ מֹשֶׁה אֶת־יָדָיו
עָלָיו, וַיִּשְׁמְעוּ אֵלָיו בְּנֵי־יִשְׂרָאֵל וַיַּעֲשׂוּ כַּאֲשֶׁר צִוָּה יְהֹוָה
אֶת־מֹשֶׁה. (Devarim 34:9)

What qualities does a good leader have?
Who do you know that would make a good leader?

Quickly get rid of people who don't want us to live a Jewish life, and destroy our enemies who want to hurt us. **Hashem, You are the Source of all blessing, who destroys enemies and humbles those who think they are superior.**

"Once it happened that Rabban Gamliel asked his assistant to call seven sages together to his attic to add a month to the calendar year and declare that year a leap year. When he arrived he counted that there were eight. He said to them all, 'Whoever is here without an invite must leave immediately!' Shmuel HaKatan stood up and said, 'It is I who came uninvited. I didn't come to be part of the process, but just to watch and to learn the halakha and how it is done.' Rabban Gamliel replied to him, 'Sit down, my son. You are worthy to be here and to be part of the process, but the halakha says that only those specifically invited can participate.' The truth of the matter was it was not Shmuel HaKatan who was the uninvited participant, but one of the others. He only said he was not invited to save that person embarrassment!"

"Shmuel HaKatan used to say: בִּנְפֹל אוֹיִבְךָ אַל תִּשְׂמָח."

(Pirkei Avot 4:24; Mishlei 24:17)

The author of this *berakha* was Shmuel HaKatan.

Why do you think he was known by that name?

Why did the Rabbis choose him to write this *berakha*?

1 לַמִּינִים וְלַמַּלְשִׁינִים אַל תְּהִי תִקְוָה

2 וְכָל הַזֵּדִים כְּרֶגַע יֹאבֵדוּ

3 וְכָל אוֹיְבֶיךָ וְכָל שׂוֹנְאֶיךָ מְהֵרָה יִכָּרֵתוּ

4 וּמַלְכוּת הָרִשְׁעָה מְהֵרָה תְעַקֵּר וּתְשַׁבֵּר

5 וּתְכַלֵּם וְתַכְנִיעֵם בִּמְהֵרָה בְיָמֵינוּ.

6 בָּרוּךְ אַתָּה יְהֹוָה

7 **שׁוֹבֵר אוֹיְבִים וּמַכְנִיעַ זֵדִים.**

Show kindness to people who are righteous, and wise, and good, and also to us. Reward all those who believe in You. **Hashem, You are the Source of all blessing, who supports and believes in righteous people.**

"Moshe was a shepherd, and Hashem tested him to see if he would be a good leader, by watching how he cared for his flock of sheep. When Moshe was looking after Yitro's sheep in the desert, a lamb ran away and Moshe followed it. The lamb hid in a shady spot under a rock. In that spot was a pool of water, and the lamb drank thirstily from it. When Moshe found the young lamb he said to it, 'I didn't know that you ran away because you were thirsty. You must be tired as well!' So he carried the lamb back to the flock on his shoulders. Hashem said, 'Because Moshe showed such love and compassion to this little lamb, he will be the leader to tend to My flock – the Children of Israel.'"

1 עַל הַצַּדִּיקִים וְעַל הַחֲסִידִים
2 וְעַל שְׁאֵרִית עַמְּךָ בֵּית יִשְׂרָאֵל וְעַל זִקְנֵיהֶם
3 וְעַל פְּלֵטַת בֵּית סוֹפְרֵיהֶם וְעַל גֵּרֵי הַצֶּדֶק וְעָלֵינוּ
4 יֶהֱמוּ נָא רַחֲמֶיךָ יְהוָה אֱלֹהֵינוּ
5 וְתֵן שָׂכָר טוֹב לְכָל הַבּוֹטְחִים בְּשִׁמְךָ בֶּאֱמֶת
6 וְשִׂים חֶלְקֵנוּ עִמָּהֶם
7 וּלְעוֹלָם לֹא נֵבוֹשׁ כִּי בְךָ בָּטָחְנוּ
8 וְעַל חַסְדְּךָ הַגָּדוֹל בֶּאֱמֶת נִשְׁעָנְנוּ.
9 בָּרוּךְ אַתָּה יְהוָה
10 **מִשְׁעָן וּמִבְטָח לַצַּדִּיקִים.**

שְׁאַל אָבִיךָ וְיַגֵּדְךָ, זְקֵנֶיךָ וְיֹאמְרוּ לָךְ.
(Devarim 32:7)

What can we learn from older people?

Can you think of something you have learned from talking to an older person?

Can we learn things from younger people too?

Please return to Yerushalayim and live there as You promised. Rebuild Your Temple there now and have it last forever. Put a king there who is a descendant of King David. **Hashem, You are the Source of all blessing, who rebuilds Yerushalayim.**

"Once, after the destruction of the Beit HaMikdash, Rabban Gamliel, Rabbi Elazar ben Azaria, Rabbi Yehoshua, and Rabbi Akiva were walking on Mount Scopus in Yerushalayim. When they reached the top and saw Har HaBayit where the Beit HaMikdash once stood, they noticed a fox leaving from where the Kodesh HaKodashim used to be. Rabbi Akiva began to laugh while his friends were crying at what they had seen. They asked Rabbi Akiva, 'How can you laugh at such a time, when a lowly fox is walking around the holiest place on earth, a place where only the Kohen Gadol could enter on the holiest day of the year?!' Rabbi Akiva replied, 'Now that I have seen the prophecies of the destruction of the Beit HaMikdash fulfilled, I know the prophecies of redemption and return will be fulfilled. As it says in Zekharia: "One day old men and women will once again sit in peace in the streets of Jerusalem."'"

לְשָׁנָה הַבָּאָה
בִּירוּשָׁלַיִם הַבְּנוּיָה

Isn't Yerushalayim rebuilt already? So what are we still praying for?

תִּשְׁכּוֹן בְּתוֹךְ יְרוּשָׁלַיִם עִירְךָ כַּאֲשֶׁר דִּבַּרְתָּ
וְכִסֵּא דָוִד עַבְדְּךָ מְהֵרָה בְּתוֹכָהּ תָּכִין
וּבְנֵה אוֹתָהּ בִּנְיַן עוֹלָם בִּמְהֵרָה בְיָמֵינוּ.
בָּרוּךְ אַתָּה יְהֹוָה

בּוֹנֵה יְרוּשָׁלָיִם.

Bring back the Kingdom of David's family, because we hope for You to bring the Mashiaḥ every day. **Hashem, You are the Source of all blessing, who already started saving us.**

Once upon a time, Hashem called for the Melekh HaMashiaḥ to tell him that the time had come for the final redemption. So the Mashiaḥ got dressed in his very best clothes, and entered the first Beit Kenesset he came to, to announce the good news. Everyone there immediately stopped their learning and stared at him in disbelief. One person called out, "That cannot be the Mashiaḥ. Just look at his hat… it has pinches and the brim is down!" So the Mashiaḥ changed his hat, and put the brim up, and traveled to the next shul on the way. But there he was also received with surprise. "What a strange thought, Mashiaḥ wearing a hat!" they said. "If you were really the Mashiaḥ you would have a knitted kippa!" So the Mashiaḥ took off his hat and placed a knitted kippa on his head, for he didn't mind what he wore on his head. At the next shul they said to him, "Who ever heard of a Mashiaḥ without a black hat?" "But I have a black hat," he replied. And as he placed it on his head they all laughed and said, "The Mashiaḥ wearing a hat with pinches and the brim down!" With sadness in his eyes the Mashiaḥ realized that his time had not yet come, and he began his journey back to heaven. As he was leaving, Jews of every type ran after him crying, "Wait! Don't leave. It was their fault!" But the Mashiaḥ just continued slowly and sadly walking, saying, "Don't you see? Hashem loves each and every one of you. But my time will only come when you do too!"

אֶת צֶמַח דָּוִד עַבְדְּךָ מְהֵרָה תַצְמִיחַ
וְקַרְנוֹ תָּרוּם בִּישׁוּעָתֶךָ
כִּי לִישׁוּעָתְךָ קִוִּינוּ כָּל הַיּוֹם.
בָּרוּךְ אַתָּה יְהֹוָה

מַצְמִיחַ קֶרֶן יְשׁוּעָה.

Hashem, please listen to our prayers, and accept them with kindness and understanding.

Hashem, You are the Source of all blessing, who listens to prayer.

"Here one should turn to Hashem with all of his needs, whether big or small … in his own words."

What do you want to ask Hashem for today?

In 1932 Rabbi Soloveitchik prayed to Hashem to allow him to stay in Europe with his family and friends. His life instead brought him to America. When he heard news of the Shoah in Europe that began in 1939 he realized that while Hashem always listens to our tefillot, He knows what is best for us better than we do ourselves, and sometimes decides not to answer them how we would wish. But He always listens.

1 שְׁמַע קוֹלֵנוּ יְהֹוָה אֱלֹהֵינוּ

2 אָב הָרַחֲמָן חוּס וְרַחֵם עָלֵינוּ

3 וְקַבֵּל בְּרַחֲמִים וּבְרָצוֹן אֶת תְּפִלָּתֵנוּ

4 כִּי אֵל שׁוֹמֵעַ תְּפִלּוֹת וְתַחֲנוּנִים אָתָּה

5 וּמִלְּפָנֶיךָ מַלְכֵּנוּ רֵיקָם אַל תְּשִׁיבֵנוּ

6 חָנֵּנוּ וַעֲנֵנוּ וּשְׁמַע תְּפִלָּתֵנוּ

7 כִּי אַתָּה שׁוֹמֵעַ תְּפִלַּת כָּל פֶּה.

8 בָּרוּךְ אַתָּה יְהֹוָה

9 **שׁוֹמֵעַ תְּפִלָּה.**

Reintroduce the service in Your Temple, and accept with love the sacrifices and prayers of Israel.

Hashem, You are the Source of all blessing, who returns to Tziyon.

Once, a long time ago, two brothers lived on a hill. One had a large family, and the other lived alone. They farmed together, and shared their produce equally each year. But one year, the unmarried brother decided that it was unfair that he should take an equal share because he had only one mouth to feed, while his brother had a large family. That night he secretly placed half of his share on his brother's pile. Meanwhile his brother was sad thinking about his unmarried, lonely brother, with no one to look after him in his old age. That very same night he too decided to secretly place half of his share on his brother's pile, so that at least he would have more wealth. The next morning, neither brother could understand why their piles were the exact same size. They tried that night again, but the same thing happened. On the third night they bumped into each other trying once more and realized what had been happening, dropped their produce and embraced. When Hashem saw this selfless act of brotherly love and kindness, He chose this spot to house His home on earth, and that is where the future Temple would be built.

רְצֵה יְהֹוָה אֱלֹהֵינוּ בְּעַמְּךָ יִשְׂרָאֵל וְלִתְפִלָּתָם שְׁעֵה
וְהָשֵׁב הָעֲבוֹדָה לִדְבִיר בֵּיתֶךָ
וְאִשֵּׁי יִשְׂרָאֵל וּתְפִלָּתָם מְהֵרָה בְּאַהֲבָה תְקַבֵּל בְּרָצוֹן
וּתְהִי לְרָצוֹן תָּמִיד עֲבוֹדַת יִשְׂרָאֵל עַמֶּךָ.

On Rosh Ḥodesh and Ḥol HaMo'ed add יַעֲלֶה וְיָבוֹא:

אֱלֹהֵינוּ וֵאלֹהֵי אֲבוֹתֵינוּ, יַעֲלֶה וְיָבוֹא, יַגִּיעַ, יֵרָאֶה וְיֵרָצֶה, יִשָּׁמַע, יִפָּקֵד וְיִזָּכֵר זִכְרוֹנֵנוּ וְזִכְרוֹן אֲבוֹתֵינוּ, זִכְרוֹן יְרוּשָׁלַיִם עִירָךְ, וְזִכְרוֹן מָשִׁיחַ בֶּן דָּוִד עַבְדָּךְ, וְזִכְרוֹן כָּל עַמְּךָ בֵּית יִשְׂרָאֵל, לְפָנֶיךָ, לִפְלֵטָה לְטוֹבָה לְחֵן, לְחֶסֶד וּלְרַחֲמִים לְחַיִּים טוֹבִים וּלְשָׁלוֹם, בְּיוֹם

Rosh Ḥodesh	*Pesaḥ*	*Sukkot*
רֹאשׁ הַחֹדֶשׁ הַזֶּה	חַג הַמַּצּוֹת הַזֶּה	חַג הַסֻּכּוֹת הַזֶּה
	בְּיוֹם מִקְרָא קֹדֶשׁ הַזֶּה	בְּיוֹם מִקְרָא קֹדֶשׁ הַזֶּה

לְרַחֵם בּוֹ עָלֵינוּ וּלְהוֹשִׁיעֵנוּ. זָכְרֵנוּ יְהֹוָה אֱלֹהֵינוּ בּוֹ לְטוֹבָה, וּפָקְדֵנוּ בוֹ לִבְרָכָה, וְהוֹשִׁיעֵנוּ בוֹ לְחַיִּים טוֹבִים. בִּדְבַר יְשׁוּעָה וְרַחֲמִים חוּס וְחָנֵּנוּ וַחֲמוֹל וְרַחֵם עָלֵינוּ וְהוֹשִׁיעֵנוּ, כִּי אֵלֶיךָ עֵינֵינוּ, כִּי אֵל מֶלֶךְ חַנּוּן וְרַחוּם אָתָּה.

וְאַתָּה בְּרַחֲמֶיךָ הָרַבִּים תַּחְפֹּץ בָּנוּ וְתִרְצֵנוּ
וְתֶחֱזֶינָה עֵינֵינוּ בְּשׁוּבְךָ לְצִיּוֹן בְּרַחֲמִים.
בָּרוּךְ אַתָּה יְהֹוָה
הַמַּחֲזִיר שְׁכִינָתוֹ לְצִיּוֹן.

We thank You, Hashem, because You are our God and the God of our ancestors from generation to generation. We thank You because our lives are in Your hands, for Your miracles that You make for us every day.

"Who is a rich person? Someone who is happy with what they have."
(Pirkei Avot 4:1)

Think about all the things you should say thank you to Hashem for.

Is it a long list?

Now say thank you!

During Israel's War of Independence in 1948 a famous miracle occurred in the Arizal's synagogue in the holy city of Tzefat. The synagogue was full of people while the battle for the city was going on around them outside. During the tefilla, a bomb exploded just outside the synagogue, spraying debris everywhere, including into the synagogue. Miraculously, just as the worshipers by the bima bowed their heads for the blessing of Modim, a piece of metal flew directly above their heads, and lodged itself in the bima. Bowing their heads saved their lives. The hole it made can still be seen today, reminding visitors of this miracle, and the need to thank Hashem for so much.

מוֹדִים אֲנַֽחְנוּ לָךְ,
שָׁאַתָּה הוּא יְהֹוָה אֱלֹהֵֽינוּ
וֵאלֹהֵי אֲבוֹתֵֽינוּ לְעוֹלָם וָעֶד.
צוּרֵֽנוּ, צוּר חַיֵּֽינוּ וּמָגֵן יִשְׁעֵֽנוּ
אַתָּה הוּא לְדוֹר וָדוֹר
נוֹדֶה לְּךָ וּנְסַפֵּר תְּהִלָּתֶֽךָ
עַל חַיֵּֽינוּ הַמְּסוּרִים בְּיָדֶֽךָ
וְעַל נִשְׁמוֹתֵֽינוּ הַפְּקוּדוֹת לָךְ
וְעַל נִסֶּֽיךָ שֶׁבְּכָל יוֹם עִמָּֽנוּ
וְעַל נִפְלְאוֹתֶֽיךָ וְטוֹבוֹתֶֽיךָ שֶׁבְּכָל עֵת
עֶֽרֶב וָבֹֽקֶר וְצָהֳרָֽיִם.
הַטּוֹב, כִּי לֹא כָלוּ רַחֲמֶֽיךָ
הַמְרַחֵם, כִּי לֹא תַֽמּוּ חֲסָדֶֽיךָ
כִּי מֵעוֹלָם קִוִּֽינוּ לָךְ.

We also thank You for the miracles, and for saving us, and for the victories in battle, which You did for our ancestors in those days at this time.

What is the difference between נִסִּים (miracles) and נִפְלָאוֹת (wonders)?

Which is more impressive?

Have you witnessed any miracles in your life? Think about them and say thank you to Hashem.

Say עַל הַנִּסִּים *on Ḥanukka and Purim.*

עַל הַנִּסִּים וְעַל הַפֻּרְקָן וְעַל הַגְּבוּרוֹת וְעַל הַתְּשׁוּעוֹת וְעַל הַנִּפְלָאוֹת וְעַל הַנֶּחָמוֹת שֶׁעָשִׂיתָ לַאֲבוֹתֵינוּ בַּיָּמִים הָהֵם בַּזְּמַן הַזֶּה.

Ḥanukka

בִּימֵי מַתִּתְיָה בֶּן יוֹחָנָן כֹּהֵן גָּדוֹל חַשְׁמוֹנַאי וּבָנָיו, כְּשֶׁעָמְדָה מַלְכוּת יָוָן הָרְשָׁעָה עַל עַמְּךָ יִשְׂרָאֵל לְשַׁכְּחָם תּוֹרָתֶךָ וּלְהַעֲבִירָם מֵחֻקֵּי רְצוֹנֶךָ, וְאַתָּה בְּרַחֲמֶיךָ הָרַבִּים עָמַדְתָּ לָהֶם בְּעֵת צָרָתָם, רַבְתָּ אֶת רִיבָם, דַּנְתָּ אֶת דִּינָם, נָקַמְתָּ אֶת נִקְמָתָם, מָסַרְתָּ גִבּוֹרִים בְּיַד חַלָּשִׁים, וְרַבִּים בְּיַד מְעַטִּים, וּרְשָׁעִים בְּיַד צַדִּיקִים, וּטְמֵאִים בְּיַד טְהוֹרִים, וְזֵדִים בְּיַד עוֹסְקֵי תוֹרָתֶךָ. לְךָ עָשִׂיתָ שֵׁם גָּדוֹל וְקָדוֹשׁ בְּעוֹלָמֶךָ, וּלְעַמְּךָ יִשְׂרָאֵל עָשִׂיתָ תְּשׁוּעָה גְדוֹלָה וּפֻרְקָן כְּהַיּוֹם הַזֶּה. וְאַחַר כָּךְ בָּאוּ בָנֶיךָ לִדְבִיר בֵּיתֶךָ, וּפִנּוּ אֶת הֵיכָלֶךָ, וְטִהֲרוּ אֶת מִקְדָּשֶׁךָ, וְהִדְלִיקוּ נֵרוֹת בְּחַצְרוֹת קָדְשֶׁךָ, וְקָבְעוּ שְׁמוֹנַת יְמֵי חֲנֻכָּה אֵלּוּ, בְּהַלֵּל וּבְהוֹדָאָה, וְעָשִׂיתָ עִמָּהֶם נִסִּים וְנִפְלָאוֹת, וְנוֹדֶה לְשִׁמְךָ הַגָּדוֹל, סֶלָה.

Purim

בִּימֵי מָרְדְּכַי וְאֶסְתֵּר בְּשׁוּשַׁן הַבִּירָה, כְּשֶׁעָמַד עֲלֵיהֶם הָמָן הָרָשָׁע, בִּקֵּשׁ לְהַשְׁמִיד לַהֲרֹג וּלְאַבֵּד אֶת־כָּל־הַיְּהוּדִים מִנַּעַר וְעַד־זָקֵן טַף וְנָשִׁים בְּיוֹם אֶחָד, בִּשְׁלוֹשָׁה עָשָׂר לְחֹדֶשׁ שְׁנֵים־עָשָׂר, הוּא חֹדֶשׁ אֲדָר, וּשְׁלָלָם לָבוֹז: וְאַתָּה בְּרַחֲמֶיךָ הָרַבִּים הֵפַרְתָּ אֶת עֲצָתוֹ, וְקִלְקַלְתָּ אֶת מַחֲשַׁבְתּוֹ, וַהֲשֵׁבוֹתָ לּוֹ גְּמוּלוֹ בְּרֹאשׁוֹ, וְתָלוּ אוֹתוֹ וְאֶת בָּנָיו עַל הָעֵץ, וְעָשִׂיתָ עִמָּהֶם נִסִּים וְנִפְלָאוֹת, וְנוֹדֶה לְשִׁמְךָ הַגָּדוֹל, סֶלָה.

All people should thank You, because You save and help people.

Hashem, You are the Source of all blessing, the One who is good and the One people should thank.

Eric's ears pricked up as he left synagogue in Pittsburgh one Shabbat morning and heard guests speaking Hebrew. He couldn't resist approaching the young couple and talking to them in his rusty Hebrew. The couple explained that they had just been transferred from Israel for work. The man's father was also with them visiting from Israel, and he was fascinated by Eric's Hebrew. Eric explained that he had volunteered in Israel during the War of Independence in 1948 as a second lieutenant in the Twelfth Brigade, Seventh Regiment. The man was dumbfounded. "I have been looking for you for fifty-two years, so I could thank you for saving my life!" said the man with growing emotion. The Egyptian army was advancing through the Negev, and the front-line units were low on ammunition and taking heavy casualties. Eric's platoon was sent to rescue the injured soldiers, and he personally saved a man's life, carrying him to safety. Eric had never thought to find out the man's name and always wondered what became of him. That injured soldier was today looking Eric in the eye and finally thanking him for saving his life!

וְעַל כֻּלָּם
יִתְבָּרַךְ וְיִתְרוֹמַם וְיִתְנַשֵּׂא תָּמִיד שִׁמְךָ מַלְכֵּנוּ
לְעוֹלָם וָעֶד
וְכָל הַחַיִּים יוֹדְוּךָ סֶּלָה

Between Rosh HaShana and Yom Kippur add these words:

וּכְתֹב לְחַיִּים טוֹבִים כָּל בְּנֵי בְרִיתֶךָ.

וִיהַלְלוּ וִיבָרְכוּ אֶת שִׁמְךָ הַגָּדוֹל בֶּאֱמֶת
לְעוֹלָם כִּי טוֹב
הָאֵל יְשׁוּעָתֵנוּ וְעֶזְרָתֵנוּ סֶלָה, הָאֵל הַטּוֹב.
בָּרוּךְ אַתָּה יְהוָה
הַטּוֹב שִׁמְךָ וּלְךָ נָאֶה לְהוֹדוֹת.

Give peace, goodness, and blessing, life, grace, kindness and care to us and all Your people of Israel. Bless us as one. **Hashem, You are the Source of all blessing, who blesses His people with peace.**

"The world stands on three things: on justice, truth, and peace."
(Pirkei Avot 1:18)

Why do you think the Amida ends with a prayer for peace?

Sometimes I would like to ask God why there is so much hate in the world. And why people fight and countries go to war. Sometimes I would like to ask God why He doesn't do something about it.

Well, why don't you ask Him?

Because I am afraid that God might ask me the same question…

How would you answer if God asked you these questions?

What can you do today to bring more peace into the world?

שִׂים שָׁלוֹם טוֹבָה וּבְרָכָה
חַיִּים חֵן וָחֶסֶד
צְדָקָה וְרַחֲמִים עָלֵינוּ וְעַל כָּל יִשְׂרָאֵל עַמֶּךָ.
וּבָרְכֵנוּ אָבִינוּ כֻּלָּנוּ כְּאֶחָד בְּאוֹר פָּנֶיךָ
כִּי בְאוֹר פָּנֶיךָ נָתַתָּ לָּנוּ יְהוָֹה אֱלֹהֵינוּ תּוֹרָה וְחַיִּים
אַהֲבָה וָחֶסֶד, צְדָקָה וְרַחֲמִים, בְּרָכָה וְשָׁלוֹם.
וְטוֹב בְּעֵינֶיךָ לְבָרְכֵנוּ וּלְבָרֵךְ אֶת כָּל עַמְּךָ יִשְׂרָאֵל
בְּרֹב עֹז וְשָׁלוֹם.

Between Rosh HaShana and Yom Kippur add these words:

וּבְסֵפֶר חַיִּים, בְּרָכָה וְשָׁלוֹם, וּפַרְנָסָה טוֹבָה וִישׁוּעָה וְנֶחָמָה, וּגְזֵרוֹת טוֹבוֹת
נִזָּכֵר וְנִכָּתֵב לְפָנֶיךָ אֲנַחְנוּ וְכָל עַמְּךָ יִשְׂרָאֵל, לְחַיִּים טוֹבִים וּלְשָׁלוֹם.

בָּרוּךְ אַתָּה יְהוָֹה
הַמְבָרֵךְ אֶת עַמּוֹ
יִשְׂרָאֵל בַּשָּׁלוֹם.
אָמֵן.

יִהְיוּ לְרָצוֹן אִמְרֵי־פִי וְהֶגְיוֹן לִבִּי לְפָנֶיךָ, יְהוָֹה צוּרִי וְגֹאֲלִי:

Hashem makes peace in heaven. We ask that He make peace for us and for all of Israel. Amen!

"Be from the students of Aharon, loving peace and chasing peace, loving people and bringing them close to the Torah."

(Pirkei Avot 1:12)

What do you think it takes to bring peace? How will you help bring peace to your world today?

"Aharon was famous for loving peace. When he saw two people having an argument he wanted to help them make up with each other. He would sit with one of them and tell them that the other is upset that he hurt his feelings, but that the person is too embarrassed to say that. Aharon would continue to describe the other person's feelings until the person's anger disappeared and he was ready to make peace with the other. Then Aharon would go and sit with the other, and say the same, until he was also ready to make peace. Then they would seek each other out and hug."

אֱלֹהַי

נְצֹר לְשׁוֹנִי מֵרָע וּשְׂפָתַי מִדַּבֵּר מִרְמָה
וְלִמְקַלְלַי נַפְשִׁי תִדֹּם, וְנַפְשִׁי כֶּעָפָר לַכֹּל תִּהְיֶה.
פְּתַח לִבִּי בְּתוֹרָתֶךָ, וְאַחֲרֵי מִצְוֹתֶיךָ תִּרְדֹּף נַפְשִׁי.
וְכָל הַקָּמִים עָלַי לְרָעָה
מְהֵרָה הָפֵר עֲצָתָם וְקַלְקֵל מַחְשְׁבוֹתָם.
יִהְיוּ כְּמֹץ לִפְנֵי־רְוּחַ וּמַלְאַךְ יְהוָה דּוֹחֶה:
עֲשֵׂה לְמַעַן שְׁמֶךָ, עֲשֵׂה לְמַעַן יְמִינֶךָ
עֲשֵׂה לְמַעַן תּוֹרָתֶךָ, עֲשֵׂה לְמַעַן קְדֻשָּׁתֶךָ.
לְמַעַן יֵחָלְצוּן יְדִידֶיךָ, הוֹשִׁיעָה יְמִינְךָ וַעֲנֵנִי:
יִהְיוּ לְרָצוֹן אִמְרֵי־פִי וְהֶגְיוֹן לִבִּי לְפָנֶיךָ, יְהוָה צוּרִי וְגֹאֲלִי:

As you finish the עֲמִידָה you should stop and think that you have just had the opportunity and honor to stand before Hashem. To be respectful, bow as you take three steps back. Then bow to the left, right and center as the pictures show.

Between Rosh HaShana and Yom Kippur say הַשָּׁלוֹם *instead of* שָׁלוֹם*.*

עֹשֶׂה שָׁלוֹם / הַשָּׁלוֹם / בִּמְרוֹמָיו
הוּא בְּרַחֲמָיו יַעֲשֶׂה שָׁלוֹם עָלֵינוּ
וְעַל כָּל עַמּוֹ יִשְׂרָאֵל
וְאִמְרוּ אָמֵן.

Our Father, our King, we have sinned, be forgiving to us.
Our Father, our King, You are our only King!

A long time ago, when there were no fire engines and fire alarms, and buildings were made of wood, a small fire could spread to the whole town. One town built a tower so a watchman could blow his bugle loudly to warn the residents that there was a fire in the town. This way, everyone would drop what they were doing as soon as they heard the bugle and run to help put out the fire. Once a boy from a village came to stay in the town. When he heard the noise of the bugle he asked the innkeeper about it. When the innkeeper explained, the boy said to himself, "What an amazing idea." So on his way home he bought a bugle and returned to his village. When he got there he showed the villagers what he had bought. He set fire to the straw roof of the nearest hut, and told the villagers not to worry, the fire will be out in no time, just watch. He began to blow his bugle with gusto, but with no success. The fire refused to obey the sound of his bugle, and instead quickly spread. The villagers screamed at the boy, "Did you think just the sound of the bugle would put out the fire? It is only a wakeup call for those asleep or at work to come and help put out the fire!"

Between Rosh HaShana and Yom Kippur we say אָבִינוּ מַלְכֵּנוּ.
We open the אֲרוֹן קֹדֶשׁ *and stand for this* תְּפִלָּה.

1 **אָבִינוּ מַלְכֵּנוּ,** חָטָאנוּ לְפָנֶיךָ רַחֵם עָלֵינוּ.

2 אָבִינוּ מַלְכֵּנוּ, אֵין לָנוּ מֶלֶךְ אֶלָּא אָתָּה.

3 אָבִינוּ מַלְכֵּנוּ, עֲשֵׂה עִמָּנוּ לְמַעַן שְׁמֶךָ.

4 אָבִינוּ מַלְכֵּנוּ, קְרַע רֹעַ גְּזַר דִּינֵנוּ.

5 אָבִינוּ מַלְכֵּנוּ, שְׁלַח רְפוּאָה שְׁלֵמָה לְכָל חוֹלֵי עַמֶּךָ.

6 אָבִינוּ מַלְכֵּנוּ, כָּתְבֵנוּ בְּסֵפֶר חַיִּים טוֹבִים.

7 אָבִינוּ מַלְכֵּנוּ, כָּתְבֵנוּ בְּסֵפֶר צַדִּיקִים וַחֲסִידִים.

8 אָבִינוּ מַלְכֵּנוּ, כָּתְבֵנוּ בְּסֵפֶר יְשָׁרִים וּתְמִימִים.

9 אָבִינוּ מַלְכֵּנוּ, כָּתְבֵנוּ בְּסֵפֶר פַּרְנָסָה וְכַלְכָּלָה טוֹבָה.

10 אָבִינוּ מַלְכֵּנוּ, כָּתְבֵנוּ בְּסֵפֶר מְחִילָה וּסְלִיחָה וְכַפָּרָה.

11 אָבִינוּ מַלְכֵּנוּ, כָּתְבֵנוּ בְּסֵפֶר גְּאֻלָּה וִישׁוּעָה.

12 אָבִינוּ מַלְכֵּנוּ, חָנֵּנוּ וַעֲנֵנוּ.

13 אָבִינוּ מַלְכֵּנוּ, הַחֲזִירֵנוּ בִּתְשׁוּבָה שְׁלֵמָה לְפָנֶיךָ.

14 אָבִינוּ מַלְכֵּנוּ, שְׁמַע קוֹלֵנוּ חוּס וְרַחֵם עָלֵינוּ.

15 אָבִינוּ מַלְכֵּנוּ, עֲשֵׂה לְמַעַנְךָ אִם לֹא לְמַעֲנֵנוּ.

16 אָבִינוּ מַלְכֵּנוּ, קַבֵּל בְּרַחֲמִים וּבְרָצוֹן אֶת תְּפִלָּתֵנוּ.

17 אָבִינוּ מַלְכֵּנוּ, אַל תְּשִׁיבֵנוּ רֵיקָם מִלְּפָנֶיךָ.

Hashem is a blessing for us, and gave the Torah to us, His nation, the Jewish People. We are happy that we know we are Hashem's nation.

When Joseph celebrated his bar mitzva in Bergen-Belsen concentration camp in 1944, he read from a tiny Sefer Torah that his teacher had kept hidden throughout the war. It was barely four inches in height. Afterwards, everyone congratulated Joseph, and some even gave him gifts. He received a small bar of chocolate, a pack of playing cards, and a very special gift that would remain with him until he was an old man. The rabbi gave him the tiny Sefer Torah, on condition that if he survived, he must tell the story of his bar mitzva. A few months later the rabbi died, but Joseph escaped. After the war he made his way to Israel and witnessed the birth of the Jewish State. He later became a professor of physics, and was part of the team that sent Israel's first astronaut, Ilan Ramon, into space. When he told Ilan the story of the tiny Sefer Torah, he asked him if he could take it with him into space. In a live telecast from aboard the space shuttle Columbia, Ilan held up the Sefer Torah and told its story to millions of people, and explained that the Sefer Torah represented the Jewish people's ability to survive, and go from the darkest of days to reach periods of hope and faith. Joseph knew then that he had kept his promise to the rabbi.

On Mondays and Thursdays and other special days such as Rosh Ḥodesh, we take the סֵפֶר תּוֹרָה *out of the* אֲרוֹן קֹדֶשׁ *and read from it.*

בָּרוּךְ הַמָּקוֹם שֶׁנָּתַן תּוֹרָה לְעַמּוֹ יִשְׂרָאֵל
בָּרוּךְ הוּא.

אַשְׁרֵי הָעָם שֶׁכָּכָה לּוֹ אַשְׁרֵי הָעָם שֶׁיהוָה אֱלֹהָיו:

גַּדְּלוּ לַיהוָה אִתִּי, וּנְרוֹמְמָה שְׁמוֹ יַחְדָּו:

רוֹמְמוּ יְהוָה אֱלֹהֵינוּ
וְהִשְׁתַּחֲווּ לַהֲדֹם רַגְלָיו קָדוֹשׁ הוּא:
רוֹמְמוּ יְהוָה אֱלֹהֵינוּ
וְהִשְׁתַּחֲווּ לְהַר קָדְשׁוֹ כִּי־קָדוֹשׁ יְהוָה אֱלֹהֵינוּ:

As the סֵפֶר תּוֹרָה *is returned to the* אֲרוֹן קֹדֶשׁ *say these verses.*

יְהַלְלוּ אֶת־שֵׁם יְהוָה, כִּי־נִשְׂגָּב שְׁמוֹ ,לְבַדּוֹ, הוֹדוֹ עַל־אֶרֶץ וְשָׁמָיִם: וַיָּרֶם קֶרֶן לְעַמּוֹ, תְּהִלָּה לְכָל חֲסִידָיו, לִבְנֵי יִשְׂרָאֵל עַם קְרֹבוֹ הַלְלוּיָהּ: יְהוָה הוּא הָאֱלֹהִים, יְהוָה הוּא הָאֱלֹהִים: בַּשָּׁמַיִם מִמַּעַל וְעַל־הָאָרֶץ מִתָּחַת, אֵין עוֹד: אֵין־כָּמוֹךָ בָאֱלֹהִים, אֲדֹנָי, וְאֵין כְּמַעֲשֶׂיךָ: וּבְנֻחֹה יֹאמַר, שׁוּבָה יְהוָה רִבֲבוֹת אַלְפֵי יִשְׂרָאֵל: הֲשִׁיבֵנוּ יְהוָה אֵלֶיךָ וְנָשׁוּבָה, חַדֵּשׁ יָמֵינוּ כְּקֶדֶם:

1 אַשְׁרֵי יוֹשְׁבֵי בֵיתֶךָ, עוֹד יְהַלְלוּךָ סֶּלָה:

2 אַשְׁרֵי הָעָם שֶׁכָּכָה לּוֹ, אַשְׁרֵי הָעָם שֶׁיְהֹוָה אֱלֹהָיו:

3 תְּהִלָּה לְדָוִד

4 אֲרוֹמִמְךָ אֱלוֹהַי הַמֶּלֶךְ, וַאֲבָרְכָה שִׁמְךָ לְעוֹלָם וָעֶד:

5 בְּכָל־יוֹם אֲבָרְכֶךָּ, וַאֲהַלְלָה שִׁמְךָ לְעוֹלָם וָעֶד:

6 גָּדוֹל יְהֹוָה וּמְהֻלָּל מְאֹד, וְלִגְדֻלָּתוֹ אֵין חֵקֶר:

7 דּוֹר לְדוֹר יְשַׁבַּח מַעֲשֶׂיךָ, וּגְבוּרֹתֶיךָ יַגִּידוּ:

8 הֲדַר כְּבוֹד הוֹדֶךָ, וְדִבְרֵי נִפְלְאֹתֶיךָ אָשִׂיחָה:

9 וֶעֱזוּז נוֹרְאֹתֶיךָ יֹאמֵרוּ, וּגְדוּלָּתְךָ אֲסַפְּרֶנָּה:

10 זֵכֶר רַב־טוּבְךָ יַבִּיעוּ, וְצִדְקָתְךָ יְרַנֵּנוּ:

11 חַנּוּן וְרַחוּם יְהֹוָה, אֶרֶךְ אַפַּיִם וּגְדָל־חָסֶד:

12 טוֹב־יְהֹוָה לַכֹּל, וְרַחֲמָיו עַל־כָּל־מַעֲשָׂיו:

13 יוֹדוּךָ יְהֹוָה כָּל־מַעֲשֶׂיךָ, וַחֲסִידֶיךָ יְבָרְכוּכָה:

14 כְּבוֹד מַלְכוּתְךָ יֹאמֵרוּ, וּגְבוּרָתְךָ יְדַבֵּרוּ:

לְהוֹדִיעַ לִבְנֵי הָאָדָם גְּבוּרֹתָיו, וּכְבוֹד הֲדַר מַלְכוּתוֹ:

מַלְכוּתְךָ מַלְכוּת כָּל־עֹלָמִים וּמֶמְשַׁלְתְּךָ בְּכָל־דּוֹר וָדֹר: 1

סוֹמֵךְ יְהוָה לְכָל־הַנֹּפְלִים, וְזוֹקֵף לְכָל־הַכְּפוּפִים: 1

עֵינֵי־כֹל אֵלֶיךָ יְשַׂבֵּרוּ וְאַתָּה נוֹתֵן־לָהֶם אֶת־אָכְלָם בְּעִתּוֹ: 1

פּוֹתֵחַ אֶת־יָדֶךָ, וּמַשְׂבִּיעַ לְכָל־חַי רָצוֹן: 1

צַדִּיק יְהוָה בְּכָל־דְּרָכָיו, וְחָסִיד בְּכָל־מַעֲשָׂיו: 2

קָרוֹב יְהוָה לְכָל־קֹרְאָיו, לְכֹל אֲשֶׁר יִקְרָאֻהוּ בֶאֱמֶת: 2

רְצוֹן־יְרֵאָיו יַעֲשֶׂה, וְאֶת־שַׁוְעָתָם יִשְׁמַע, וְיוֹשִׁיעֵם: 2

שׁוֹמֵר יְהוָה אֶת־כָּל־אֹהֲבָיו, וְאֵת כָּל־הָרְשָׁעִים יַשְׁמִיד: 2

תְּהִלַּת יְהוָה יְדַבֶּר פִּי וִיבָרֵךְ כָּל־בָּשָׂר שֵׁם קָדְשׁוֹ לְעוֹלָם וָעֶד: 24

וַאֲנַחְנוּ נְבָרֵךְ יָהּ מֵעַתָּה וְעַד־עוֹלָם, הַלְלוּיָהּ: 2

"Shammai would eat for Shabbat every day of the week. What does that mean? If he found a tasty piece of meat in the market he would buy it and say, 'This will be for Shabbat!' But, on the next day if he found an even better piece of meat he would buy it for Shabbat, and eat the first one that day. So for Shammai, he was focused on Shabbat starting already on Sunday!"

Why do you think we mention Shabbat before each of these songs?

Each day the Levi'im would sing a different song from סֵפֶר תְּהִלִּים *in the* בֵּית הַמִּקְדָּשׁ*. Say the beginning of the song for today.*

Sunday:

1 הַיּוֹם יוֹם אֶחָד בְּשַׁבַּת קֹדֶשׁ, הַשִּׁיר שֶׁהָיוּ הַלְוִיִּם אוֹמְרִים עַל הַדּוּכָן:

2 לְדָוִד מִזְמוֹר, לַיהוָה הָאָרֶץ וּמְלוֹאָהּ, תֵּבֵל וְיֹשְׁבֵי בָהּ:

Monday

3 הַיּוֹם יוֹם שֵׁנִי בְּשַׁבַּת קֹדֶשׁ, הַשִּׁיר שֶׁהָיוּ הַלְוִיִּם אוֹמְרִים עַל הַדּוּכָן:

4 שִׁיר מִזְמוֹר לִבְנֵי־קֹרַח:

5 גָּדוֹל יְהוָה וּמְהֻלָּל מְאֹד, בְּעִיר אֱלֹהֵינוּ, הַר־קָדְשׁוֹ:

Tuesday

6 הַיּוֹם יוֹם שְׁלִישִׁי בְּשַׁבַּת קֹדֶשׁ, הַשִּׁיר שֶׁהָיוּ הַלְוִיִּם אוֹמְרִים עַל הַדּוּכָן:

7 מִזְמוֹר לְאָסָף, אֱלֹהִים נִצָּב בַּעֲדַת־אֵל, בְּקֶרֶב אֱלֹהִים יִשְׁפֹּט:

Wednesday:

8 הַיּוֹם יוֹם רְבִיעִי בְּשַׁבַּת קֹדֶשׁ, הַשִּׁיר שֶׁהָיוּ הַלְוִיִּם אוֹמְרִים עַל הַדּוּכָן:

9 אֵל־נְקָמוֹת יְהוָה, אֵל נְקָמוֹת הוֹפִיעַ:

Thursday:

10 הַיּוֹם יוֹם חֲמִישִׁי בְּשַׁבַּת קֹדֶשׁ, הַשִּׁיר שֶׁהָיוּ הַלְוִיִּם אוֹמְרִים עַל הַדּוּכָן:

11 לַמְנַצֵּחַ עַל־הַגִּתִּית לְאָסָף:

12 הַרְנִינוּ לֵאלֹהִים עוּזֵּנוּ, הָרִיעוּ לֵאלֹהֵי יַעֲקֹב:

Friday:

13 הַיּוֹם יוֹם הַשִּׁשִּׁי בְּשַׁבַּת קֹדֶשׁ, הַשִּׁיר שֶׁהָיוּ הַלְוִיִּם אוֹמְרִים עַל הַדּוּכָן:

14 יְהוָה מָלָךְ, גֵּאוּת לָבֵשׁ, לָבֵשׁ יְהוָה עֹז הִתְאַזָּר, אַף־תִּכּוֹן

15 תֵּבֵל בַּל־תִּמּוֹט:

Between Rosh Ḥodesh Elul and Yom Kippur, and on Hoshana Rabba, say these verses from סֵפֶר תְּהִלִּים.

16 אַחַת שָׁאַלְתִּי מֵאֵת־יְהוָה, אוֹתָהּ אֲבַקֵּשׁ שִׁבְתִּי בְּבֵית־

17 יְהוָה כָּל־יְמֵי חַיַּי, לַחֲזוֹת בְּנֹעַם־יְהוָה וּלְבַקֵּר בְּהֵיכָלוֹ:

We must praise the Ruler of the universe, and tell how great Hashem is, the Creator of all things.

He is our God, no one else. He is our King, no one else. Hashem is our God in heaven and on earth.

וְעַתָּה אִם־שָׁמוֹעַ תִּשְׁמְעוּ
בְּקֹלִי וּשְׁמַרְתֶּם אֶת־בְּרִיתִי,
וִהְיִיתֶם לִי סְגֻלָּה מִכָּל־הָעַמִּים
כִּי־לִי כָּל־הָאָרֶץ. (Shemot 19:5)

What's so special about being a Jew?

וְאַתֶּם תִּהְיוּ־לִי מַמְלֶכֶת
כֹּהֲנִים וְגוֹי קָדוֹשׁ.

(Shemot 19:6)

What do you think is the most important message Judaism has for the world?

We stand when we say עָלֵינוּ.

עָלֵינוּ לְשַׁבֵּחַ לַאֲדוֹן הַכֹּל, לָתֵת גְּדֻלָּה לְיוֹצֵר בְּרֵאשִׁית

שֶׁלֹּא עָשָׂנוּ כְּגוֹיֵי הָאֲרָצוֹת, וְלֹא שָׂמָנוּ כְּמִשְׁפְּחוֹת הָאֲדָמָה

שֶׁלֹּא שָׂם חֶלְקֵנוּ כָּהֶם וְגוֹרָלֵנוּ כְּכָל הֲמוֹנָם.

שֶׁהֵם מִשְׁתַּחֲוִים לְהֶבֶל וָרִיק וּמִתְפַּלְּלִים אֶל־אֵל לֹא יוֹשִׁיעַ.

וַאֲנַחְנוּ מִשְׁתַּחֲוִים לִפְנֵי מֶלֶךְ מַלְכֵי הַמְּלָכִים

הַקָּדוֹשׁ בָּרוּךְ הוּא

שֶׁהוּא נוֹטֶה שָׁמַיִם וְיוֹסֵד אָרֶץ

וּמוֹשַׁב יְקָרוֹ בַּשָּׁמַיִם מִמַּעַל, וּשְׁכִינַת עֻזּוֹ בְּגָבְהֵי מְרוֹמִים.

הוּא אֱלֹהֵינוּ, וְאֵין עוֹד אַחֵר

אֱמֶת מַלְכֵּנוּ, וְאֶפֶס זוּלָתוֹ

כַּכָּתוּב בַּתּוֹרָה

וְיָדַעְתָּ הַיּוֹם וַהֲשֵׁבֹתָ אֶל־לְבָבֶךָ

כִּי יְהוָה הוּא הָאֱלֹהִים בַּשָּׁמַיִם מִמַּעַל וְעַל־הָאָרֶץ מִתָּחַת

אֵין עוֹד:

Therefore we hope that You will let us see Your amazing power, when all evil and misunderstanding will be removed from the world, and the world will be perfect with every person recognizing You as King.

Aaron Feuerstein owned a textile mill in a small town in Massachusetts, at a time when most of the textile mills had closed down because it was cheaper to have them in other countries such as India and Mexico. His mill was destroyed in a fire, and most people assumed he would take this opportunity to take the insurance money and close it down. But the mill had employed 1,800 people from the local town, who would all be out of a job if the mill closed. Aaron felt a responsibility to them, and refused to close the mill. Not only did he rebuild the mill, making their jobs safe, but he paid them full salaries while the mill was being rebuilt and they couldn't work. Aaron had made a tremendous Kiddush Hashem and made the world a better place.

עַל כֵּן נְקַוֶּה לְּךָ, יְהֹוָה אֱלֹהֵינוּ, לִרְאוֹת מְהֵרָה בְּתִפְאֶרֶת עֻזֶּךָ

לְהַעֲבִיר גִּלּוּלִים מִן הָאָרֶץ וְהָאֱלִילִים כָּרוֹת יִכָּרֵתוּן

לְתַקֵּן עוֹלָם בְּמַלְכוּת שַׁדַּי

וְכָל בְּנֵי בָשָׂר יִקְרְאוּ בִשְׁמֶךָ לְהַפְנוֹת אֵלֶיךָ כָּל רִשְׁעֵי אָרֶץ

יַכִּירוּ וְיֵדְעוּ כָּל יוֹשְׁבֵי תֵבֵל

כִּי לְךָ תִּכְרַע כָּל בֶּרֶךְ, תִּשָּׁבַע כָּל לָשׁוֹן.

לְפָנֶיךָ יְהֹוָה אֱלֹהֵינוּ יִכְרְעוּ וְיִפֹּלוּ, וְלִכְבוֹד שִׁמְךָ יְקָר יִתֵּנוּ

וִיקַבְּלוּ כֻלָּם אֶת עוֹל מַלְכוּתֶךָ

וְתִמְלֹךְ עֲלֵיהֶם מְהֵרָה לְעוֹלָם וָעֶד

כִּי הַמַּלְכוּת שֶׁלְּךָ הִיא וּלְעוֹלְמֵי עַד תִּמְלוֹךְ בְּכָבוֹד

כַּכָּתוּב בְּתוֹרָתֶךָ, יְהֹוָה יִמְלֹךְ לְעֹלָם וָעֶד:

וְנֶאֱמַר, וְהָיָה יְהֹוָה לְמֶלֶךְ עַל־כָּל־הָאָרֶץ

בַּיּוֹם הַהוּא יִהְיֶה יְהֹוָה אֶחָד וּשְׁמוֹ אֶחָד:

שַׁבָּת

Shabbat

לֵיל שַׁבָּת — Shabbat Evening

הַדְלָקַת נֵרוֹת	148	Candle Lighting
קַבָּלַת שַׁבָּת	150	Kabbalat Shabbat
מַעֲרִיב לְשַׁבָּת	154	Ma'ariv for Shabbat
קִדּוּשׁ לְלֵיל שַׁבָּת	174	Kiddush for Shabbat Evening

יוֹם שַׁבָּת — Shabbat Morning

נִשְׁמַת	180	Nishmat
קְרִיאַת שְׁמַע וּבִרְכוֹתֶיהָ	186	The Shema and Its Blessings
עֲמִידָה לְשַׁבָּת	199	The Amida for Shabbat
קְרִיאַת הַתּוֹרָה	210	Reading of the Torah
מוּסָף לְשַׁבָּת	216	Musaf for Shabbat
קִדּוּשׁ לְיוֹם שַׁבָּת	230	Kiddush for Shabbat Morning
הַבְדָּלָה	234	Havdala

Just before Shabbat begins, light the Shabbat candles.
Then cover your eyes and say this בְּרָכָה.

1 בָּרוּךְ אַתָּה יְהוָה, אֱלֹהֵינוּ מֶלֶךְ הָעוֹלָם

2 אֲשֶׁר קִדְּשָׁנוּ בְּמִצְוֹתָיו וְצִוָּנוּ

3 לְהַדְלִיק נֵר שֶׁל שַׁבָּת.

Once there was a king who wished to discover the sweetest music in the world. He brought together all the musicians in his kingdom so he could listen to each play their instrument one at a time. But no single melody stood out to him as the sweetest. Then he asked all the musicians to play at once, but the noise was almost unbearable, until an old lady came forward and set two candles down in front of the king. The king demanded silence as he watched the old woman say the בְּרָכָה *on the candles and welcome in the Shabbat Queen. The king asked for the meaning of her actions, and she explained that the sweetest music of all is the sound of the rest and peace of Shabbat.*

Many communities sing this song about our love for Hashem before קַבָּלַת שַׁבָּת.

יְדִיד נֶפֶשׁ, אָב הָרַחֲמָן, מְשׁוֹךְ עַבְדְּךָ אֶל רְצוֹנָךְ.
יָרוּץ עַבְדְּךָ כְּמוֹ אַיָּל, יִשְׁתַּחֲוֶה מוּל הֲדָרָךְ.
כִּי יֶעֱרַב לוֹ יְדִידוּתָךְ, מִנֹּפֶת צוּף וְכָל טָעַם.
כִּי יֶעֱרַב לוֹ יְדִידוּתָךְ, מִנֹּפֶת צוּף וְכָל טָעַם.

הָדוּר, נָאֶה, זִיו הָעוֹלָם, נַפְשִׁי חוֹלַת אַהֲבָתָךְ.
אָנָּא, אֵל נָא, רְפָא נָא לָהּ, בְּהַרְאוֹת לָהּ נֹעַם זִיוָךְ.
אָז תִּתְחַזֵּק וְתִתְרַפֵּא, וְהָיְתָה לָךְ שִׁפְחַת עוֹלָם.
אָז תִּתְחַזֵּק וְתִתְרַפֵּא, וְהָיְתָה לָךְ שִׁפְחַת עוֹלָם.

וָתִיק, יֶהֱמוּ רַחֲמֶיךָ, וְחוּס נָא עַל בֵּן אוֹהֲבָךְ.
כִּי זֶה כַּמֶּה נִכְסֹף נִכְסַף לִרְאוֹת בְּתִפְאֶרֶת עֻזָּךְ.
אָנָּא, אֵלִי, מַחְמַד לִבִּי, חוּשָׁה נָּא, וְאַל תִּתְעַלָּם.
אָנָּא, אֵלִי, מַחְמַד לִבִּי, חוּשָׁה נָּא, וְאַל תִּתְעַלָּם.

הִגָּלֶה נָא וּפְרֹשׂ, חָבִיב, עָלַי אֶת סֻכַּת שְׁלוֹמָךְ.
תָּאִיר אֶרֶץ מִכְּבוֹדָךְ, נָגִילָה וְנִשְׂמְחָה בָךְ.
מַהֵר, אָהוּב, כִּי בָא מוֹעֵד, וְחָנֵּנִי כִּימֵי עוֹלָם.
מַהֵר, אָהוּב, כִּי בָא מוֹעֵד, וְחָנֵּנִי כִּימֵי עוֹלָם.

Come, my love, to welcome the bride, let's welcome Shabbat!

לְכָה דוֹדִי לִקְרַאת כַּלָּה, פְּנֵי שַׁבָּת נְקַבְּלָה. 1
לְכָה דוֹדִי לִקְרַאת כַּלָּה, פְּנֵי שַׁבָּת נְקַבְּלָה. 2

שָׁמוֹר וְזָכוֹר בְּדִבּוּר אֶחָד 3
הִשְׁמִיעָנוּ אֵל הַמְיֻחָד 4
יְהֹוָה אֶחָד וּשְׁמוֹ אֶחָד 5
לְשֵׁם וּלְתִפְאֶרֶת וְלִתְהִלָּה. 6
לְכָה דוֹדִי לִקְרַאת כַּלָּה, פְּנֵי שַׁבָּת נְקַבְּלָה. 7

לִקְרַאת שַׁבָּת לְכוּ וְנֵלְכָה 8
כִּי הִיא מְקוֹר הַבְּרָכָה 9
מֵרֹאשׁ מִקֶּדֶם נְסוּכָה 10
סוֹף מַעֲשֶׂה בְּמַחֲשָׁבָה תְּחִלָּה. 11
לְכָה דוֹדִי לִקְרַאת כַּלָּה, פְּנֵי שַׁבָּת נְקַבְּלָה. 12

מִקְדַּשׁ מֶלֶךְ עִיר מְלוּכָה
קוּמִי צְאִי מִתּוֹךְ הַהֲפֵכָה
רַב לָךְ שֶׁבֶת בְּעֵמֶק הַבָּכָא
וְהוּא יַחֲמֹל עָלַיִךְ חֶמְלָה.
לְכָה דוֹדִי לִקְרַאת כַּלָּה, פְּנֵי שַׁבָּת נְקַבְּלָה.

הִתְנַעֲרִי, מֵעָפָר קוּמִי
לִבְשִׁי בִּגְדֵי תִפְאַרְתֵּךְ עַמִּי
עַל יַד בֶּן יִשַׁי בֵּית הַלַּחְמִי
קָרְבָה אֶל נַפְשִׁי, גְּאָלָהּ.
לְכָה דוֹדִי לִקְרַאת כַּלָּה, פְּנֵי שַׁבָּת נְקַבְּלָה.

הִתְעוֹרְרִי הִתְעוֹרְרִי
כִּי בָא אוֹרֵךְ קוּמִי אוֹרִי
עוּרִי עוּרִי, שִׁיר דַּבֵּרִי
כְּבוֹד יְהוָה עָלַיִךְ נִגְלָה.
לְכָה דוֹדִי לִקְרַאת כַּלָּה, פְּנֵי שַׁבָּת נְקַבְּלָה.

לֹא תֵבֹשִׁי וְלֹא תִכָּלְמִי
מַה תִּשְׁתּוֹחֲחִי וּמַה תֶּהֱמִי
בָּךְ יֶחֱסוּ עֲנִיֵּי עַמִּי
וְנִבְנְתָה עִיר עַל תִּלָּהּ.
לְכָה דוֹדִי לִקְרַאת כַּלָּה, פְּנֵי שַׁבָּת נְקַבְּלָה.

וְהָיוּ לִמְשִׁסָּה שֹׁאסָיִךְ
וְרָחֲקוּ כָּל מְבַלְּעָיִךְ
יָשִׂישׂ עָלַיִךְ אֱלֹהָיִךְ
כִּמְשׂוֹשׂ חָתָן עַל כַּלָּה.
לְכָה דוֹדִי לִקְרַאת כַּלָּה, פְּנֵי שַׁבָּת נְקַבְּלָה.

יָמִין וּשְׂמֹאל תִּפְרֹצִי
וְאֶת יְהוָה תַּעֲרִיצִי
עַל יַד אִישׁ בֶּן פַּרְצִי
וְנִשְׂמְחָה וְנָגִילָה.
לְכָה דוֹדִי לִקְרַאת כַּלָּה, פְּנֵי שַׁבָּת נְקַבְּלָה.

At this point we stand and turn to face the back of the בֵּית כְּנֶסֶת *and welcome the bride – Shabbat. Bow to welcome her at the words* בּוֹאִי כַלָּה *and then turn to face forward.*

בּוֹאִי בְשָׁלוֹם עֲטֶרֶת בַּעְלָהּ
גַּם בְּשִׂמְחָה בְּרִנָּה וּבְצָהֳלָה
תּוֹךְ אֱמוּנֵי עַם סְגֻלָּה
בּוֹאִי כַלָּה, בּוֹאִי כַלָּה.

Say quietly תּוֹךְ אֱמוּנֵי עַם סְגֻלָּה
בּוֹאִי כַלָּה, שַׁבָּת מַלְכְּתָא.

"Rabbi Ḥanina would put his cloak on and stand as the sun was setting on Erev Shabbat and call, 'Come let's go and welcome the Shabbat Queen.' Rabbi Yannai would do the same and say, 'Come in, Bride. Come in, Bride.'"

What do Shabbat, a queen, and a bride all have in common?

לְמַעַן אַחַי וְרֵעָי אֲדַבְּרָה־נָּא שָׁלוֹם בָּךְ: לְמַעַן בֵּית יְהֹוָה אֱלֹהֵינוּ אֲבַקְשָׁה טוֹב לָךְ: וּרְאֵה־בָנִים לְבָנֶיךָ שָׁלוֹם עַל־יִשְׂרָאֵל: שָׁלוֹם רָב לְאֹהֲבֵי תוֹרָתֶךָ, וְאֵין־לָמוֹ מִכְשׁוֹל: יְהֹוָה עֹז לְעַמּוֹ יִתֵּן, יְהֹוָה יְבָרֵךְ אֶת־עַמּוֹ בַשָּׁלוֹם:

מִזְמוֹר שִׁיר לְיוֹם הַשַּׁבָּת: טוֹב לְהֹדוֹת לַיהֹוָה, וּלְזַמֵּר לְשִׁמְךָ עֶלְיוֹן: לְהַגִּיד בַּבֹּקֶר חַסְדֶּךָ, וֶאֱמוּנָתְךָ בַּלֵּילוֹת: עֲלֵי־עָשׂוֹר וַעֲלֵי־נָבֶל, עֲלֵי הִגָּיוֹן בְּכִנּוֹר: כִּי שִׂמַּחְתַּנִי יְהֹוָה בְּפָעֳלֶךָ, בְּמַעֲשֵׂי יָדֶיךָ אֲרַנֵּן: מַה־גָּדְלוּ מַעֲשֶׂיךָ יְהֹוָה, מְאֹד עָמְקוּ מַחְשְׁבֹתֶיךָ: אִישׁ־בַּעַר לֹא יֵדָע, וּכְסִיל לֹא־יָבִין אֶת־זֹאת: בִּפְרֹחַ רְשָׁעִים כְּמוֹ עֵשֶׂב, וַיָּצִיצוּ כָּל־פֹּעֲלֵי אָוֶן לְהִשָּׁמְדָם עֲדֵי־עַד: וְאַתָּה מָרוֹם לְעֹלָם יְהֹוָה: כִּי הִנֵּה אֹיְבֶיךָ יְהֹוָה, כִּי־הִנֵּה אֹיְבֶיךָ יֹאבֵדוּ יִתְפָּרְדוּ כָּל־פֹּעֲלֵי אָוֶן: וַתָּרֶם כִּרְאֵים קַרְנִי, בַּלֹּתִי בְּשֶׁמֶן רַעֲנָן: וַתַּבֵּט עֵינִי בְּשׁוּרָי, בַּקָּמִים עָלַי מְרֵעִים תִּשְׁמַעְנָה אָזְנָי: צַדִּיק כַּתָּמָר יִפְרָח, כְּאֶרֶז בַּלְּבָנוֹן יִשְׂגֶּה: שְׁתוּלִים בְּבֵית יְהֹוָה, בְּחַצְרוֹת אֱלֹהֵינוּ יַפְרִיחוּ: עוֹד יְנוּבוּן בְּשֵׂיבָה, דְּשֵׁנִים וְרַעֲנַנִּים יִהְיוּ: לְהַגִּיד כִּי־יָשָׁר יְהֹוָה, צוּרִי, וְלֹא־עַוְלָתָה בּוֹ:

בָּרוּךְ אַתָּה יְהוָה, אֱלֹהֵינוּ מֶלֶךְ הָעוֹלָם
אֲשֶׁר בִּדְבָרוֹ מַעֲרִיב עֲרָבִים בְּחָכְמָה
פּוֹתֵחַ שְׁעָרִים בִּתְבוּנָה
מְשַׁנֶּה עִתִּים וּמַחֲלִיף אֶת הַזְּמַנִּים
וּמְסַדֵּר אֶת הַכּוֹכָבִים בְּמִשְׁמְרוֹתֵיהֶם בָּרָקִיעַ כִּרְצוֹנוֹ.
בּוֹרֵא יוֹמָם וָלָיְלָה
גּוֹלֵל אוֹר מִפְּנֵי חֹשֶׁךְ וְחֹשֶׁךְ מִפְּנֵי אוֹר
הַמַּעֲבִיר יוֹם וּמֵבִיא לָיְלָה
וּמַבְדִּיל בֵּין יוֹם וּבֵין לָיְלָה
יְהוָה צְבָאוֹת שְׁמוֹ:
בָּרוּךְ אַתָּה יְהוָה, הַמַּעֲרִיב עֲרָבִים.

אַהֲבַת עוֹלָם בֵּית יִשְׂרָאֵל עַמְּךָ אָהָבְתָּ
תּוֹרָה וּמִצְוֹת חֻקִּים וּמִשְׁפָּטִים אוֹתָנוּ לִמַּדְתָּ
עַל כֵּן יְהוָה אֱלֹהֵינוּ בְּשָׁכְבֵנוּ וּבְקוּמֵנוּ נָשִׂיחַ בְּחֻקֶּיךָ
וְנִשְׂמַח וְנַעֲלֹז בְּדִבְרֵי תַלְמוּד תּוֹרָתֶךָ
וּמִצְוֹתֶיךָ וְחֻקּוֹתֶיךָ לְעוֹלָם וָעֶד
כִּי הֵם חַיֵּינוּ וְאֹרֶךְ יָמֵינוּ וּבָהֶם נֶהְגֶּה יוֹמָם וָלָיְלָה.
וְאַהֲבָתְךָ לֹא תָסוּר מִמֶּנּוּ לְעוֹלָמִים.
בָּרוּךְ אַתָּה יְהוָה, אוֹהֵב אֶת עַמּוֹ יִשְׂרָאֵל.

It is a special מִצְוָה to say the שְׁמַע every morning and evening. Say the first first verse aloud while covering your eyes with your right hand. Say line 2 quietly to yourself.

שְׁמַע יִשְׂרָאֵל יְהֹוָה אֱלֹהֵינוּ, יְהֹוָה ׀ אֶחָד:

בָּרוּךְ שֵׁם כְּבוֹד מַלְכוּתוֹ לְעוֹלָם וָעֶד.

וְאָהַבְתָּ אֵת יְהֹוָה אֱלֹהֶיךָ, בְּכָל־לְבָבְךָ וּבְכָל־נַפְשְׁךָ וּבְכָל־
מְאֹדֶךָ: וְהָיוּ הַדְּבָרִים הָאֵלֶּה, אֲשֶׁר אָנֹכִי מְצַוְּךָ הַיּוֹם,
עַל־לְבָבֶךָ: וְשִׁנַּנְתָּם לְבָנֶיךָ וְדִבַּרְתָּ בָּם, בְּשִׁבְתְּךָ בְּבֵיתֶךָ
וּבְלֶכְתְּךָ בַדֶּרֶךְ, וּבְשָׁכְבְּךָ וּבְקוּמֶךָ: וּקְשַׁרְתָּם לְאוֹת עַל־יָדֶךָ
וְהָיוּ לְטֹטָפֹת בֵּין עֵינֶיךָ: וּכְתַבְתָּם עַל־מְזֻזוֹת בֵּיתֶךָ וּבִשְׁעָרֶיךָ:

It once happened on the battlefield between two warring nations, that Jew faced Jew in mortal combat. As one of the Jewish soldiers ran for cover into a foxhole, the other called out, "Surrender, or I'll shoot." The hiding soldier covered his eyes, and crying, recited the words: "Shema Yisrael, Hashem Eloheinu, Hashem Eḥad." As the other soldier heard this, he replied, "Barukh shem kevod malkhuto le'olam va'ed," laid down his gun and extended a hand, and they embraced as brothers.

וְהָיָ֗ה אִם־שָׁמֹ֤עַ תִּשְׁמְעוּ֙ אֶל־מִצְוֺתַ֔י אֲשֶׁ֧ר אָנֹכִ֛י מְצַוֶּ֥ה אֶתְכֶ֖ם הַיּ֑וֹם, לְאַהֲבָ֞ה אֶת־יְהֹוָ֤ה אֱלֹהֵיכֶם֙ וּלְעָבְד֔וֹ, בְּכָל־לְבַבְכֶ֖ם וּבְכָל־נַפְשְׁכֶֽם׃ וְנָתַתִּ֧י מְטַר־אַרְצְכֶ֛ם בְּעִתּ֖וֹ, יוֹרֶ֣ה וּמַלְק֑וֹשׁ, וְאָסַפְתָּ֣ דְגָנֶ֔ךָ וְתִירֹשְׁךָ֖ וְיִצְהָרֶֽךָ׃ וְנָתַתִּ֛י עֵ֥שֶׂב בְּשָׂדְךָ֖ לִבְהֶמְתֶּ֑ךָ, וְאָכַלְתָּ֖ וְשָׂבָֽעְתָּ׃ הִשָּׁמְר֣וּ לָכֶ֔ם פֶּ֥ן־יִפְתֶּ֖ה לְבַבְכֶ֑ם, וְסַרְתֶּ֗ם וַעֲבַדְתֶּם֙ אֱלֹהִ֣ים אֲחֵרִ֔ים וְהִשְׁתַּחֲוִיתֶ֖ם לָהֶֽם׃ וְחָרָ֨ה אַף־יְהֹוָ֜ה בָּכֶ֗ם, וְעָצַ֤ר אֶת־הַשָּׁמַ֙יִם֙ וְלֹא־יִהְיֶ֣ה מָטָ֔ר, וְהָ֣אֲדָמָ֔ה לֹ֥א תִתֵּ֖ן אֶת־יְבוּלָ֑הּ, וַאֲבַדְתֶּ֣ם מְהֵרָ֗ה מֵעַל֙ הָאָ֣רֶץ הַטֹּבָ֔ה אֲשֶׁ֥ר יְהֹוָ֖ה נֹתֵ֥ן לָכֶֽם׃ וְשַׂמְתֶּם֙ אֶת־דְּבָרַ֣י אֵ֔לֶּה עַל־לְבַבְכֶ֖ם וְעַל־נַפְשְׁכֶ֑ם, וּקְשַׁרְתֶּ֨ם אֹתָ֤ם לְאוֹת֙ עַל־יֶדְכֶ֔ם, וְהָי֥וּ לְטוֹטָפֹ֖ת בֵּ֥ין עֵינֵיכֶֽם׃ וְלִמַּדְתֶּ֥ם אֹתָ֛ם אֶת־בְּנֵיכֶ֖ם לְדַבֵּ֣ר בָּ֑ם, בְּשִׁבְתְּךָ֤ בְּבֵיתֶ֙ךָ֙ וּבְלֶכְתְּךָ֣ בַדֶּ֔רֶךְ, וּבְשָׁכְבְּךָ֖ וּבְקוּמֶֽךָ׃ וּכְתַבְתָּ֛ם עַל מְזוּז֥וֹת בֵּיתֶ֖ךָ וּבִשְׁעָרֶֽיךָ׃ לְמַ֨עַן יִרְבּ֤וּ יְמֵיכֶם֙ וִימֵ֣י בְנֵיכֶ֔ם עַ֚ל הָאֲדָמָ֔ה אֲשֶׁ֨ר נִשְׁבַּ֧ע יְהֹוָ֛ה לַאֲבֹתֵיכֶ֖ם לָתֵ֣ת לָהֶ֑ם, כִּימֵ֥י הַשָּׁמַ֖יִם עַל־הָאָֽרֶץ׃

וַיֹּאמֶר יְהֹוָה אֶל־מֹשֶׁה לֵּאמֹר: דַּבֵּר אֶל־בְּנֵי יִשְׂרָאֵל וְאָמַרְתָּ אֲלֵהֶם, וְעָשׂוּ לָהֶם צִיצִת עַל־כַּנְפֵי בִגְדֵיהֶם לְדֹרֹתָם, וְנָתְנוּ עַל־צִיצִת הַכָּנָף פְּתִיל תְּכֵלֶת: וְהָיָה לָכֶם לְצִיצִת, וּרְאִיתֶם אֹתוֹ וּזְכַרְתֶּם אֶת־כָּל־מִצְוֹת יְהֹוָה וַעֲשִׂיתֶם אֹתָם, וְלֹא תָתוּרוּ אַחֲרֵי לְבַבְכֶם וְאַחֲרֵי עֵינֵיכֶם, אֲשֶׁר־אַתֶּם זֹנִים אַחֲרֵיהֶם: לְמַעַן תִּזְכְּרוּ וַעֲשִׂיתֶם אֶת־כָּל־מִצְוֹתָי, וִהְיִיתֶם קְדֹשִׁים לֵאלֹהֵיכֶם: אֲנִי יְהֹוָה אֱלֹהֵיכֶם, אֲשֶׁר הוֹצֵאתִי אֶתְכֶם מֵאֶרֶץ מִצְרַיִם, לִהְיוֹת לָכֶם לֵאלֹהִים, אֲנִי יְהֹוָה אֱלֹהֵיכֶם:

אֱמֶת

יְהֹוָה אֱלֹהֵיכֶם אֱמֶת

The Children of Israel must keep Shabbat in every generation as an agreement between them and Hashem forever. Keeping Shabbat is a sign – it shows that we believe that Hashem created the world in six days and then stopped and rested on the seventh.

We stand for this תְּפִלָּה, which is said aloud together.

וְשָׁמְרוּ בְנֵי־יִשְׂרָאֵל אֶת־הַשַּׁבָּת
לַעֲשׂוֹת אֶת־הַשַּׁבָּת לְדֹרֹתָם בְּרִית עוֹלָם:
בֵּינִי וּבֵין בְּנֵי יִשְׂרָאֵל, אוֹת הִוא לְעֹלָם
כִּי־שֵׁשֶׁת יָמִים עָשָׂה יְהוָה אֶת־הַשָּׁמַיִם וְאֶת־הָאָרֶץ
וּבַיּוֹם הַשְּׁבִיעִי שָׁבַת וַיִּנָּפַשׁ:

The עֲמִידָה is the climax of our תְּפִלָּה where we stand before Hashem and open our hearts in prayer. You should mouth the words of the עֲמִידָה but without a sound. We learn this from the prayer of Ḥanna when she prayed to have a child. Take three steps forward and begin saying the עֲמִידָה while standing with your feet together.

1 אֲדֹנָי, שְׂפָתַי תִּפְתָּח, וּפִי יַגִּיד תְּהִלָּתֶךָ:

2 בָּרוּךְ אַתָּה יְהֹוָה

3 אֱלֹהֵינוּ וֵאלֹהֵי אֲבוֹתֵינוּ

4 אֱלֹהֵי אַבְרָהָם, אֱלֹהֵי יִצְחָק, וֵאלֹהֵי יַעֲקֹב

5 הָאֵל הַגָּדוֹל הַגִּבּוֹר וְהַנּוֹרָא, אֵל עֶלְיוֹן

6 גּוֹמֵל חֲסָדִים טוֹבִים, קוֹנֵה הַכֹּל

7 וְזוֹכֵר חַסְדֵי אָבוֹת

8 וּמֵבִיא גוֹאֵל לִבְנֵי בְנֵיהֶם לְמַעַן שְׁמוֹ בְּאַהֲבָה.

Between Rosh HaShana and Yom Kippur add these words:

זָכְרֵנוּ לְחַיִּים, מֶלֶךְ חָפֵץ בַּחַיִּים כָּתְבֵנוּ בְּסֵפֶר הַחַיִּים, לְמַעַנְךָ אֱלֹהִים חַיִּים.

9 מֶלֶךְ עוֹזֵר וּמוֹשִׁיעַ וּמָגֵן.

10 בָּרוּךְ אַתָּה יְהֹוָה

11 מָגֵן אַבְרָהָם.

אַתָּה גִּבּוֹר לְעוֹלָם, אֲדֹנָי
מְחַיֵּה מֵתִים אַתָּה, רַב לְהוֹשִׁיעַ

Between Simḥat Torah and Pesaḥ add these words:

מַשִּׁיב הָרוּחַ וּמוֹרִיד הַגֶּשֶׁם

If you are in Israel between Pesaḥ and Shemini Atzeret add these words:

מוֹרִיד הַטָּל

מְכַלְכֵּל חַיִּים בְּחֶסֶד, מְחַיֵּה מֵתִים בְּרַחֲמִים רַבִּים
סוֹמֵךְ נוֹפְלִים, וְרוֹפֵא חוֹלִים, וּמַתִּיר אֲסוּרִים
וּמְקַיֵּם אֱמוּנָתוֹ לִישֵׁנֵי עָפָר.
מִי כָמוֹךָ, בַּעַל גְּבוּרוֹת
וּמִי דּוֹמֶה לָּךְ
מֶלֶךְ, מֵמִית וּמְחַיֶּה וּמַצְמִיחַ יְשׁוּעָה.

Between Rosh HaShana and Yom Kippur add these words:

מִי כָמוֹךָ אָב הָרַחֲמָן, זוֹכֵר יְצוּרָיו בְּרַחֲמִים לְחַיִּים.

וְנֶאֱמָן אַתָּה לְהַחֲיוֹת מֵתִים.
בָּרוּךְ אַתָּה יְהוָה
מְחַיֵּה הַמֵּתִים.

1 אַתָּה קָדוֹשׁ וְשִׁמְךָ קָדוֹשׁ

2 וּקְדוֹשִׁים בְּכָל יוֹם יְהַלְלוּךָ סֶּלָה.

3 בָּרוּךְ אַתָּה יְהוָה

4 **הָאֵל הַקָּדוֹשׁ.**

Between Rosh HaShana and Yom Kippur change the ending of this בְּרָכָה to these words:

הַמֶּלֶךְ הַקָּדוֹשׁ.

Eliezer had a trusty cow that worked hard for him all week long. When it came to Shabbat they both rested from a hard week of work. The time came when Eliezer had to sell his cow, and he got a good price from his non-Jewish neighbor. After a few days the neighbor returned with the cow, frustrated and angry. "Your cow is hard working," said the neighbor, "but every Saturday she refuses to work. I tried everything but she only works for six days a week! I demand a refund." Eliezer then whispered something into the ear of the cow, who immediately got up and returned to her new owner's field to begin working. Shocked, the man asked Eliezer what he told the cow. Eliezer told him that he explained to the cow that she no longer belonged to a Jew and so it was now okay for her to work on Shabbat. The non-Jew was so moved by this, that he pledged to learn more about his Creator and promised that he too would allow the cow to rest every Shabbat.

1 **אַתָּה קִדַּשְׁתָּ** אֶת יוֹם הַשְּׁבִיעִי לִשְׁמֶךָ

2 תַּכְלִית מַעֲשֵׂה שָׁמַיִם וָאָרֶץ

3 וּבֵרַכְתּוֹ מִכָּל הַיָּמִים, וְקִדַּשְׁתּוֹ מִכָּל הַזְּמַנִּים

4 וְכֵן כָּתוּב בְּתוֹרָתֶךָ:

5 **וַיְכֻלּוּ הַשָּׁמַיִם**

6 וְהָאָרֶץ וְכָל־צְבָאָם:

7 וַיְכַל אֱלֹהִים בַּיּוֹם הַשְּׁבִיעִי

8 מְלַאכְתּוֹ אֲשֶׁר עָשָׂה

9 וַיִּשְׁבֹּת בַּיּוֹם הַשְּׁבִיעִי

10 מִכָּל־מְלַאכְתּוֹ אֲשֶׁר עָשָׂה:

11 וַיְבָרֶךְ אֱלֹהִים אֶת־יוֹם הַשְּׁבִיעִי, וַיְקַדֵּשׁ אֹתוֹ

12 כִּי בוֹ שָׁבַת מִכָּל־מְלַאכְתּוֹ, אֲשֶׁר־בָּרָא אֱלֹהִים לַעֲשׂוֹת

It is written in Your Torah: Hashem finished creating the heaven and the earth on the seventh day, and then rested from all the work He had done. And Hashem blessed it – He made it special.

"More than the Jews have kept Shabbat, Shabbat has kept the Jews."

What does Shabbat do for you?

"The Mashiaḥ will come if all Jews keep just one Shabbat, because Shabbat is equal to all the other mitzvot."

Why do you think Shabbat is equal to all the other mitzvot?

אֱלֹהֵינוּ וֵאלֹהֵי אֲבוֹתֵינוּ, רְצֵה נָא בִמְנוּחָתֵנוּ.
קַדְּשֵׁנוּ בְּמִצְוֹתֶיךָ, שִׂים חֶלְקֵנוּ בְּתוֹרָתֶךָ
שַׂבְּעֵנוּ מִטּוּבֶךָ, שַׂמֵּחַ נַפְשֵׁנוּ בִּישׁוּעָתֶךָ.
וְטַהֵר לִבֵּנוּ לְעָבְדְּךָ בֶּאֱמֶת.
וְהַנְחִילֵנוּ, יְהוָֹה אֱלֹהֵינוּ
בְּאַהֲבָה וּבְרָצוֹן שַׁבַּת קָדְשֶׁךָ
וְיָנוּחוּ בָהּ כָּל יִשְׂרָאֵל מְקַדְּשֵׁי שְׁמֶךָ.
בָּרוּךְ אַתָּה יְהוָֹה

מְקַדֵּשׁ הַשַּׁבָּת.

רְצֵה יְהֹוָה אֱלֹהֵינוּ בְּעַמְּךָ יִשְׂרָאֵל וְלִתְפִלָּתָם שְׁעֵה
וְהָשֵׁב הָעֲבוֹדָה לִדְבִיר בֵּיתֶךָ
וְאִשֵּׁי יִשְׂרָאֵל וּתְפִלָּתָם מְהֵרָה בְּאַהֲבָה תְקַבֵּל בְּרָצוֹן
וּתְהִי לְרָצוֹן תָּמִיד עֲבוֹדַת יִשְׂרָאֵל עַמֶּךָ.

On Rosh Ḥodesh and Ḥol HaMo'ed add יַעֲלֶה וְיָבוֹא:

אֱלֹהֵינוּ וֵאלֹהֵי אֲבוֹתֵינוּ, יַעֲלֶה וְיָבוֹא, יַגִּיעַ, יֵרָאֶה וְיֵרָצֶה, יִשָּׁמַע, יִפָּקֵד וְיִזָּכֵר זִכְרוֹנֵנוּ וְזִכְרוֹן אֲבוֹתֵינוּ, זִכְרוֹן יְרוּשָׁלַיִם עִירֶךָ, וְזִכְרוֹן מָשִׁיחַ בֶּן דָּוִד עַבְדֶּךָ, וְזִכְרוֹן כָּל עַמְּךָ בֵּית יִשְׂרָאֵל, לְפָנֶיךָ, לִפְלֵיטָה לְטוֹבָה לְחֵן, לְחֶסֶד וּלְרַחֲמִים לְחַיִּים טוֹבִים וּלְשָׁלוֹם, בְּיוֹם

Sukkot	*Pesaḥ*	*Rosh Ḥodesh*
חַג הַסֻּכּוֹת הַזֶּה	חַג הַמַּצּוֹת הַזֶּה	רֹאשׁ הַחֹדֶשׁ הַזֶּה
בְּיוֹם מִקְרָא קֹדֶשׁ הַזֶּה	בְּיוֹם מִקְרָא קֹדֶשׁ הַזֶּה	

לְרַחֵם בּוֹ עָלֵינוּ וּלְהוֹשִׁיעֵנוּ. זָכְרֵנוּ יְהֹוָה אֱלֹהֵינוּ בּוֹ לְטוֹבָה, וּפָקְדֵנוּ בוֹ לִבְרָכָה, וְהוֹשִׁיעֵנוּ בוֹ לְחַיִּים טוֹבִים. בִּדְבַר יְשׁוּעָה וְרַחֲמִים חוּס וְחָנֵּנוּ וַחֲמֹל וְרַחֵם עָלֵינוּ וְהוֹשִׁיעֵנוּ, כִּי אֵלֶיךָ עֵינֵינוּ, כִּי אֵל מֶלֶךְ חַנּוּן וְרַחוּם אָתָּה.

וְאַתָּה בְּרַחֲמֶיךָ הָרַבִּים תַּחְפֹּץ בָּנוּ וְתִרְצֵנוּ
וְתֶחֱזֶינָה עֵינֵינוּ בְּשׁוּבְךָ לְצִיּוֹן בְּרַחֲמִים.
בָּרוּךְ אַתָּה יְהֹוָה
הַמַּחֲזִיר שְׁכִינָתוֹ לְצִיּוֹן.

We thank You, Hashem, because You are our God and the God of our ancestors from generation to generation. We thank You because our lives are in Your hands, for Your miracles that You make for us every day.

מוֹדִים אֲנַחְנוּ לָךְ
שָׁאַתָּה הוּא יְהֹוָה אֱלֹהֵינוּ
וֵאלֹהֵי אֲבוֹתֵינוּ לְעוֹלָם וָעֶד.
צוּרֵנוּ, צוּר חַיֵּינוּ וּמָגֵן יִשְׁעֵנוּ
אַתָּה הוּא לְדוֹר וָדוֹר
נוֹדֶה לְּךָ וּנְסַפֵּר תְּהִלָּתֶךָ
עַל חַיֵּינוּ הַמְּסוּרִים בְּיָדֶךָ
וְעַל נִשְׁמוֹתֵינוּ הַפְּקוּדוֹת לָךְ
וְעַל נִסֶּיךָ שֶׁבְּכָל יוֹם עִמָּנוּ
וְעַל נִפְלְאוֹתֶיךָ וְטוֹבוֹתֶיךָ
שֶׁבְּכָל עֵת, עֶרֶב וָבֹקֶר וְצָהֳרָיִם.
הַטּוֹב, כִּי לֹא כָלוּ רַחֲמֶיךָ
הַמְרַחֵם, כִּי לֹא תַמּוּ חֲסָדֶיךָ
כִּי מֵעוֹלָם קִוִּינוּ לָךְ.

During Ḥanukka say עַל הַנִּסִּים.

עַל הַנִּסִּים וְעַל הַפֻּרְקָן וְעַל הַגְּבוּרוֹת וְעַל הַתְּשׁוּעוֹת וְעַל הַנִּפְלָאוֹת
וְעַל הַנֶּחָמוֹת שֶׁעָשִׂיתָ לַאֲבוֹתֵינוּ בַּיָּמִים הָהֵם בַּזְּמַן הַזֶּה.

בִּימֵי מַתִּתְיָה בֶּן יוֹחָנָן כֹּהֵן גָּדוֹל חַשְׁמוֹנַאי וּבָנָיו, כְּשֶׁעָמְדָה מַלְכוּת יָוָן הָרְשָׁעָה עַל עַמְּךָ יִשְׂרָאֵל לְשַׁכְּחָם תּוֹרָתֶךָ וּלְהַעֲבִירָם מֵחֻקֵּי רְצוֹנֶךָ, וְאַתָּה בְּרַחֲמֶיךָ הָרַבִּים עָמַדְתָּ לָהֶם בְּעֵת צָרָתָם, רַבְתָּ אֶת רִיבָם, דַּנְתָּ אֶת דִּינָם, נָקַמְתָּ אֶת נִקְמָתָם, מָסַרְתָּ גִבּוֹרִים בְּיַד חַלָּשִׁים, וְרַבִּים בְּיַד מְעַטִּים, וּרְשָׁעִים בְּיַד צַדִּיקִים, וּטְמֵאִים בְּיַד טְהוֹרִים, וְזֵדִים בְּיַד עוֹסְקֵי תוֹרָתֶךָ. לְךָ עָשִׂיתָ שֵׁם גָּדוֹל וְקָדוֹשׁ בְּעוֹלָמֶךָ, וּלְעַמְּךָ יִשְׂרָאֵל עָשִׂיתָ תְּשׁוּעָה גְדוֹלָה וּפֻרְקָן כְּהַיּוֹם הַזֶּה. וְאַחַר כָּךְ בָּאוּ בָנֶיךָ לִדְבִיר בֵּיתֶךָ, וּפִנּוּ אֶת הֵיכָלֶךָ, וְטִהֲרוּ אֶת מִקְדָּשֶׁךָ, וְהִדְלִיקוּ נֵרוֹת בְּחַצְרוֹת קָדְשֶׁךָ, וְקָבְעוּ שְׁמוֹנַת יְמֵי חֲנֻכָּה אֵלּוּ, בְּהַלֵּל וּבְהוֹדָאָה, וְעָשִׂיתָ עִמָּהֶם נִסִּים וְנִפְלָאוֹת, וְנוֹדֶה לְשִׁמְךָ הַגָּדוֹל, סֶלָה.

וְעַל כֻּלָּם
יִתְבָּרַךְ וְיִתְרוֹמַם וְיִתְנַשֵּׂא תָּמִיד שִׁמְךָ מַלְכֵּנוּ לְעוֹלָם וָעֶ
וְכָל הַחַיִּים יוֹדוּךָ סֶּלָה

Between Rosh HaShana and Yom Kippur add these words:

וּכְתֹב לְחַיִּים טוֹבִים כָּל בְּנֵי בְרִיתֶךָ.

וִיהַלְלוּ וִיבָרְכוּ אֶת שִׁמְךָ הַגָּדוֹל בֶּאֱמֶת לְעוֹלָם כִּי טוֹב
הָאֵל יְשׁוּעָתֵנוּ וְעֶזְרָתֵנוּ סֶלָה, הָאֵל הַטּוֹב.
בָּרוּךְ אַתָּה יְהוָה
הַטּוֹב שִׁמְךָ וּלְךָ נָאֶה לְהוֹדוֹת.

שִׂים שָׁלוֹם טוֹבָה וּבְרָכָה
חַיִּים חֵן וָחֶסֶד, צְדָקָה וְרַחֲמִים
עָלֵינוּ וְעַל כָּל יִשְׂרָאֵל עַמֶּךָ.
וּבָרְכֵנוּ אָבִינוּ כֻּלָּנוּ כְּאֶחָד בְּאוֹר פָּנֶיךָ
כִּי בְאוֹר פָּנֶיךָ נָתַתָּ לָּנוּ, יְהוָה אֱלֹהֵינוּ
תּוֹרָה וְחַיִּים, אַהֲבָה וָחֶסֶד, צְדָקָה וְרַחֲמִים, בְּרָכָה וְשָׁלוֹם.
וְטוֹב בְּעֵינֶיךָ לְבָרְכֵנוּ, וּלְבָרֵךְ אֶת כָּל עַמְּךָ יִשְׂרָאֵל
בְּרֹב עֹז וְשָׁלוֹם.

Between Rosh HaShana and Yom Kippur add these words:

וּבְסֵפֶר חַיִּים, בְּרָכָה וְשָׁלוֹם, וּפַרְנָסָה טוֹבָה, וִישׁוּעָה וְנֶחָמָה, וּגְזֵרוֹת טוֹבוֹת,
נִזָּכֵר וְנִכָּתֵב לְפָנֶיךָ, אֲנַחְנוּ וְכָל עַמְּךָ יִשְׂרָאֵל, לְחַיִּים טוֹבִים וּלְשָׁלוֹם.

בָּרוּךְ אַתָּה יְהוָה
הַמְבָרֵךְ אֶת עַמּוֹ
יִשְׂרָאֵל בַּשָּׁלוֹם. אָמֵן

יִהְיוּ לְרָצוֹן אִמְרֵי־פִי וְהֶגְיוֹן לִבִּי לְפָנֶיךָ, יְהוָה צוּרִי וְגֹאֲלִי:

Why do you think these two *berakhot* follow each other?
How do you think saying "thank you" can lead to peace?

1 # אֱלֹהַי

2 נְצֹר לְשׁוֹנִי מֵרָע וּשְׂפָתַי מִדַּבֵּר מִרְמָה

3 וְלִמְקַלְלַי נַפְשִׁי תִדֹּם, וְנַפְשִׁי כֶּעָפָר לַכֹּל תִּהְיֶה.

4 פְּתַח לִבִּי בְּתוֹרָתֶךָ, וְאַחֲרֵי מִצְוֹתֶיךָ תִּרְדֹּף נַפְשִׁי.

5 וְכָל הַקָּמִים עָלַי לְרָעָה

6 מְהֵרָה הָפֵר עֲצָתָם וְקַלְקֵל מַחְשְׁבוֹתָם.

7 יִהְיוּ כְּמֹץ לִפְנֵי־רוּחַ וּמַלְאַךְ יְהֹוָה דּוֹחֶה:

8 עֲשֵׂה לְמַעַן שְׁמֶךָ, עֲשֵׂה לְמַעַן יְמִינֶךָ

9 עֲשֵׂה לְמַעַן תּוֹרָתֶךָ, עֲשֵׂה לְמַעַן קְדֻשָּׁתֶךָ.

10 לְמַעַן יֵחָלְצוּן יְדִידֶיךָ, הוֹשִׁיעָה יְמִינְךָ וַעֲנֵנִי:

11 יִהְיוּ לְרָצוֹן אִמְרֵי־פִי וְהֶגְיוֹן לִבִּי לְפָנֶיךָ, יְהֹוָה צוּרִי וְגֹאֲלִי:

"If you only have enough money to buy either Shabbat candles, or wine for *kiddush*, or Ḥanukkah candles, then you should buy Shabbat candles because they create *Shalom Bayit*."

How can the Shabbat candles provide *shalom* in your house?

How can you provide *shalom* in your house this Shabbat?

As you finish the עֲמִידָה you should stop and think that you have just had the opportunity and honor to stand before Hashem. To be respectful, bow as you take three steps back. Then bow to the left, right and center as the pictures show.

Between Rosh HaShana and Yom Kippur say הַשָּׁלוֹם *instead of* שָׁלוֹם.

12 עֹשֶׂה שָׁלוֹם / הַשָּׁלוֹם / בִּמְרוֹמָיו

13 הוּא בְּרַחֲמָיו יַעֲשֶׂה שָׁלוֹם עָלֵינוּ

14 וְעַל כָּל עַמּוֹ יִשְׂרָאֵל

15 וְאִמְרוּ אָמֵן.

We must praise the Ruler of the universe, and tell how great Hashem is, the Creator of all things.
He is our God, no one else. He is our King, no one else.
Hashem is our God in heaven and on earth.

We stand when we say עָלֵינוּ.

1 **עָלֵינוּ** לְשַׁבֵּחַ לַאֲדוֹן הַכֹּל, לָתֵת גְּדֻלָּה לְיוֹצֵר בְּרֵאשִׁית

2 שֶׁלֹּא עָשָׂנוּ כְּגוֹיֵי הָאֲרָצוֹת, וְלֹא שָׂמָנוּ כְּמִשְׁפְּחוֹת הָאֲדָמָה

3 שֶׁלֹּא שָׂם חֶלְקֵנוּ כָּהֶם וְגוֹרָלֵנוּ כְּכָל הֲמוֹנָם.

4 שֶׁהֵם מִשְׁתַּחֲוִים לְהֶבֶל וָרִיק וּמִתְפַּלְלִים אֶל־אֵל לֹא יוֹשִׁיעַ

5 וַאֲנַחְנוּ מִשְׁתַּחֲוִים לִפְנֵי מֶלֶךְ מַלְכֵי הַמְּלָכִים

6 הַקָּדוֹשׁ בָּרוּךְ הוּא

7 שֶׁהוּא נוֹטֶה שָׁמַיִם וְיוֹסֵד אָרֶץ

8 וּמוֹשַׁב יְקָרוֹ בַּשָּׁמַיִם מִמַּעַל

9 וּשְׁכִינַת עֻזּוֹ בְּגָבְהֵי מְרוֹמִים.

10 הוּא אֱלֹהֵינוּ, וְאֵין עוֹד אַחֵר

11 אֱמֶת מַלְכֵּנוּ, וְאֶפֶס זוּלָתוֹ

12 כַּכָּתוּב בַּתּוֹרָה, וְיָדַעְתָּ הַיּוֹם וַהֲשֵׁבֹתָ אֶל־לְבָבֶךָ

13 כִּי יְהוָה הוּא הָאֱלֹהִים בַּשָּׁמַיִם מִמַּעַל

14 וְעַל־הָאָרֶץ מִתָּחַת אֵין עוֹד:

עַל כֵּן נְקַוֶּה לְּךָ, יְהֹוָה אֱלֹהֵינוּ
לִרְאוֹת מְהֵרָה בְּתִפְאֶרֶת עֻזֶּךָ
לְהַעֲבִיר גִּלּוּלִים מִן הָאָרֶץ, וְהָאֱלִילִים כָּרוֹת יִכָּרֵתוּן
לְתַקֵּן עוֹלָם בְּמַלְכוּת שַׁדַּי
וְכָל בְּנֵי בָשָׂר יִקְרְאוּ בִשְׁמֶךָ לְהַפְנוֹת אֵלֶיךָ כָּל רִשְׁעֵי אָרֶץ
יַכִּירוּ וְיֵדְעוּ כָּל יוֹשְׁבֵי תֵבֵל
כִּי לְךָ תִכְרַע כָּל בֶּרֶךְ, תִּשָּׁבַע כָּל לָשׁוֹן.
לְפָנֶיךָ יְהֹוָה אֱלֹהֵינוּ יִכְרְעוּ וְיִפֹּלוּ
וְלִכְבוֹד שִׁמְךָ יְקָר יִתֵּנוּ
וִיקַבְּלוּ כֻלָּם אֶת עֹל מַלְכוּתֶךָ
וְתִמְלֹךְ עֲלֵיהֶם מְהֵרָה לְעוֹלָם וָעֶד
כִּי הַמַּלְכוּת שֶׁלְּךָ הִיא, וּלְעוֹלְמֵי עַד תִּמְלֹךְ בְּכָבוֹד
כַּכָּתוּב בְּתוֹרָתֶךָ, יְהֹוָה יִמְלֹךְ לְעֹלָם וָעֶד:
וְנֶאֱמַר, וְהָיָה יְהֹוָה לְמֶלֶךְ עַל-כָּל-הָאָרֶץ
בַּיּוֹם הַהוּא יִהְיֶה יְהֹוָה אֶחָד וּשְׁמוֹ אֶחָד:

At the end of תְּפִלַּת עַרְבִית *on Shabbat we say* אֲדוֹן עוֹלָם *or* יִגְדַּל *(page 27/29).*

Many families bless their children on Friday night with these בְּרָכוֹת.

For sons:

1 יְשִׂמְךָ אֱלֹהִים

2 כְּאֶפְרַיִם וְכִמְנַשֶּׁה:

For daughters:

יְשִׂימֵךְ אֱלֹהִים

כְּשָׂרָה רִבְקָה רָחֵל וְלֵאָה.

3 יְבָרֶכְךָ יְהֹוָה וְיִשְׁמְרֶךָ:

4 יָאֵר יְהֹוָה פָּנָיו אֵלֶיךָ וִיחֻנֶּךָּ:

5 יִשָּׂא יְהֹוָה פָּנָיו אֵלֶיךָ וְיָשֵׂם לְךָ שָׁלוֹם:

What do you think your parents think about when they give you a blessing?

What do you think about when you get a blessing?

This poem is said when we come home from the בֵּית כְּנֶסֶת on Friday night, to welcome and say farewell to the two angels that the Rabbis tell us accompany us on the way home. Some families say each verse three times.

שָׁלוֹם עֲלֵיכֶם
מַלְאֲכֵי הַשָּׁרֵת מַלְאֲכֵי עֶלְיוֹן
מִמֶּלֶךְ מַלְכֵי הַמְּלָכִים
הַקָּדוֹשׁ בָּרוּךְ הוּא.

בּוֹאֲכֶם לְשָׁלוֹם
מַלְאֲכֵי הַשָּׁלוֹם מַלְאֲכֵי עֶלְיוֹן
מִמֶּלֶךְ מַלְכֵי הַמְּלָכִים
הַקָּדוֹשׁ בָּרוּךְ הוּא.

בָּרְכוּנִי לְשָׁלוֹם
מַלְאֲכֵי הַשָּׁלוֹם מַלְאֲכֵי עֶלְיוֹן
מִמֶּלֶךְ מַלְכֵי הַמְּלָכִים
הַקָּדוֹשׁ בָּרוּךְ הוּא.

בְּשִׁבְתְּכֶם לְשָׁלוֹם
מַלְאֲכֵי הַשָּׁלוֹם מַלְאֲכֵי עֶלְיוֹן
מִמֶּלֶךְ מַלְכֵי הַמְּלָכִים
הַקָּדוֹשׁ בָּרוּךְ הוּא.

צֵאתְכֶם לְשָׁלוֹם
מַלְאֲכֵי הַשָּׁלוֹם מַלְאֲכֵי עֶלְיוֹן
מִמֶּלֶךְ מַלְכֵי הַמְּלָכִים
הַקָּדוֹשׁ בָּרוּךְ הוּא.

כִּי מַלְאָכָיו יְצַוֶּה־לָּךְ
לִשְׁמָרְךָ בְּכָל־דְּרָכֶיךָ:
יְהוָה יִשְׁמָר־צֵאתְךָ וּבוֹאֶךָ
מֵעַתָּה וְעַד־עוֹלָם:

"Two angels walk with a person on Friday night on his way home from the Beit Kenesset, one good and one bad. When he arrives at home and finds his house warm and light and ready for Shabbat, the good angel says, 'May you have another Shabbat like this one,' and the bad angel is forced to say, 'Amen.' If the house is not ready for Shabbat, the bad angel says, 'May you have another Shabbat like this one,' and the good angel is forced to answer, 'Amen' against his will."

The Shabbat meal on Friday night begins with קִדּוּשׁ - announcing that it is now the holy day of Shabbat.

יוֹם הַשִּׁשִּׁי: וַיְכֻלּוּ הַשָּׁמַיִם וְהָאָרֶץ וְכָל־צְבָאָם:
וַיְכַל אֱלֹהִים בַּיּוֹם הַשְּׁבִיעִי מְלַאכְתּוֹ אֲשֶׁר עָשָׂה
וַיִּשְׁבֹּת בַּיּוֹם הַשְּׁבִיעִי מִכָּל־מְלַאכְתּוֹ אֲשֶׁר עָשָׂה:
וַיְבָרֶךְ אֱלֹהִים אֶת־יוֹם הַשְּׁבִיעִי, וַיְקַדֵּשׁ אֹתוֹ
כִּי בוֹ שָׁבַת מִכָּל־מְלַאכְתּוֹ
אֲשֶׁר־בָּרָא אֱלֹהִים, לַעֲשׂוֹת:

סַבְרִי מָרָנָן

Everyone says:

לְחַיִּים

בָּרוּךְ אַתָּה יְהֹוָה, אֱלֹהֵינוּ מֶלֶךְ הָעוֹלָם
בּוֹרֵא פְּרִי הַגָּפֶן.

"One day a man was wandering from place to place when he passed a beautiful palace that was lit up. He said to himself, 'How can the palace be abandoned with no one taking care of it?' At that very moment the owner of the palace peeped out from the top floor and called to him, 'I am the owner!' This is like Avraham's journey to find Hashem. He looked at the world and wondered how there could be no one to look after it, and at that moment Hashem called to him and said, 'I am the Creator of the world!'"

בָּרוּךְ אַתָּה יְהֹוָה אֱלֹהֵינוּ מֶלֶךְ הָעוֹלָם
אֲשֶׁר קִדְּשָׁנוּ בְּמִצְוֹתָיו, וְרָצָה בָנוּ
וְשַׁבַּת קָדְשׁוֹ בְּאַהֲבָה וּבְרָצוֹן הִנְחִילָנוּ
זִכָּרוֹן לְמַעֲשֵׂה בְרֵאשִׁית
תְּחִלָּה לְמִקְרָאֵי קֹדֶשׁ, זֵכֶר לִיצִיאַת מִצְרָיִם
וְשַׁבַּת קָדְשְׁךָ בְּאַהֲבָה וּבְרָצוֹן הִנְחַלְתָּנוּ.
בָּרוּךְ אַתָּה יְהֹוָה, מְקַדֵּשׁ הַשַּׁבָּת.

Many people like to sing special Shabbat songs (זְמִירוֹת) at their Shabbat meals. There are some here on pages 176–179 and others on pages 231–233.

מְנוּחָה וְשִׂמְחָה אוֹר לַיְּהוּדִים
יוֹם שַׁבָּתוֹן, יוֹם מַחֲמַדִּים
שׁוֹמְרָיו וְזוֹכְרָיו הֵמָּה מְעִידִים
כִּי לְשִׁשָּׁה כֹּל בְּרוּאִים וְעוֹמְדִים.

שְׁמֵי שָׁמַיִם, אֶרֶץ וְיַמִּים
כָּל צְבָא מָרוֹם גְּבוֹהִים וְרָמִים
תַּנִּין וְאָדָם וְחַיַּת רְאֵמִים
כִּי בְּיָהּ יְהֹוָה צוּר עוֹלָמִים.

"Rabbi Yehuda HaNasi and the Emperor Antonius were good friends. Antonius once joined Rabbi Yehuda and his family for their Shabbat meal, and had a wonderful time. He particularly enjoyed the Shabbat food which tasted like nothing he had ever had in his whole life, despite the food being cold because cooking on Shabbat is forbidden. He promised Rabbi Yehuda that he would visit again soon. When he came next time, it was during the week, and Rabbi Yehuda served him piping hot, tasty food. But Antonius did not enjoy the food as much as the previous visit. When he mentioned this, Rabbi Yehuda explained that the hot food was missing one vital ingredient. 'What can it be?' Antonius asked, offering to have it sent from the royal kitchens. 'Your kitchens will certainly not have this, explained Rabbi Yehuda. 'This special spice is called "Shabbat!"'"

9 הוּא אֲשֶׁר דִּבֶּר לְעַם סְגֻלָּתוֹ
10 שָׁמוֹר לְקַדְּשׁוֹ מִבּוֹאוֹ עַד צֵאתוֹ
11 שַׁבַּת קֹדֶשׁ יוֹם חֶמְדָּתוֹ
12 כִּי בוֹ שָׁבַת אֵל מִכָּל מְלַאכְתּוֹ.

13 בְּמִצְוַת שַׁבָּת אֵל יַחֲלִיצָךְ
14 קוּם קְרָא אֵלָיו, יָחִישׁ לְאַמְּצָךְ
15 נִשְׁמַת כָּל חַי וְגַם נַעֲרִיצָךְ
16 אֱכֹל בְּשִׂמְחָה כִּי כְבָר רָצָךְ.

17 בְּמִשְׁנֶה לֶחֶם וְקִדּוּשׁ רַבָּה
18 בְּרֹב מַטְעַמִּים וְרוּחַ נְדִיבָה
19 יִזְכּוּ לְרַב טוּב הַמִּתְעַנְּגִים בָּהּ
20 בְּבִיאַת גּוֹאֵל לְחַיֵּי הָעוֹלָם הַבָּא.

1 צוּר מִשֶּׁלּוֹ אָכַלְנוּ   בָּרְכוּ אֱמוּנַי
2 שָׂבַעְנוּ וְהוֹתַרְנוּ   כִּדְבַר יְהֹוָה.
3 הַזָּן אֶת עוֹלָמוֹ   רוֹעֵנוּ אָבִינוּ
4 אָכַלְנוּ אֶת לַחְמוֹ   וְיֵינוֹ שָׁתִינוּ
5 עַל כֵּן נוֹדֶה לִשְׁמוֹ   וּנְהַלְלוֹ בְּפִינוּ
6 אָמַרְנוּ וְעָנִינוּ   אֵין קָדוֹשׁ כַּיהֹוָה.
7 צוּר מִשֶּׁלּוֹ אָכַלְנוּ, בָּרְכוּ אֱמוּנַי, שָׂבַעְנוּ וְהוֹתַרְנוּ כִּדְבַר יְהֹוָה.

8 בְּשִׁיר וְקוֹל תּוֹדָה   נְבָרֵךְ אֱלֹהֵינוּ
9 עַל אֶרֶץ חֶמְדָּה   שֶׁהִנְחִיל לַאֲבוֹתֵינוּ
10 מָזוֹן וְצֵידָה   הִשְׂבִּיעַ לְנַפְשֵׁנוּ
11 חַסְדּוֹ גָּבַר עָלֵינוּ   וֶאֱמֶת יְהֹוָה.
12 צוּר מִשֶּׁלּוֹ אָכַלְנוּ, בָּרְכוּ אֱמוּנַי, שָׂבַעְנוּ וְהוֹתַרְנוּ כִּדְבַר יְהֹוָה.

"Yosef was so famous for honoring Shabbat, that he became known as 'Yosef-who-honors-Shabbat.' A fortune-teller once told a non-Jew that he would lose all his wealth to Yosef. To try and protect his riches, the man sold everything he owned and bought with the money a precious pearl which he placed in the hat that he always wore. Once he was crossing a river in a boat, and a gust of wind blew his hat into the water and a fish swallowed the pearl. On Erev Shabbat just as the sun was setting, the fish was caught and taken to market. The fisherman wondered who will buy a fish so late in the day? The people said to him, 'Go bring it to Yosef, he always buys the tastiest food for Shabbat.' Yosef bought the fish for his Shabbat meal, and while preparing it he found the pearl. They said about Yosef, 'Whoever gives to Shabbat, Shabbat repays him!'"

13 רַחֵם בְּחַסְדֶּךָ   עַל עַמְּךָ צוּרֵנוּ
14 עַל צִיּוֹן מִשְׁכַּן כְּבוֹדֶךָ   זְבוּל בֵּית תִּפְאַרְתֵּנוּ
15 בֶּן דָּוִד עַבְדֶּךָ   יָבוֹא וְיִגְאָלֵנוּ
16 רוּחַ אַפֵּינוּ   מְשִׁיחַ יְהֹוָה.
17 צוּר מִשֶּׁלּוֹ אָכַלְנוּ, בָּרְכוּ אֱמוּנַי, שָׂבַעְנוּ וְהוֹתַרְנוּ כִּדְבַר יְהֹוָה.

18 יִבָּנֶה הַמִּקְדָּשׁ   עִיר צִיּוֹן תְּמַלֵּא
19 וְשָׁם נָשִׁיר שִׁיר חָדָשׁ   וּבִרְנָנָה נַעֲלֶה
20 הָרַחֲמָן הַנִּקְדָּשׁ   יִתְבָּרַךְ וְיִתְעַלֶּה
21 עַל כּוֹס יַיִן מָלֵא   כְּבִרְכַּת יְהֹוָה.
22 צוּר מִשֶּׁלּוֹ אָכַלְנוּ, בָּרְכוּ אֱמוּנַי, שָׂבַעְנוּ וְהוֹתַרְנוּ כִּדְבַר יְהֹוָה.

After the meal we say בִּרְכַּת הַמָּזוֹן *on page 266, thanking Hashem for the meal.*

For the beginning of תְּפִלַּת שַׁחֲרִית*, turn to pages 9–61.*
Then continue here with נִשְׁמַת*.*

נִשְׁמַת כָּל חַי

תְּבָרֵךְ אֶת שִׁמְךָ, יְהֹוָה אֱלֹהֵינוּ
וְרוּחַ כָּל בָּשָׂר תְּפָאֵר וּתְרוֹמֵם זִכְרְךָ מַלְכֵּנוּ תָּמִיד.
מִן הָעוֹלָם וְעַד הָעוֹלָם אַתָּה אֵל
וּמִבַּלְעָדֶיךָ אֵין לָנוּ מֶלֶךְ גּוֹאֵל וּמוֹשִׁיעַ
פּוֹדֶה וּמַצִּיל וְעוֹנֶה וּמְרַחֵם
בְּכָל עֵת צָרָה וְצוּקָה, אֵין לָנוּ מֶלֶךְ עוֹזֵר וְסוֹמֵךְ אֶלָּא אָתָּה
אֱלֹהֵי הָרִאשׁוֹנִים וְהָאַחֲרוֹנִים
אֱלוֹהַּ כָּל בְּרִיּוֹת, אֲדוֹן כָּל תּוֹלָדוֹת
הַמְהֻלָּל בְּכָל הַתִּשְׁבָּחוֹת
הַמְנַהֵג עוֹלָמוֹ בְּחֶסֶד וּבְרִיּוֹתָיו בְּרַחֲמִים.
וַיהֹוָה אֱלֹהִים אֱמֶת, לֹא יָנוּם וְלֹא יִישָׁן
הַמְעוֹרֵר יְשֵׁנִים וְהַמֵּקִיץ נִרְדָּמִים

מְחַיֵּה מֵתִים, וְרוֹפֵא חוֹלִים
פּוֹקֵחַ עִוְרִים, וְזוֹקֵף כְּפוּפִים.
הַמֵּשִׂיחַ אִלְּמִים וְהַמְפַעְנֵחַ נֶעֱלָמִים
וּלְךָ לְבַדְּךָ אֲנַחְנוּ מוֹדִים.
וְאִלּוּ פִינוּ מָלֵא שִׁירָה כַּיָּם
וּלְשׁוֹנֵנוּ רִנָּה כַּהֲמוֹן גַּלָּיו
וְשִׂפְתוֹתֵינוּ שֶׁבַח כְּמֶרְחֲבֵי רָקִיעַ
וְעֵינֵינוּ מְאִירוֹת כַּשֶּׁמֶשׁ וְכַיָּרֵחַ
וְיָדֵינוּ פְרוּשׂוֹת כְּנִשְׁרֵי שָׁמָיִם
וְרַגְלֵינוּ קַלּוֹת כָּאַיָּלוֹת
אֵין אֲנַחְנוּ מַסְפִּיקִין לְהוֹדוֹת לְךָ, יְהוָה אֱלֹהֵינוּ
וּלְבָרֵךְ אֶת שִׁמְךָ, מַלְכֵּנוּ
עַל אַחַת מֵאֶלֶף אַלְפֵי אֲלָפִים
וְרֹב רִבֵּי רְבָבוֹת פְּעָמִים הַטּוֹבוֹת
נִסִּים וְנִפְלָאוֹת שֶׁעָשִׂיתָ עִמָּנוּ וְעִם אֲבוֹתֵינוּ מִלְּפָנִים
מִמִּצְרַיִם גְּאַלְתָּנוּ, יְהוָה אֱלֹהֵינוּ, מִבֵּית עֲבָדִים פְּדִיתָנוּ
בְּרָעָב זַנְתָּנוּ, וּבְשָׂבָע כִּלְכַּלְתָּנוּ
מֵחֶרֶב הִצַּלְתָּנוּ, מִדֶּבֶר מִלַּטְתָּנוּ

32 וּמֵחֳלָאִים רָעִים וְרַבִּים דִּלִּיתָנוּ.
33 עַד הֵנָּה עֲזָרוּנוּ רַחֲמֶיךָ, וְלֹא עֲזָבוּנוּ חֲסָדֶיךָ
34 עַל כֵּן, אֵבָרִים שֶׁפִּלַּגְתָּ בָּנוּ
35 וְרוּחַ וּנְשָׁמָה שֶׁנָּפַחְתָּ בְּאַפֵּינוּ
36 וְלָשׁוֹן אֲשֶׁר שַׂמְתָּ בְּפִינוּ
37 הֵן הֵם יוֹדוּ וִיבָרְכוּ וִישַׁבְּחוּ וִיפָאֲרוּ
38 אֶת שִׁמְךָ מַלְכֵּנוּ תָּמִיד

כָּל עַצְמוֹתַי תֹּאמַרְנָה יְהוָֹה מִי כָמוֹךָ (Tehillim 35:10)

"All of my bones will say 'Who is like You Hashem?'"

How can we use our actual bodies to pray to Hashem?

כִּי כָל פֶּה לְךָ יוֹדֶה, וְכָל לָשׁוֹן לְךָ תְשַׁבֵּחַ

וְכָל עַיִן לְךָ תְצַפֶּה

וְכָל בֶּרֶךְ לְךָ תִכְרַע

וְכָל קוֹמָה לְפָנֶיךָ תִשְׁתַּחֲוֶה

וְהַלְּבָבוֹת יִירָאוּךָ

וְכָל קֶרֶב וּכְלָיוֹת יְזַמְּרוּ לִשְׁמֶךָ

כַּדָּבָר שֶׁנֶּאֱמַר

כָּל עַצְמֹתַי תֹּאמַרְנָה יְהֹוָה מִי כָמוֹךָ

מַצִּיל עָנִי מֵחָזָק מִמֶּנּוּ, וְעָנִי וְאֶבְיוֹן מִגֹּזְלוֹ:

שַׁוְעַת עֲנִיִּים אַתָּה תִשְׁמַע, צַעֲקַת הַדַּל תַּקְשִׁיב וְתוֹשִׁיעַ.

One Friday night Rabbi Avraham Ibn Ezra once had a dream. An angel in the form of a man stood in front of him holding out a sealed letter. As the Ibn Ezra opened the letter he realized it was from Shabbat! The letter asked that Shabbat, the eternal covenant, be observed in a way that is unique from the other days of the week. Shabbat then promised to look after the Ibn Ezra just as he had observed Shabbat from his youth. But the letter ends with criticism of the Ibn Ezra. Shaking he pleaded with the angel to explain to him his sin. The angel replied that one of his students had become careless in his Shabbat observance. From that day on the Ibn Ezra was careful to not only observe Shabbat himself, but to ensure those he could influence to do the same

1 # וְכָתוּב

2 רַנְּנוּ צַדִּיקִים בַּיהוָה, לַיְשָׁרִים נָאוָה תְהִלָּה:

3 בְּפִי יְ שָׁרִים תִּתְ ר וֹמָם

4 וּבְשִׂפְתֵי צַ דִּיקִים תִּתְ בָּ רַךְ

5 וּבִלְשׁוֹן חֲ סִידִים תִּתְ קַ דָּשׁ

6 וּבְקֶרֶב קְ דוֹשִׁים תִּתְ הַ לָּל

7 בְּמִקְהֲלוֹת רִבְבוֹת עַמְּךָ בֵּית יִשְׂרָאֵל

8 שֶׁכֵּן חוֹבַת כָּל הַיְצוּרִים

9 לְפָנֶיךָ יְהוָה אֱלֹהֵינוּ

10 וֵאלֹהֵי אֲבוֹתֵינוּ

11 לְהוֹדוֹת, לְהַלֵּל, לְשַׁבֵּחַ

12 לְפָאֵר, לְרוֹמֵם, לְהַדֵּר וּלְנַצֵּחַ

13 עַל כָּל דִּבְרֵי שִׁירוֹת וְתִשְׁבָּחוֹת

14 דָּוִד בֶּן יִשַׁי, עַבְדְּךָ מְשִׁיחֶךָ.

Everything living that You, Hashem, created must thank, praise, compliment, honor, and bless, even more than the songs and praises of Your servant David ben Yishai.

Why do you think we use the words of David HaMelekh, and not our own, to praise Hashem?

וּבְכֵן יִשְׁתַּבַּח

שִׁמְךָ לָעַד, מַלְכֵּנוּ
הָאֵל הַמֶּלֶךְ הַגָּדוֹל וְהַקָּדוֹשׁ בַּשָּׁמַיִם וּבָאָרֶץ
כִּי לְךָ נָאֶה, יְהֹוָה אֱלֹהֵינוּ וֵאלֹהֵי אֲבוֹתֵינוּ לְעוֹלָם וָעֶד
שִׁיר וּשְׁבָחָה, הַלֵּל וְזִמְרָה
עֹז וּמֶמְשָׁלָה, נֶצַח, גְּדֻלָּה וּגְבוּרָה
תְּהִלָּה וְתִפְאֶרֶת, קְדֻשָּׁה וּמַלְכוּת
בְּרָכוֹת וְהוֹדָאוֹת לְשִׁמְךָ הַגָּדוֹל וְהַקָּדוֹשׁ
וּמֵעוֹלָם עַד־עוֹלָם אַתָּה אֵל:

בָּרוּךְ אַתָּה יְהֹוָה
מֶלֶךְ גָּדוֹל וּמְהֻלָּל בַּתִּשְׁבָּחוֹת
אֵל הַהוֹדָאוֹת, אֲדוֹן הַנִּפְלָאוֹת
בּוֹרֵא כָּל הַנְּשָׁמוֹת, רִבּוֹן כָּל הַמַּעֲשִׂים
הַבּוֹחֵר בְּשִׁירֵי זִמְרָה
מֶלֶךְ, אֵל, חַי הָעוֹלָמִים. אָמֵן.

The next section of תְּפִלַּת שַׁחֲרִית is the שְׁמַע and its בְּרָכוֹת. There are two בְּרָכוֹת before and one after the שְׁמַע. We sit from here until the עֲמִידָה.

Hashem, You create light and darkness, and make peace in the world. You created absolutely everything.

בָּרוּךְ אַתָּה יְהֹוָה
אֱלֹהֵינוּ מֶלֶךְ הָעוֹלָם
יוֹצֵר אוֹר וּבוֹרֵא חֹשֶׁךְ
עֹשֶׂה שָׁלוֹם וּבוֹרֵא אֶת הַכֹּל.

All people will thank You.

All people will praise You.

All people will say about You: nothing is as holy as Hashem!

הַכֹּל יוֹדוּךָ וְהַכֹּל יְשַׁבְּחוּךָ
וְהַכֹּל יֹאמְרוּ אֵין קָדוֹשׁ כַּיהוה
הַכֹּל יְרוֹמְמוּךָ סֶּלָה, יוֹצֵר הַכֹּל.
הָאֵל הַפּוֹתֵחַ בְּכָל יוֹם
דַּלְתוֹת שַׁעֲרֵי מִזְרָח
וּבוֹקֵעַ חַלּוֹנֵי רָקִיעַ
מוֹצִיא חַמָּה מִמְּקוֹמָהּ
וּלְבָנָה מִמְּכוֹן שִׁבְתָּהּ
וּמֵאִיר לָעוֹלָם כֻּלּוֹ וּלְיוֹשְׁבָיו
שֶׁבָּרָא בְּמִדַּת הָרַחֲמִים.

With kindness You give light to the earth and to all the people that live here.

1 הַמֵּאִיר לָאָרֶץ וְלַדָּרִים עָלֶיהָ בְּרַחֲמִים

2 וּבְטוּבוֹ מְחַדֵּשׁ בְּכָל יוֹם תָּמִיד מַעֲשֵׂה בְרֵאשִׁית.

3 מָה־רַבּוּ מַעֲשֶׂיךָ, יְהוָה, כֻּלָּם בְּחָכְמָה עָשִׂיתָ

4 מָלְאָה הָאָרֶץ קִנְיָנֶךָ:

5 הַמֶּלֶךְ הַמְרוֹמָם לְבַדּוֹ מֵאָז

6 הַמְשֻׁבָּח וְהַמְפֹאָר וְהַמִּתְנַשֵּׂא מִימוֹת עוֹלָם.

7 אֱלֹהֵי עוֹלָם

8 בְּרַחֲמֶיךָ הָרַבִּים רַחֵם עָלֵינוּ

9 אֲדוֹן עֻזֵּנוּ, צוּר מִשְׂגַּבֵּנוּ, מָגֵן יִשְׁעֵנוּ, מִשְׂגָּב בַּעֲדֵנוּ.

10 אֵין עֲרוֹךְ לָךְ.

11 וְאֵין זוּלָתָךְ.

12 אֶפֶס בִּלְתָּךְ.

13 וּמִי דּוֹמֶה לָּךְ.

14 אֵין עֲרוֹךְ לָךְ, יְהוָה אֱלֹהֵינוּ, בָּעוֹלָם הַזֶּה

15 וְאֵין זוּלָתָךְ, מַלְכֵּנוּ, לְחַיֵּי הָעוֹלָם הַבָּא

16 אֶפֶס בִּלְתָּךְ, גּוֹאֲלֵנוּ, לִימוֹת הַמָּשִׁיחַ

17 וּמִי דּוֹמֶה לָּךְ, מוֹשִׁיעֵנוּ, לִתְחִיַּת הַמֵּתִים.

אֵל אָדוֹן עַל כָּל הַמַּעֲשִׂים

בָּרוּךְ וּמְבֹרָךְ בְּפִי כָּל הַנְּשָׁמָה

גָּדְלוֹ וְטוּבוֹ מָלֵא עוֹלָם
דַּעַת וּתְבוּנָה סוֹבְבִים הוֹדוֹ.

הַמִּתְגָּאֶה עַל חַיּוֹת הַקֹּדֶשׁ
וְנֶהְדָּר בְּכָבוֹד עַל הַמֶּרְכָּבָה

זְכוּת וּמִישׁוֹר לִפְנֵי כִסְאוֹ
חֶסֶד וְרַחֲמִים לִפְנֵי כְבוֹדוֹ.

טוֹבִים מְאוֹרוֹת שֶׁבָּרָא אֱלֹהֵינוּ
יְצָרָם בְּדַעַת בְּבִינָה וּבְהַשְׂכֵּל

כֹּחַ וּגְבוּרָה נָתַן בָּהֶם
לִהְיוֹת מוֹשְׁלִים בְּקֶרֶב תֵּבֵל.

Hashem, You created the world.

Hashem, every person blesses You.

Hashem, Your greatness and goodness can be seen everywhere.

Hashem, Your knowledge and wisdom is everywhere.

"Sunshine and Shabbat … are a taste of the World to Come."

What do Shabbat and sunshine have in common that they are both considered a taste of the World to Come?

13 מְלֵאִים זִיו וּמְפִיקִים נֹגַהּ
14 נָאֶה זִיוָם בְּכָל הָעוֹלָם

15 שְׂמֵחִים בְּצֵאתָם שָׂשִׂים בְּבוֹאָם
16 עוֹשִׂים בְּאֵימָה רְצוֹן קוֹנֵיהֶם.

17 פְּאֵר וְכָבוֹד נוֹתְנִים לִשְׁמוֹ
18 צָהֳלָה וְרִנָּה לְזֵכֶר מַלְכוּתוֹ

19 קָרָא לַשֶּׁמֶשׁ וַיִּזְרַח אוֹר
20 רָאָה וְהִתְקִין צוּרַת הַלְּבָנָה.

21 שֶׁבַח נוֹתְנִים לוֹ כָּל צְבָא מָרוֹם
22 תִּפְאֶרֶת וּגְדֻלָּה שְׂרָפִים וְחַיּוֹת וְאוֹפַנֵּי הַקֹּדֶשׁ.

> Hashem, You rested from creating the world on the seventh day. Then You sat on Your throne and created Shabbat as a wonderful day of rest.

לָאֵל אֲשֶׁר שָׁבַת מִכָּל הַמַּעֲשִׂים
וּבַיּוֹם הַשְּׁבִיעִי נִתְעַלָּה וְיָשַׁב עַל כִּסֵּא כְבוֹדוֹ.
תִּפְאֶרֶת עָטָה לְיוֹם הַמְּנוּחָה
עֹנֶג קָרָא לְיוֹם הַשַּׁבָּת.
זֶה שִׁיר שֶׁבַח שֶׁל יוֹם הַשְּׁבִיעִי
שֶׁבּוֹ שָׁבַת אֵל מִכָּל מְלַאכְתּוֹ.
וְיוֹם הַשְּׁבִיעִי מְשַׁבֵּחַ וְאוֹמֵר
מִזְמוֹר שִׁיר לְיוֹם הַשַּׁבָּת:

לְפִיכָךְ יְפָאֲרוּ לָאֵל כָּל יְצוּרָיו
שֶׁבַח וִיקָר וּגְדֻלָּה וְכָבוֹד יִתְּנוּ לַמֶּלֶךְ יוֹצֵר כֹּל
הַמַּנְחִיל מְנוּחָה לְעַמּוֹ יִשְׂרָאֵל
בְּיוֹם שַׁבַּת קֹדֶשׁ.
שִׁמְךָ יְהֹוָה אֱלֹהֵינוּ יִתְקַדַּשׁ
וְזִכְרְךָ יִתְפָּאַר מַלְכֵּנוּ
בַּשָּׁמַיִם מִמַּעַל וְעַל הָאָרֶץ מִתָּחַת
עַל כָּל שֶׁבַח מַעֲשֵׂה יָדֶיךָ
וְעַל מְאוֹרֵי אוֹר שֶׁיָּצַרְתָּ, הֵמָּה יְפָאֲרוּךָ סֶּלָה.

תִּתְבָּרַךְ לָנֶצַח

צוּרֵנוּ מַלְכֵּנוּ וְגוֹאֲלֵנוּ, בּוֹרֵא קְדוֹשִׁים

יִשְׁתַּבַּח שִׁמְךָ לָעַד

מַלְכֵּנוּ, יוֹצֵר מְשָׁרְתִים

וַאֲשֶׁר מְשָׁרְתָיו כֻּלָּם, עוֹמְדִים בְּרוּם עוֹלָם

וּמַשְׁמִיעִים בְּיִרְאָה יַחַד בְּקוֹל

דִּבְרֵי אֱלֹהִים חַיִּים וּמֶלֶךְ עוֹלָם.

כֻּלָּם אֲהוּבִים   כֻּלָּם בְּרוּרִים

כֻּלָּם גִּבּוֹרִים   כֻּלָּם קְדוֹשִׁים

כֻּלָּם עוֹשִׂים בְּאֵימָה וּבְיִרְאָה רְצוֹן קוֹנֵיהֶם

וְכֻלָּם פּוֹתְחִים אֶת פִּיהֶם

בִּקְדֻשָּׁה וּבְטָהֳרָה בְּשִׁירָה וּבְזִמְרָה

וּמְבָרְכִין   וּמְשַׁבְּחִין   וּמְפָאֲרִין

וּמַקְדִּישִׁין   וּמַעֲרִיצִין   וּמַמְלִיכִין

We describe Hashem here as our Rock, our King, our Savior, and the Creator of the angels.

What do these descriptions have in common with each other?

How are they different?

אֶת שֵׁם הָאֵל
הַמֶּלֶךְ הַגָּדוֹל, הַגִּבּוֹר וְהַנּוֹרָא
קָדוֹשׁ הוּא.
וְכֻלָּם מְקַבְּלִים עֲלֵיהֶם עֹל מַלְכוּת שָׁמַיִם זֶה מִזֶּה
וְנוֹתְנִים רְשׁוּת זֶה לָזֶה
לְהַקְדִּישׁ לְיוֹצְרָם בְּנַחַת רוּחַ
בְּשָׂפָה בְרוּרָה וּבִנְעִימָה
קְדֻשָּׁה כֻּלָּם כְּאֶחָד
עוֹנִים בְּאֵימָה וְאוֹמְרִים בְּיִרְאָה

These words are said together aloud:

קָדוֹשׁ ׀ קָדוֹשׁ קָדוֹשׁ יְהוָה צְבָאוֹת
מְלֹא כָל־הָאָרֶץ כְּבוֹדוֹ:

וְהָאוֹפַנִּים וְחַיּוֹת הַקֹּדֶשׁ
בְּרַעַשׁ גָּדוֹל מִתְנַשְּׂאִים לְעֻמַּת הַשְּׂרָפִים
לְעֻמָּתָם מְשַׁבְּחִים וְאוֹמְרִים

These words are said together aloud:

בָּרוּךְ כְּבוֹד־יְהוָה מִמְּקוֹמוֹ:

לְאֵל בָּרוּךְ נְעִימוֹת יִתֵּנוּ
לְמֶלֶךְ אֵל חַי וְקַיָּם, זְמִירוֹת יֹאמֵרוּ וְתִשְׁבָּחוֹת יַשְׁמִיעוּ
כִּי הוּא לְבַדּוֹ מָרוֹם וְקָדוֹשׁ
פּוֹעֵל גְּבוּרוֹת, עוֹשֶׂה חֲדָשׁוֹת
בַּעַל מִלְחָמוֹת, זוֹרֵעַ צְדָקוֹת
מַצְמִיחַ יְשׁוּעוֹת, בּוֹרֵא רְפוּאוֹת
נוֹרָא תְהִלּוֹת, אֲדוֹן הַנִּפְלָאוֹת
הַמְחַדֵּשׁ בְּטוּבוֹ בְּכָל יוֹם תָּמִיד
מַעֲשֵׂה בְרֵאשִׁית
כָּאָמוּר
לְעֹשֵׂה אוֹרִים גְּדֹלִים, כִּי לְעוֹלָם חַסְדּוֹ:
בָּרוּךְ אַתָּה יְהֹוָה יוֹצֵר הַמְּאוֹרוֹת.

Only Hashem is truly holy and does mighty things and creates new things, makes war and justice, saves us and heals us, and makes breathtaking miracles.

Why do you think sometimes people say the same words over and over?

Now think about why the angels might repeat that Hashem is holy three times.

אַהֲבַת עוֹלָם אֲהַבְתָּנוּ, יְהוָה אֱלֹהֵינוּ
חֶמְלָה גְדוֹלָה וִיתֵרָה חָמַלְתָּ עָלֵינוּ.
אָבִינוּ מַלְכֵּנוּ
בַּעֲבוּר שִׁמְךָ הַגָּדוֹל וּבַעֲבוּר אֲבוֹתֵינוּ שֶׁבָּטְחוּ בְךָ
וַתְּלַמְּדֵמוֹ חֻקֵּי חַיִּים, לַעֲשׂוֹת רְצוֹנְךָ בְּלֵבָב שָׁלֵם
כֵּן תְּחָנֵּנוּ אָבִינוּ, אָב הָרַחֲמָן
הַמְרַחֵם, רַחֵם נָא עָלֵינוּ
וְתֵן בְּלִבֵּנוּ בִּינָה לְהָבִין, לְהַשְׂכִּיל, לִשְׁמֹעַ
לִלְמֹד וּלְלַמֵּד, לִשְׁמֹר וְלַעֲשׂוֹת
וּלְקַיֵּם אֶת כָּל דִּבְרֵי תַלְמוּד תּוֹרָתְךָ בְּאַהֲבָה.
וְהָאֵר עֵינֵינוּ בְּתוֹרָתֶךָ, וְדַבֵּק לִבֵּנוּ בְּמִצְוֹתֶיךָ
וְיַחֵד לְבָבֵנוּ לְאַהֲבָה וּלְיִרְאָה אֶת שְׁמֶךָ
לֹא נֵבוֹשׁ וְלֹא נִכָּלֵם וְלֹא נִכָּשֵׁל לְעוֹלָם וָעֶד

Which direction do we face when we pray? Close your eyes. Relax. Imagine yourself entering the old city of Yerushalayim, through the Jaffa gate. Walking briskly and excitedly toward the Jewish Quarter, and then skipping down the stairs to the Kotel. Take a moment to stare at the Kotel from afar, with hundreds of pious Jews praying there. As you run up to the Kotel and place your hands on the cool stones of the holiest place in the world, think about the millions of Jews around the world at this instant that are facing this spot, and opening their hearts to pray to Hashem. Think about Jews in Europe facing south to pray toward Yerushalayim, Jews in South Africa facing north, Jews in Hong Kong facing west, and Jews in the United States facing east right now. Feel the power of all those *tefillot* focused on one place!

כִּי בְשֵׁם קָדְשְׁךָ הַגָּדוֹל הַגִּבּוֹר וְהַנּוֹרָא בָּטָחְנוּ
נָגִֽילָה וְנִשְׂמְחָה בִּישׁוּעָתֶֽךָ.
וְרַחֲמֶיךָ יְהֹוָה אֱלֹהֵינוּ וַחֲסָדֶֽיךָ הָרַבִּים
אַל יַעַזְבוּנוּ נֶֽצַח סֶֽלָה וָעֶד.

At this point if you are wearing צִיצִית *or a* טַלִּית *you should gather the* צִיצִיּוֹת *together in preparation for the* שְׁמַע.

מַהֵר וְהָבֵא עָלֵֽינוּ בְּרָכָה וְשָׁלוֹם
מְהֵרָה מֵאַרְבַּע כַּנְפוֹת כָּל הָאָֽרֶץ
וּשְׁבוֹר עֹל הַגּוֹיִם מֵעַל צַוָּארֵֽנוּ
וְהוֹלִיכֵֽנוּ מְהֵרָה קוֹמְמִיּוּת לְאַרְצֵֽנוּ.
כִּי אֵל פּוֹעֵל יְשׁוּעוֹת אָֽתָּה, וּבָֽנוּ בָחַֽרְתָּ מִכָּל עַם וְלָשׁוֹן
וְקֵרַבְתָּֽנוּ מַלְכֵּֽנוּ לְשִׁמְךָ הַגָּדוֹל בְּאַהֲבָה
לְהוֹדוֹת לְךָ וּלְיַחֶדְךָ, לְיִרְאָה וּלְאַהֲבָה אֶת שְׁמֶֽךָ.
בָּרוּךְ אַתָּה יְהֹוָה, הַבּוֹחֵר בְּעַמּוֹ יִשְׂרָאֵל בְּאַהֲבָה.

It is a special מִצְוָה to say the שְׁמַע every morning and evening.
Say the first first verse aloud while covering your eyes with your right hand.
Say line 2 quietly to yourself.

1 **שְׁמַע יִשְׂרָאֵל, יְהֹוָה אֱלֹהֵינוּ, יְהֹוָה ׀ אֶחָד:**

2 בָּרוּךְ שֵׁם כְּבוֹד מַלְכוּתוֹ לְעוֹלָם וָעֶד.

3 וְאָהַבְתָּ אֵת יְהֹוָה אֱלֹהֶיךָ, בְּכָל־לְבָבְךָ וּבְכָל־נַפְשְׁךָ וּבְכָל־
4 מְאֹדֶךָ: וְהָיוּ הַדְּבָרִים הָאֵלֶּה, אֲשֶׁר אָנֹכִי מְצַוְּךָ הַיּוֹם, עַל־
5 לְבָבֶךָ: וְשִׁנַּנְתָּם לְבָנֶיךָ וְדִבַּרְתָּ בָּם, בְּשִׁבְתְּךָ בְּבֵיתֶךָ
6 וּבְלֶכְתְּךָ בַדֶּרֶךְ, וּבְשָׁכְבְּךָ וּבְקוּמֶךָ: וּקְשַׁרְתָּם לְאוֹת עַל־יָדֶךָ
7 וְהָיוּ לְטֹטָפֹת בֵּין עֵינֶיךָ: וּכְתַבְתָּם עַל־מְזֻזוֹת בֵּיתֶךָ וּבִשְׁעָרֶיךָ:

Listen, Israel: Hashem is our God, Hashem is the only One.

You should love Hashem with all your heart and soul and strength. The words that I, Hashem, am telling you today should be in your heart.

וְהָיָה אִם־שָׁמֹעַ תִּשְׁמְעוּ אֶל־מִצְוֹתַי אֲשֶׁר אָנֹכִי מְצַוֶּה אֶתְכֶם הַיּוֹם, לְאַהֲבָה אֶת־יְהֹוָה אֱלֹהֵיכֶם וּלְעָבְדוֹ, בְּכָל־לְבַבְכֶם וּבְכָל־נַפְשְׁכֶם: וְנָתַתִּי מְטַר־אַרְצְכֶם בְּעִתּוֹ, יוֹרֶה וּמַלְקוֹשׁ, וְאָסַפְתָּ דְגָנֶךָ וְתִירֹשְׁךָ וְיִצְהָרֶךָ: וְנָתַתִּי עֵשֶׂב בְּשָׂדְךָ לִבְהֶמְתֶּךָ, וְאָכַלְתָּ וְשָׂבָעְתָּ: הִשָּׁמְרוּ לָכֶם פֶּן־יִפְתֶּה לְבַבְכֶם, וְסַרְתֶּם וַעֲבַדְתֶּם אֱלֹהִים אֲחֵרִים וְהִשְׁתַּחֲוִיתֶם לָהֶם: וְחָרָה אַף־יְהֹוָה בָּכֶם, וְעָצַר אֶת־הַשָּׁמַיִם וְלֹא־יִהְיֶה מָטָר, וְהָאֲדָמָה לֹא תִתֵּן אֶת־יְבוּלָהּ, וַאֲבַדְתֶּם מְהֵרָה מֵעַל הָאָרֶץ הַטֹּבָה אֲשֶׁר יְהֹוָה נֹתֵן לָכֶם: וְשַׂמְתֶּם אֶת־דְּבָרַי אֵלֶּה עַל־לְבַבְכֶם וְעַל־נַפְשְׁכֶם, וּקְשַׁרְתֶּם אֹתָם לְאוֹת עַל־יֶדְכֶם, וְהָיוּ לְטוֹטָפֹת בֵּין עֵינֵיכֶם: וְלִמַּדְתֶּם אֹתָם אֶת־בְּנֵיכֶם לְדַבֵּר בָּם, בְּשִׁבְתְּךָ בְּבֵיתֶךָ, וּבְלֶכְתְּךָ בַדֶּרֶךְ וּבְשָׁכְבְּךָ וּבְקוּמֶךָ: וּכְתַבְתָּם עַל־מְזוּזוֹת בֵּיתֶךָ וּבִשְׁעָרֶיךָ: לְמַעַן יִרְבּוּ יְמֵיכֶם וִימֵי בְנֵיכֶם עַל הָאֲדָמָה אֲשֶׁר נִשְׁבַּע יְהֹוָה לַאֲבֹתֵיכֶם לָתֵת לָהֶם, כִּימֵי הַשָּׁמַיִם עַל־הָאָרֶץ:

If you are wearing צִיצִית pass them before your eyes and kiss them when you say the words וּרְאִיתֶם אֹתוֹ and kiss them and then pass them before your eyes when you say the word עֵינֵיכֶם.

וַיֹּאמֶר יְהֹוָה אֶל־מֹשֶׁה לֵּאמֹר: דַּבֵּר אֶל־בְּנֵי יִשְׂרָאֵל וְאָמַרְתָּ אֲלֵהֶם, וְעָשׂוּ לָהֶם צִיצִת עַל־כַּנְפֵי בִגְדֵיהֶם לְדֹרֹתָם, וְנָתְנוּ עַל־צִיצִת הַכָּנָף פְּתִיל תְּכֵלֶת: וְהָיָה לָכֶם לְצִיצִת, וּרְאִיתֶם אֹתוֹ, וּזְכַרְתֶּם אֶת־כָּל־מִצְוֹת יְהֹוָה וַעֲשִׂיתֶם אֹתָם, וְלֹא תָתוּרוּ אַחֲרֵי לְבַבְכֶם וְאַחֲרֵי עֵינֵיכֶם, אֲשֶׁר־אַתֶּם זֹנִים אַחֲרֵיהֶם: לְמַעַן תִּזְכְּרוּ וַעֲשִׂיתֶם אֶת־כָּל־מִצְוֹתָי, וִהְיִיתֶם קְדֹשִׁים לֵאלֹהֵיכֶם: אֲנִי יְהֹוָה אֱלֹהֵיכֶם, אֲשֶׁר הוֹצֵאתִי אֶתְכֶם מֵאֶרֶץ מִצְרַיִם, לִהְיוֹת לָכֶם לֵאלֹהִים, אֲנִי יְהֹוָה אֱלֹהֵיכֶם:

אֱמֶת

יְהֹוָה אֱלֹהֵיכֶם אֱמֶת

For the תְּפִלּוֹת between the שְׁמַע and the עֲמִידָה turn to pages 83–89.

A young boy and his father were walking down the road one day when they passed a large rock. The boy turned to his father and asked, "Abba, do you think I can move that huge rock?" His father replied to him, "If you use all of your strength, I am sure you can, my son." So the boy tried. He heaved and he pushed and tried so hard to move the rock but it just wouldn't budge. "You were wrong," the boy said to his father in frustration. "I couldn't move it." His father put his arm around his son and said to him gently, "But you didn't use all of your strength. You didn't ask me for help."

The עֲמִידָה is the climax of our תְּפִלָּה where we stand before Hashem and open our hearts in prayer. You should mouth the words of the עֲמִידָה but without a sound. We learn this from the prayer of Ḥanna when she prayed to have a child. Take three steps forward and begin saying the עֲמִידָה while standing with your feet together.

1 אֲדֹנָי, שְׂפָתַי תִּפְתָּח, וּפִי יַגִּיד תְּהִלָּתֶךָ:

2 בָּרוּךְ אַתָּה יְהֹוָה

3 אֱלֹהֵינוּ וֵאלֹהֵי אֲבוֹתֵינוּ

4 אֱלֹהֵי אַבְרָהָם, אֱלֹהֵי יִצְחָק, וֵאלֹהֵי יַעֲקֹב

5 הָאֵל הַגָּדוֹל הַגִּבּוֹר וְהַנּוֹרָא, אֵל עֶלְיוֹן

6 גּוֹמֵל חֲסָדִים טוֹבִים, וְקוֹנֵה הַכֹּל

7 וְזוֹכֵר חַסְדֵי אָבוֹת

8 וּמֵבִיא גוֹאֵל לִבְנֵי בְנֵיהֶם, לְמַעַן שְׁמוֹ בְּאַהֲבָה.

Between Rosh HaShana and Yom Kippur add these words:

9 זָכְרֵנוּ לְחַיִּים, מֶלֶךְ חָפֵץ בַּחַיִּים, כָּתְבֵנוּ בְּסֵפֶר חַיִּים, לְמַעַנְךָ אֱלֹהִים חַיִּים.

10 מֶלֶךְ עוֹזֵר וּמוֹשִׁיעַ וּמָגֵן.

11 בָּרוּךְ אַתָּה יְהֹוָה

12 מָגֵן אַבְרָהָם.

1 אַתָּה גִּבּוֹר לְעוֹלָם, אֲדֹנָי

2 מְחַיֶּה מֵתִים אַתָּה, רַב לְהוֹשִׁיעַ

Between Pesaḥ and Shemini Atzeret add these words:	*Between Simḥat Torah and Pesaḥ add these words:*
מוֹרִיד הַטָּל	3 מַשִּׁיב הָרוּחַ וּמוֹרִיד הַגֶּשֶׁם

4 מְכַלְכֵּל חַיִּים בְּחֶסֶד, מְחַיֶּה מֵתִים בְּרַחֲמִים רַבִּים

5 סוֹמֵךְ נוֹפְלִים, וְרוֹפֵא חוֹלִים, וּמַתִּיר אֲסוּרִים

6 וּמְקַיֵּם אֱמוּנָתוֹ לִישֵׁנֵי עָפָר.

7 מִי כָמוֹךָ, בַּעַל גְּבוּרוֹת

8 וּמִי דּוֹמֶה לָּךְ

9 מֶלֶךְ, מֵמִית וּמְחַיֶּה וּמַצְמִיחַ יְשׁוּעָה.

Between Rosh HaShana and Yom Kippur add these words:

10 מִי כָמוֹךָ אַב הָרַחֲמָן, זוֹכֵר יְצוּרָיו בְּרַחֲמִים לְחַיִּים.

11 וְנֶאֱמָן אַתָּה לְהַחֲיוֹת מֵתִים.

12 בָּרוּךְ אַתָּה יְהֹוָה

13 **מְחַיֵּה הַמֵּתִים.**

1 אַתָּה קָדוֹשׁ וְשִׁמְךָ קָדוֹשׁ
2 וּקְדוֹשִׁים בְּכָל יוֹם יְהַלְלְוּךָ סֶּלָה.
3 בָּרוּךְ אַתָּה יְהֹוָה
4 **הָאֵל הַקָּדוֹשׁ.**

Between Rosh HaShana and Yom Kippur change the ending of this בְּרָכָה *to these words:*

הַמֶּלֶךְ הַקָּדוֹשׁ.

There once was a poor man who dreamed of being rich. He prayed passionately every day to win the lottery. But not once during his long life did he win the lottery, and he remained poor. When he died and went to heaven he couldn't help himself and had to ask God why He never answered his prayers and let him win the lottery. God replied to him, "My son, I may have answered your prayers. But to win the lottery, you need to buy a ticket!"

It is written in Your Torah: The Children of Israel should keep Shabbat. Shabbat is a promise and a sign between them and between Hashem forever.

יִשְׂמַח מֹשֶׁה בְּמַתְּנַת חֶלְקוֹ
כִּי עֶבֶד נֶאֱמָן קָרָאתָ לּוֹ
כְּלִיל תִּפְאֶרֶת בְּרֹאשׁוֹ נָתַתָּ
בְּעָמְדוֹ לְפָנֶיךָ עַל הַר סִינַי
שְׁנֵי לוּחוֹת אֲבָנִים הוֹרִיד בְּיָדוֹ
וְכָתוּב בָּהֶם שְׁמִירַת שַׁבָּת
וְכֵן כָּתוּב בְּתוֹרָתֶךָ

וְשָׁמְרוּ בְנֵי־יִשְׂרָאֵל אֶת־הַשַּׁבָּת
לַעֲשׂוֹת אֶת־הַשַּׁבָּת לְדֹרֹתָם בְּרִית עוֹלָם:
בֵּינִי וּבֵין בְּנֵי יִשְׂרָאֵל אוֹת הִוא לְעֹלָם
כִּי־שֵׁשֶׁת יָמִים עָשָׂה יְהֹוָה אֶת־הַשָּׁמַיִם וְאֶת־הָאָרֶץ
וּבַיּוֹם הַשְּׁבִיעִי שָׁבַת וַיִּנָּפַשׁ:

וְלֹא נְתַתּוֹ, יְהֹוָה אֱלֹהֵינוּ, לְגוֹיֵי הָאֲרָצוֹת
וְלֹא הִנְחַלְתּוֹ, מַלְכֵּנוּ, לְעוֹבְדֵי אֱלִילִים
גַּם בִּמְנוּחָתוֹ לֹא יִשְׁכְּנוּ עֲרֵלִים
כִּי לְעַמְּךָ יִשְׂרָאֵל נְתַתּוֹ בְּאַהֲבָה
לְזֶרַע יַעֲקֹב אֲשֶׁר בָּם בָּחָרְתָּ.

יִשְׂמְחוּ בְמַלְכוּתְךָ שׁוֹמְרֵי שַׁבָּת וְקוֹרְאֵי עֹנֶג
עַם מְקַדְּשֵׁי שְׁבִיעִי
כֻּלָּם יִשְׂבְּעוּ וְיִתְעַנְּגוּ מִטּוּבֶךָ
וְהַשְּׁבִיעִי רָצִיתָ בּוֹ וְקִדַּשְׁתּוֹ
חֶמְדַּת יָמִים אוֹתוֹ קָרָאתָ.

אֱלֹהֵינוּ וֵאלֹהֵי אֲבוֹתֵינוּ,
רְצֵה נָא בִמְנוּחָתֵנוּ
קַדְּשֵׁנוּ בְּמִצְוֹתֶיךָ, שִׂים חֶלְקֵנוּ בְּתוֹרָתֶךָ
שַׂבְּעֵנוּ מִטּוּבֶךָ, שַׂמֵּחַ נַפְשֵׁנוּ בִּישׁוּעָתֶךָ
וְטַהֵר לִבֵּנוּ לְעָבְדְּךָ בֶּאֱמֶת.
וְהַנְחִילֵנוּ, יְהֹוָה אֱלֹהֵינוּ
בְּאַהֲבָה וּבְרָצוֹן שַׁבַּת קָדְשֶׁךָ
וְיָנוּחוּ בוֹ כָּל יִשְׂרָאֵל מְקַדְּשֵׁי שְׁמֶךָ.
בָּרוּךְ אַתָּה יְהֹוָה

מְקַדֵּשׁ הַשַּׁבָּת.

רְצֵה יְהֹוָה אֱלֹהֵינוּ בְּעַמְּךָ יִשְׂרָאֵל וְלִתְפִלָּתָם שְׁעֵה
וְהָשֵׁב הָעֲבוֹדָה לִדְבִיר בֵּיתֶךָ
וְאִשֵּׁי יִשְׂרָאֵל וּתְפִלָּתָם מְהֵרָה בְּאַהֲבָה תְקַבֵּל בְּרָצוֹן
וּתְהִי לְרָצוֹן תָּמִיד עֲבוֹדַת יִשְׂרָאֵל עַמֶּךָ.

On Rosh Ḥodesh and Ḥol HaMo'ed add יַעֲלֶה וְיָבוֹא.

אֱלֹהֵינוּ וֵאלֹהֵי אֲבוֹתֵינוּ, יַעֲלֶה וְיָבוֹא, יַגִּיעַ, יֵרָאֶה וְיֵרָצֶה, יִשָּׁמַע, יִפָּקֵד וְיִזָּכֵר זִכְרוֹנֵנוּ וְזִכְרוֹן אֲבוֹתֵינוּ, זִכְרוֹן יְרוּשָׁלַיִם עִירָךְ, וְזִכְרוֹן מָשִׁיחַ בֶּן דָּוִד עַבְדָּךְ, וְזִכְרוֹן כָּל עַמְּךָ בֵּית יִשְׂרָאֵל, לְפָנֶיךָ, לִפְלֵיטָה לְטוֹבָה לְחֵן, לְחֶסֶד וּלְרַחֲמִים (לְחַיִּים טוֹבִים וּלְשָׁלוֹם), בְּיוֹם

Rosh Ḥodesh	*Pesaḥ*	*Sukkot*
רֹאשׁ הַחֹדֶשׁ הַזֶּה	חַג הַמַּצּוֹת הַזֶּה בְּיוֹם מִקְרָא קֹדֶשׁ הַזֶּה	חַג הַסֻּכּוֹת הַזֶּה בְּיוֹם מִקְרָא קֹדֶשׁ הַזֶּה

לְרַחֵם בּוֹ עָלֵינוּ וּלְהוֹשִׁיעֵנוּ. זָכְרֵנוּ יְהֹוָה אֱלֹהֵינוּ בּוֹ לְטוֹבָה, וּפָקְדֵנוּ בוֹ לִבְרָכָה, וְהוֹשִׁיעֵנוּ בוֹ לְחַיִּים טוֹבִים. בִּדְבַר יְשׁוּעָה וְרַחֲמִים חוּס וְחָנֵּנוּ וַחֲמֹל וְרַחֵם עָלֵינוּ וְהוֹשִׁיעֵנוּ, כִּי אֵלֶיךָ עֵינֵינוּ, כִּי אֵל מֶלֶךְ חַנּוּן וְרַחוּם אָתָּה.

וְאַתָּה בְּרַחֲמֶיךָ הָרַבִּים תַּחְפֹּץ בָּנוּ וְתִרְצֵנוּ
וְתֶחֱזֶינָה עֵינֵינוּ בְּשׁוּבְךָ לְצִיּוֹן בְּרַחֲמִים.
בָּרוּךְ אַתָּה יְהֹוָה
הַמַּחֲזִיר שְׁכִינָתוֹ לְצִיּוֹן.

Hashem, may we see You return to Yerushalayim when the Mashiaḥ comes.

Hashem, You are the Source of blessing, who returns to Yerushalayim.

מוֹדִים אֲנַחְנוּ לָךְ.
שָׁאַתָּה הוּא יְהוָה אֱלֹהֵינוּ
וֵאלֹהֵי אֲבוֹתֵינוּ לְעוֹלָם וָעֶד.
צוּרֵנוּ, צוּר חַיֵּינוּ וּמָגֵן יִשְׁעֵנוּ
אַתָּה הוּא לְדוֹר וָדוֹר
נוֹדֶה לְךָ וּנְסַפֵּר תְּהִלָּתֶךָ
עַל חַיֵּינוּ הַמְּסוּרִים בְּיָדֶךָ
וְעַל נִשְׁמוֹתֵינוּ הַפְּקוּדוֹת לָךְ.
וְעַל נִסֶּיךָ שֶׁבְּכָל יוֹם עִמָּנוּ
וְעַל נִפְלְאוֹתֶיךָ וְטוֹבוֹתֶיךָ
שֶׁבְּכָל עֵת, עֶרֶב וָבֹקֶר וְצָהֳרָיִם.
הַטּוֹב, כִּי לֹא כָלוּ רַחֲמֶיךָ
הַמְרַחֵם, כִּי לֹא תַמּוּ חֲסָדֶיךָ
כִּי מֵעוֹלָם קִוִּינוּ לָךְ.

During Ḥanukka say עַל הַנִּסִּים.

עַל הַנִּסִּים וְעַל הַפֻּרְקָן וְעַל הַגְּבוּרוֹת וְעַל הַתְּשׁוּעוֹת וְעַל הַנִּפְלָאוֹ וְעַל הַנֶּחָמוֹת שֶׁעָשִׂיתָ לַאֲבוֹתֵינוּ בַּיָּמִים הָהֵם בַּזְּמַן הַזֶּה.

בִּימֵי מַתִּתְיָה בֶּן יוֹחָנָן כֹּהֵן גָּדוֹל חַשְׁמוֹנַאי וּבָנָיו, כְּשֶׁעָמְדָה מַלְכוּ יָוָן הָרְשָׁעָה עַל עַמְּךָ יִשְׂרָאֵל לְשַׁכְּחָם תּוֹרָתֶךָ וּלְהַעֲבִירָם מֵחֻקֵּי רְצוֹנֶךָ וְאַתָּה בְּרַחֲמֶיךָ הָרַבִּים עָמַדְתָּ לָהֶם בְּעֵת צָרָתָם, רַבְתָּ אֶת רִיבָ דַּנְתָּ אֶת דִּינָם, נָקַמְתָּ אֶת נִקְמָתָם, מָסַרְתָּ גִּבּוֹרִים בְּיַד חַלָּשִׁים, וְרַבִּי בְּיַד מְעַטִּים, וּרְשָׁעִים בְּיַד צַדִּיקִים, וּטְמֵאִים בְּיַד טְהוֹרִים, וְזֵדִי בְּיַד עוֹסְקֵי תוֹרָתֶךָ. לְךָ עָשִׂיתָ שֵׁם גָּדוֹל וְקָדוֹשׁ בְּעוֹלָמֶךָ, וּלְעַמְּ יִשְׂרָאֵל עָשִׂיתָ תְּשׁוּעָה גְדוֹלָה וּפֻרְקָן כְּהַיּוֹם הַזֶּה. וְאַחַר כָּךְ בָּאוּ בָנֶי לִדְבִיר בֵּיתֶךָ, וּפִנּוּ אֶת הֵיכָלֶךָ,וְטִהֲרוּ אֶת מִקְדָּשֶׁךָ, וְהִדְלִיקוּ נֵרוֹ בְּחַצְרוֹת קָדְשֶׁךָ, וְקָבְעוּ שְׁמוֹנַת יְמֵי חֲנֻכָּה אֵלּוּ, בְּהַלֵּל וּבְהוֹדָאָה וְעָשִׂיתָ עִמָּהֶם נִסִּים וְנִפְלָאוֹת, וְנוֹדֶה לְשִׁמְךָ הַגָּדוֹל, סֶלָה.

וְעַל כֻּלָּם
יִתְבָּרַךְ וְיִתְרוֹמַם וְיִתְנַשֵּׂא תָּמִיד שִׁמְךָ מַלְכֵּנוּ לְעוֹלָם וָ
וְכָל הַחַיִּים יוֹדוּךָ סֶּלָה

Between Rosh HaShana and Yom Kippur add these words:

וּכְתֹב לְחַיִּים טוֹבִים כָּל בְּנֵי בְרִיתֶךָ.

וִיהַלְלוּ וִיבָרְכוּ אֶת שִׁמְךָ הַגָּדוֹל בֶּאֱמֶת לְעוֹלָם כִּי טוֹב
הָאֵל יְשׁוּעָתֵנוּ וְעֶזְרָתֵנוּ סֶלָה, הָאֵל הַטּוֹב.
בָּרוּךְ אַתָּה יְהֹוָה
הַטּוֹב שִׁמְךָ וּלְךָ נָאֶה לְהוֹדוֹת.

שִׂים שָׁלוֹם טוֹבָה וּבְרָכָה
חַיִּים חֵן וָחֶסֶד, צְדָקָה וְרַחֲמִים
עָלֵינוּ וְעַל כָּל יִשְׂרָאֵל עַמֶּךָ.
בָּרְכֵנוּ אָבִינוּ כֻּלָּנוּ כְּאֶחָד בְּאוֹר פָּנֶיךָ
כִּי בְאוֹר פָּנֶיךָ נָתַתָּ לָּנוּ, יְהוָה אֱלֹהֵינוּ
תּוֹרָה וְחַיִּים, אַהֲבָה וָחֶסֶד
צְדָקָה וְרַחֲמִים, בְּרָכָה וְשָׁלוֹם.
וְטוֹב בְּעֵינֶיךָ לְבָרְכֵנוּ, וּלְבָרֵךְ אֶת כָּל עַמְּךָ יִשְׂרָאֵל
בְּרֹב עֹז וְשָׁלוֹם

Between Rosh HaShana and Yom Kippur add these words:

10 וּבְסֵפֶר חַיִּים, בְּרָכָה וְשָׁלוֹם, וּפַרְנָסָה טוֹבָה, וִישׁוּעָה וְנֶחָמָה, וּגְזֵרוֹת טוֹבוֹת
11 נִזָּכֵר וְנִכָּתֵב לְפָנֶיךָ, אֲנַחְנוּ וְכָל עַמְּךָ יִשְׂרָאֵל, לְחַיִּים טוֹבִים וּלְשָׁלוֹם.

12 בָּרוּךְ אַתָּה יְהוָה
13 הַמְבָרֵךְ אֶת
14 עַמּוֹ יִשְׂרָאֵל
15 בַּשָּׁלוֹם. אָמֵן.

Give peace, goodness, and blessing, grace, kindness and care to us and all Your people of Israel. Bless us as one. **Hashem, You are the Source of all blessing, who blesses His people with peace. Amen.**

Between Rosh HaShana and Yom Kippur change the ending of this בְּרָכָה *to these words:*

בָּרוּךְ אַתָּה יְהוָה עוֹשֵׂה הַשָּׁלוֹם.

16 יִהְיוּ לְרָצוֹן אִמְרֵי־פִי וְהֶגְיוֹן לִבִּי לְפָנֶיךָ, יְהוָה צוּרִי וְגֹאֲלִי:

אֱלֹהַי

נְצֹר לְשׁוֹנִי מֵרָע וּשְׂפָתַי מִדַּבֵּר מִרְמָה
וְלִמְקַלְלַי נַפְשִׁי תִדֹּם, וְנַפְשִׁי כֶּעָפָר לַכֹּל תִּהְיֶה.
פְּתַח לִבִּי בְּתוֹרָתֶךָ, וְאַחֲרֵי מִצְוֹתֶיךָ תִּרְדֹּף נַפְשִׁי.
וְכָל הַקָּמִים עָלַי לְרָעָה
מְהֵרָה הָפֵר עֲצָתָם וְקַלְקֵל מַחְשְׁבוֹתָם.
יִהְיוּ כְּמֹץ לִפְנֵי־רוּחַ וּמַלְאַךְ יְהוָה דּוֹחֶה:
עֲשֵׂה לְמַעַן שְׁמֶךָ, עֲשֵׂה לְמַעַן יְמִינֶךָ
עֲשֵׂה לְמַעַן תּוֹרָתֶךָ, עֲשֵׂה לְמַעַן קְדֻשָּׁתֶךָ.
לְמַעַן יֵחָלְצוּן יְדִידֶיךָ, הוֹשִׁיעָה יְמִינְךָ וַעֲנֵנִי:
יִהְיוּ לְרָצוֹן אִמְרֵי־פִי וְהֶגְיוֹן לִבִּי לְפָנֶיךָ, יְהוָה צוּרִי וְגֹאֲלִי:

וְכִתְּתוּ חַרְבוֹתָם לְאִתִּים וַחֲנִיתוֹתֵיהֶם לְמַזְמֵרוֹת, לֹא־יִשָּׂא גוֹי
אֶל־גּוֹי חֶרֶב וְלֹא־יִלְמְדוּ עוֹד מִלְחָמָה. (Yeshayahu 2:4)

Why do you think we greet people on Shabbat by saying שַׁבָּת שָׁלוֹם?

What might be the deeper connection between שַׁבָּת and שָׁלוֹם?

As you finish the עֲמִידָה you should stop and think that you have just had the opportunity and honor to stand before Hashem. To be respectful, bow as you take three steps back. Then bow to the left, right and center as the pictures show

Between Rosh HaShana and Yom Kippur say הַשָּׁלוֹם *instead of* שָׁלוֹם.

12 עֹשֶׂה שָׁלוֹם / הַשָּׁלוֹם / בִּמְרוֹמָיו

13 הוּא בְּרַחֲמָיו יַעֲשֶׂה שָׁלוֹם עָלֵינוּ

14 וְעַל כָּל עַמּוֹ יִשְׂרָאֵל

15 וְאִמְרוּ אָמֵן.

We say these verses in preparation for the removing of the סֵפֶר תּוֹרָה *from the* אֲרוֹן קֹדֶשׁ.

We stand as the אֲרוֹן קֹדֶשׁ *is opened.*

1 **אַתָּה הָרְאֵתָ** לָדַעַת, כִּי יְהֹוָה הוּא הָאֱלֹהִים

2 אֵין עוֹד מִלְּבַדּוֹ:

3 אֵין־כָּמוֹךָ בָאֱלֹהִים, אֲדֹנָי, וְאֵין כְּמַעֲשֶׂיךָ:

4 יְהִי יְהֹוָה אֱלֹהֵינוּ עִמָּנוּ כַּאֲשֶׁר הָיָה עִם־אֲבֹתֵינוּ

5 אַל־יַעַזְבֵנוּ וְאַל־יִטְּשֵׁנוּ:

6 הוֹשִׁיעָה אֶת־עַמֶּךָ וּבָרֵךְ אֶת־נַחֲלָתֶךָ

7 וּרְעֵם וְנַשְּׂאֵם עַד־הָעוֹלָם:

8 וַיְהִי בִּנְסֹעַ הָאָרֹן וַיֹּאמֶר מֹשֶׁה

9 קוּמָה יְהֹוָה וְיָפֻצוּ אֹיְבֶיךָ, וְיָנֻסוּ מְשַׂנְאֶיךָ מִפָּנֶיךָ:

10 קוּמָה יְהֹוָה לִמְנוּחָתֶךָ, אַתָּה וַאֲרוֹן עֻזֶּךָ:

11 כֹּהֲנֶיךָ יִלְבְּשׁוּ־צֶדֶק, וַחֲסִידֶיךָ יְרַנֵּנוּ:

12 בַּעֲבוּר דָּוִד עַבְדֶּךָ, אַל־תָּשֵׁב פְּנֵי מְשִׁיחֶךָ:

We say these verses as the סֵפֶר תּוֹרָה *is removed from the* אֲרוֹן קֹדֶשׁ:

13 בָּרוּךְ הַמָּקוֹם שֶׁנָּתַן תּוֹרָה לְעַמּוֹ יִשְׂרָאֵל בָּרוּךְ הוּא.

14 אַשְׁרֵי הָעָם שֶׁכָּכָה לּוֹ, אַשְׁרֵי הָעָם שֶׁיְהֹוָה אֱלֹהָיו:

Hashem is a blessing for us, and gave the Torah to us, His nation, the Jewish People. We are happy that we know we are Hashem's nation.

Once the סֵפֶר תּוֹרָה *has been removed from the* אֲרוֹן קֹדֶשׁ,
we say these verses with the חַזָּן:

גַּדְּלוּ לַיהוָה אִתִּי וּנְרוֹמְמָה שְׁמוֹ יַחְדָּו:

רוֹמְמוּ יְהוָה אֱלֹהֵינוּ וְהִשְׁתַּחֲווּ לַהֲדֹם רַגְלָיו, קָדוֹשׁ הוּא: רוֹמְמוּ יְהוָה אֱלֹהֵינוּ וְהִשְׁתַּחֲווּ לְהַר קָדְשׁוֹ, כִּי־קָדוֹשׁ יְהוָה אֱלֹהֵינוּ: אֵין־קָדוֹשׁ כַּיהוָה כִּי־אֵין בִּלְתֶּךָ, וְאֵין צוּר כֵּאלֹהֵינוּ: כִּי מִי אֱלוֹהַּ מִבַּלְעֲדֵי יְהוָה, וּמִי צוּר זוּלָתִי אֱלֹהֵינוּ: תּוֹרָה צִוָּה־לָנוּ מֹשֶׁה, מוֹרָשָׁה קְהִלַּת יַעֲקֹב: עֵץ־חַיִּים הִיא לַמַּחֲזִיקִים בָּהּ, וְתֹמְכֶיהָ מְאֻשָּׁר: דְּרָכֶיהָ דַרְכֵי־נֹעַם וְכָל־נְתִיבוֹתֶיהָ שָׁלוֹם: שָׁלוֹם רָב לְאֹהֲבֵי תוֹרָתֶךָ, וְאֵין־לָמוֹ מִכְשׁוֹל: יְהוָה עֹז לְעַמּוֹ יִתֵּן, יְהוָה יְבָרֵךְ אֶת־עַמּוֹ בַשָּׁלוֹם:

כִּי שֵׁם יְהוָה אֶקְרָא, הָבוּ גֹדֶל לֵאלֹהֵינוּ:
הַכֹּל תְּנוּ עֹז לֵאלֹהִים וּתְנוּ כָבוֹד לַתּוֹרָה.

As the סֵפֶר תּוֹרָה *is lifted for all to see, we say these verses:*

וְזֹאת הַתּוֹרָה אֲשֶׁר־שָׂם מֹשֶׁה לִפְנֵי בְּנֵי יִשְׂרָאֵל:
תּוֹרָה צִוָּה־לָנוּ מֹשֶׁה, מוֹרָשָׁה קְהִלַּת יַעֲקֹב:
הָאֵל תָּמִים דַּרְכּוֹ, אִמְרַת־יְהוָה צְרוּפָה
מָגֵן הוּא לְכֹל הַחוֹסִים בּוֹ:

The weekly Parasha is now read from the סֵפֶר תּוֹרָה.

The special תְּפִלָּה for your country's government is said now.

This is a special תְּפִלָּה asking Hashem to protect the State of Israel.

אָבִינוּ שֶׁבַּשָּׁמַיִם, צוּר יִשְׂרָאֵל וְגוֹאֲלוֹ
בָּרֵךְ אֶת מְדִינַת יִשְׂרָאֵל, רֵאשִׁית צְמִיחַת גְּאֻלָּתֵנוּ.
הָגֵן עָלֶיהָ בְּאֶבְרַת חַסְדֶּךָ וּפְרֹשׂ עָלֶיהָ סֻכַּת שְׁלוֹמֶךָ
וּשְׁלַח אוֹרְךָ וַאֲמִתְּךָ לְרָאשֶׁיהָ, שָׂרֶיהָ וְיוֹעֲצֶיהָ
וְתַקְּנֵם בְּעֵצָה טוֹבָה מִלְּפָנֶיךָ.

חַזֵּק אֶת יְדֵי מְגִנֵּי אֶרֶץ קָדְשֵׁנוּ, וְהַנְחִילֵם אֱלֹהֵינוּ
יְשׁוּעָה וַעֲטֶרֶת נִצָּחוֹן תְּעַטְּרֵם, וְנָתַתָּ שָׁלוֹם בָּאָרֶץ
וְשִׂמְחַת עוֹלָם לְיוֹשְׁבֶיהָ.

וְאֶת אַחֵינוּ כָּל בֵּית יִשְׂרָאֵל, פְּקָד נָא בְּכָל אַרְצוֹת
פְּזוּרֵיהֶם, וְתוֹלִיכֵם מְהֵרָה קוֹמְמִיּוּת לְצִיּוֹן עִירֶךָ
וְלִירוּשָׁלַיִם מִשְׁכַּן שְׁמֶךָ.

Hashem, please look after the State of Israel, it's leaders, our people that live there, and especially all the soldiers that protect and fight for Israel. Please Hashem bring peace to Israel now.

This is a special תְּפִלָּה asking Hashem to protect Israel's Defense Forces.

מִי שֶׁבֵּרַךְ אֲבוֹתֵינוּ אַבְרָהָם יִצְחָק וְיַעֲקֹב הוּא יְבָרֵךְ אֶת חַיָּלֵי צְבָא הַהֲגָנָה לְיִשְׂרָאֵל וְאַנְשֵׁי כֹּחוֹת הַבִּטָּחוֹן, הָעוֹמְדִים עַל מִשְׁמַר אַרְצֵנוּ וְעָרֵי אֱלֹהֵינוּ, מִגְּבוּל הַלְּבָנוֹן וְעַד מִדְבַּר מִצְרַיִם וּמִן הַיָּם הַגָּדוֹל עַד לְבוֹא הָעֲרָבָה וּבְכָל מָקוֹם שֶׁהֵם, בַּיַּבָּשָׁה, בָּאֲוִיר וּבַיָּם. יִתֵּן יְהֹוָה אֶת אוֹיְבֵינוּ הַקָּמִים עָלֵינוּ נִגָּפִים לִפְנֵיהֶם. הַקָּדוֹשׁ בָּרוּךְ הוּא יִשְׁמֹר וְיַצִּיל אֶת חַיָּלֵינוּ מִכָּל צָרָה וְצוּקָה וּמִכָּל נֶגַע וּמַחֲלָה, וְיִשְׁלַח בְּרָכָה וְהַצְלָחָה בְּכָל מַעֲשֵׂי יְדֵיהֶם. יַדְבֵּר שׂוֹנְאֵינוּ תַּחְתֵּיהֶם וִיעַטְּרֵם בְּכֶתֶר יְשׁוּעָה וּבַעֲטֶרֶת נִצָּחוֹן. וִיקֻיַּם בָּהֶם הַכָּתוּב: כִּי יְהֹוָה אֱלֹהֵיכֶם הַהֹלֵךְ עִמָּכֶם לְהִלָּחֵם לָכֶם עִם־אֹיְבֵיכֶם לְהוֹשִׁיעַ אֶתְכֶם: וְנֹאמַר אָמֵן.

Hashem will be King of the universe forever. Hashem will be our God, the God of Israel, for ever and ever.

We say these verses as the סֵפֶר תּוֹרָה *is returned to the* אֲרוֹן קֹדֶשׁ.

The חַזָּן *takes the* סֵפֶר תּוֹרָה *and says:*

1 יִמְלֹךְ יְהוָה לְעוֹלָם,

2 אֱלֹהַיִךְ צִיּוֹן לְדֹר וָדֹר, הַלְלוּיָהּ:

We then repeat the verse:

3 יִמְלֹךְ יְהוָה לְעוֹלָם

4 אֱלֹהַיִךְ צִיּוֹן לְדֹר וָדֹר, הַלְלוּיָהּ:

"The Maggid of Mezeritch used to say that grown-ups should learn three things from children: Always be happy, never sit still and do nothing, and when you want something, ask for it over and over and with lots of energy."

What could you teach a grown-up today?

"Keriat HaTorah is a reenactment of the original experience of Matan Torah."

Why do you think we read the Torah in public?

Why not just at home on our own?

As the סֵפֶר תּוֹרָה is returned to the אֲרוֹן קֹדֶשׁ we say these verses:

מִזְמוֹר לְדָוִד, הָבוּ לַיהוָה בְּנֵי אֵלִים, הָבוּ לַיהוָה כָּבוֹד וָעֹז: 1
הָבוּ לַיהוָה כְּבוֹד שְׁמוֹ, הִשְׁתַּחֲווּ לַיהוָה בְּהַדְרַת־קֹדֶשׁ: 2
קוֹל יְהוָה עַל־הַמָּיִם, אֵל־הַכָּבוֹד הִרְעִים, יְהוָה עַל־מַיִם רַבִּים: 3
קוֹל־יְהוָה בַּכֹּחַ, קוֹל יְהוָה בֶּהָדָר: 4
קוֹל יְהוָה שֹׁבֵר אֲרָזִים, וַיְשַׁבֵּר יְהוָה אֶת־אַרְזֵי הַלְּבָנוֹן: 5
וַיַּרְקִידֵם כְּמוֹ־עֵגֶל, לְבָנוֹן וְשִׂרְיוֹן כְּמוֹ בֶן־רְאֵמִים: 6
קוֹל־יְהוָה חֹצֵב לַהֲבוֹת אֵשׁ: 7
קוֹל יְהוָה יָחִיל מִדְבָּר, יָחִיל יְהוָה מִדְבַּר קָדֵשׁ: 8
קוֹל יְהוָה יְחוֹלֵל אַיָּלוֹת וַיֶּחֱשֹׂף יְעָרוֹת 9
וּבְהֵיכָלוֹ, כֻּלּוֹ אֹמֵר כָּבוֹד: 10
יְהוָה לַמַּבּוּל יָשָׁב, וַיֵּשֶׁב יְהוָה מֶלֶךְ לְעוֹלָם: 11
יְהוָה עֹז לְעַמּוֹ יִתֵּן, יְהוָה יְבָרֵךְ אֶת־עַמּוֹ בַשָּׁלוֹם: 12

Once the סֵפֶר תּוֹרָה has been replaced in the אֲרוֹן קֹדֶשׁ we say these verses:

שׁוּבָה לִמְעוֹנָךְ וּשְׁכֹן בְּבֵית מַאֲוָיָךְ 13
כִּי כָל פֶּה וְכָל לָשׁוֹן יִתְּנוּ הוֹד וְהָדָר לְמַלְכוּתָךְ. 14
וּבְנֻחֹה יֹאמַר, שׁוּבָה יְהוָה רִבְבוֹת אַלְפֵי יִשְׂרָאֵל 15
הֲשִׁיבֵנוּ יְהוָה אֵלֶיךָ וְנָשׁוּבָה, חַדֵּשׁ יָמֵינוּ כְּקֶדֶם: 16

תְּפִלַּת מוּסָף is said on special days such as Shabbat and Yom Tov, in place of the קׇרְבַּן מוּסָף in the בֵּית הַמִּקְדָּשׁ. Just as all other עֲמִידוֹת, you should mouth the words to the עֲמִידָה but without a sound. We learn this from the prayer of Ḥanna when she prayed to have a child. Take three steps forward and begin saying the עֲמִידָה while standing with your feet together.

1 אֲדֹנָי, שְׂפָתַי תִּפְתָּח, וּפִי יַגִּיד תְּהִלָּתֶךָ:

2 בָּרוּךְ אַתָּה יְהֹוָה

3 אֱלֹהֵינוּ וֵאלֹהֵי אֲבוֹתֵינוּ

4 אֱלֹהֵי אַבְרָהָם, אֱלֹהֵי יִצְחָק, וֵאלֹהֵי יַעֲקֹב

5 הָאֵל הַגָּדוֹל הַגִּבּוֹר וְהַנּוֹרָא, אֵל עֶלְיוֹן

6 גּוֹמֵל חֲסָדִים טוֹבִים, וְקוֹנֵה הַכֹּל

7 וְזוֹכֵר חַסְדֵי אָבוֹת

8 וּמֵבִיא גוֹאֵל לִבְנֵי בְנֵיהֶם לְמַעַן שְׁמוֹ בְּאַהֲבָה.

Between Rosh HaShana and Yom Kippur add these words:

9 זָכְרֵנוּ לְחַיִּים, מֶלֶךְ חָפֵץ בַּחַיִּים, כָּתְבֵנוּ בְּסֵפֶר חַיִּים, לְמַעַנְךָ אֱלֹהִים חַיִּים.

10 מֶלֶךְ עוֹזֵר וּמוֹשִׁיעַ וּמָגֵן.

11 בָּרוּךְ

12 אַתָּה

13 יְהֹוָה

14 מָגֵן אַבְרָהָם.

You are the God of heaven, who acts with kindness, and You created everything. You remember the lives of our ancestors, and will lovingly bring Mashiaḥ to us their descendants. **Hashem, You are the Source of all blessing, who remembers the lives of our ancestors.**

1 אַתָּה גִּבּוֹר לְעוֹלָם, אֲדֹנָי

2 מְחַיֵּה מֵתִים אַתָּה, רַב לְהוֹשִׁיעַ

Between Simḥat Torah and Pesaḥ add these words:

3 מַשִּׁיב הָרוּחַ וּמוֹרִיד הַגֶּשֶׁם

Between Pesaḥ and Shemini Atzeret add these words:

מוֹרִיד הַטָּל

4 מְכַלְכֵּל חַיִּים בְּחֶסֶד, מְחַיֵּה מֵתִים בְּרַחֲמִים רַבִּים

5 סוֹמֵךְ נוֹפְלִים, וְרוֹפֵא חוֹלִים, וּמַתִּיר אֲסוּרִים

6 וּמְקַיֵּם אֱמוּנָתוֹ לִישֵׁנֵי עָפָר.

7 מִי כָמְוֹךָ, בַּעַל גְּבוּרוֹת

8 וּמִי דּוֹמֶה לָּךְ, מֶלֶךְ מֵמִית וּמְחַיֶּה וּמַצְמִיחַ יְשׁוּעָה.

Between Rosh HaShana and Yom Kippur add these words:

9 מִי כָמְוֹךָ אָב הָרַחֲמִים, זוֹכֵר יְצוּרָיו בְּרַחֲמִים לְחַיִּים.

10 וְנֶאֱמָן אַתָּה לְהַחֲיוֹת מֵתִים. בָּרוּךְ אַתָּה יְהֹוָה

11 **מְחַיֵּה הַמֵּתִים.**

12 אַתָּה קָדוֹשׁ וְשִׁמְךָ קָדוֹשׁ

13 וּקְדוֹשִׁים בְּכָל יוֹם יְהַלְלְוּךָ סֶּלָה. בָּרוּךְ אַתָּה יְהֹוָה

14 **הָאֵל הַקָּדוֹשׁ.**

Between Rosh HaShana and Yom Kippur change the ending of this בְּרָכָה *to these words:*

הַמֶּלֶךְ הַקָּדוֹשׁ.

תִּכַּנְתָּ שַׁבָּת, רָצִיתָ קָרְבְּנוֹתֶיהָ

צִוִּיתָ פֵּרוּשֶׁיהָ עִם סִדּוּרֵי נְסָכֶיהָ

מְעַנְּגֶיהָ לְעוֹלָם כָּבוֹד יִנְחָלוּ

טוֹעֲמֶיהָ חַיִּים זָכוּ

וְגַם הָאוֹהֲבִים דְּבָרֶיהָ גְּדֻלָּה בָּחָרוּ

אָז מִסִּינַי נִצְטַוּוּ צִוּוּיֵי פְעָלֶיהָ כָּרָאוּי.

יְהִי רָצוֹן מִלְּפָנֶיךָ, יְהוָה אֱלֹהֵינוּ וֵאלֹהֵי אֲבוֹתֵינוּ

שֶׁתַּעֲלֵנוּ בְשִׂמְחָה לְאַרְצֵנוּ, וְתִטָּעֵנוּ בִּגְבוּלֵנוּ

וְשָׁם נַעֲשֶׂה לְפָנֶיךָ אֶת קָרְבְּנוֹת חוֹבוֹתֵינוּ

תְּמִידִים כְּסִדְרָם וּמוּסָפִים כְּהִלְכָתָם.

"The world is like a human eye. The white of the eye is the ocean surrounding the world; the iris is the continent; the pupil is Jerusalem; and the image in the pupil is the Holy Temple."

What do you think it means that Yerushalayim is the eye of the universe?

Close your eyes, and imagine you are there.

אֶת מוּסַף יוֹם הַשַּׁבָּת הַזֶּה
נַעֲשֶׂה וְנַקְרִיב לְפָנֶיךָ בְּאַהֲבָה כְּמִצְוַת רְצוֹנֶךָ
כְּמוֹ שֶׁכָּתַבְתָּ עָלֵינוּ בְּתוֹרָתְךָ עַל יְדֵי מֹשֶׁה עַבְדְּךָ
כָּאָמוּר

וּבְיוֹם הַשַּׁבָּת

שְׁנֵי־כְבָשִׂים בְּנֵי־שָׁנָה תְּמִימִם
וּשְׁנֵי עֶשְׂרֹנִים סֹלֶת מִנְחָה בְּלוּלָה בַשֶּׁמֶן וְנִסְכּוֹ:
עֹלַת שַׁבַּת בְּשַׁבַּתּוֹ, עַל־עֹלַת הַתָּמִיד וְנִסְכָּהּ:

יִשְׂמְחוּ בְמַלְכוּתְךָ שׁוֹמְרֵי שַׁבָּת וְקוֹרְאֵי עֹנֶג
עַם מְקַדְּשֵׁי שְׁבִיעִי, כֻּלָּם יִשְׂבְּעוּ וְיִתְעַנְּגוּ מִטּוּבֶךָ
וְהַשְּׁבִיעִי רָצִיתָ בּוֹ וְקִדַּשְׁתּוֹ
חֶמְדַּת יָמִים אוֹתוֹ קָרָאתָ, זֵכֶר לְמַעֲשֵׂה בְרֵאשִׁית.

אֱלֹהֵינוּ וֵאלֹהֵי אֲבוֹתֵינוּ, רְצֵה בִמְנוּחָתֵנוּ
קַדְּשֵׁנוּ בְּמִצְוֹתֶיךָ, שִׂים חֶלְקֵנוּ בְּתוֹרָתֶךָ
שַׂבְּעֵנוּ מִטּוּבֶךָ, שַׂמֵּחַ נַפְשֵׁנוּ בִּישׁוּעָתֶךָ
וְטַהֵר לִבֵּנוּ לְעָבְדְּךָ בֶּאֱמֶת
וְהַנְחִילֵנוּ, יְהֹוָה אֱלֹהֵינוּ, בְּאַהֲבָה וּבְרָצוֹן שַׁבַּת קָדְשֶׁךָ
וְיָנוּחוּ בוֹ כָּל יִשְׂרָאֵל מְקַדְּשֵׁי שְׁמֶךָ
בָּרוּךְ אַתָּה יְהֹוָה

מְקַדֵּשׁ הַשַּׁבָּת.

רְצֵה יְהֹוָה אֱלֹהֵינוּ בְּעַמְּךָ יִשְׂרָאֵל וְלִתְפִלָּתָם שְׁעֵה
וְהָשֵׁב הָעֲבוֹדָה לִדְבִיר בֵּיתֶךָ
וְאִשֵּׁי יִשְׂרָאֵל וּתְפִלָּתָם מְהֵרָה בְּאַהֲבָה תְקַבֵּל בְּרָצוֹן
וּתְהִי לְרָצוֹן תָּמִיד עֲבוֹדַת יִשְׂרָאֵל עַמֶּךָ.
וְאַתָּה בְּרַחֲמֶיךָ הָרַבִּים תַּחְפֹּץ בָּנוּ וְתִרְצֵנוּ
וְתֶחֱזֶינָה עֵינֵינוּ בְּשׁוּבְךָ לְצִיּוֹן בְּרַחֲמִים.
בָּרוּךְ אַתָּה יְהֹוָה

הַמַּחֲזִיר שְׁכִינָתוֹ לְצִיּוֹן.

מוֹדִים אֲנַחְנוּ לָךְ.

שָׁאַתָּה הוּא יְהֹוָה אֱלֹהֵינוּ
וֵאלֹהֵי אֲבוֹתֵינוּ לְעוֹלָם וָעֶד.
צוּרֵנוּ, צוּר חַיֵּינוּ וּמָגֵן יִשְׁעֵנוּ
אַתָּה הוּא לְדוֹר וָדוֹר.
נוֹדֶה לְךָ וּנְסַפֵּר תְּהִלָּתֶךָ
עַל חַיֵּינוּ הַמְּסוּרִים בְּיָדֶךָ
וְעַל נִשְׁמוֹתֵינוּ הַפְּקוּדוֹת לָךְ.
וְעַל נִסֶּיךָ שֶׁבְּכָל יוֹם עִמָּנוּ
וְעַל נִפְלְאוֹתֶיךָ וְטוֹבוֹתֶיךָ
שֶׁבְּכָל עֵת, עֶרֶב וָבֹקֶר וְצָהֳרָיִם.
הַטּוֹב, כִּי לֹא כָלוּ רַחֲמֶיךָ
הַמְּרַחֵם, כִּי לֹא תַמּוּ חֲסָדֶיךָ
כִּי מֵעוֹלָם קִוִּינוּ לָךְ.

Hashem, understand that we are resting on Shabbat because You have asked us to. Make us holy by helping us keep Your mitzvot and Your Torah. Because You love us, give us the ability to keep Your holy Shabbat, just like our generations before us.

During Ḥanukka say עַל הַנִּסִּים.

עַל הַנִּסִּים וְעַל הַפֻּרְקָן וְעַל הַגְּבוּרוֹת וְעַל הַתְּשׁוּעוֹת וְעַל הַנִּפְלָאוֹ
וְעַל הַנֶּחָמוֹת שֶׁעָשִׂיתָ לַאֲבוֹתֵינוּ בַּיָּמִים הָהֵם בַּזְּמַן הַזֶּה.

בִּימֵי מַתִּתְיָה בֶּן יוֹחָנָן כֹּהֵן גָּדוֹל חַשְׁמוֹנַאי וּבָנָיו, כְּשֶׁעָמְדָה מַלְכוּ
יָוָן הָרְשָׁעָה עַל עַמְּךָ יִשְׂרָאֵל לְשַׁכְּחָם תּוֹרָתֶךָ וּלְהַעֲבִירָם מֵחֻקֵּי רְצוֹנֶךָ
וְאַתָּה בְּרַחֲמֶיךָ הָרַבִּים עָמַדְתָּ לָהֶם בְּעֵת צָרָתָם, רַבְתָּ אֶת רִיבָם, דַּנְ
אֶת דִּינָם, נָקַמְתָּ אֶת נִקְמָתָם, מָסַרְתָּ גִבּוֹרִים בְּיַד חַלָּשִׁים, וְרַבִּים בְּיַ
מְעַטִּים, וּרְשָׁעִים בְּיַד צַדִּיקִים, וּטְמֵאִים בְּיַד טְהוֹרִים, וְזֵדִים בְּיַד עוֹסְקֵ
תוֹרָתֶךָ. לְךָ עָשִׂיתָ שֵׁם גָּדוֹל וְקָדוֹשׁ בְּעוֹלָמֶךָ, וּלְעַמְּךָ יִשְׂרָאֵל עָשִׂיתָ תְּשׁוּעָ
גְדוֹלָה וּפֻרְקָן כְּהַיּוֹם הַזֶּה. וְאַחַר כָּךְ בָּאוּ בָנֶיךָ לִדְבִיר בֵּיתֶךָ, וּפִנּוּ אֶ
הֵיכָלֶךָ, וְטִהֲרוּ אֶת מִקְדָּשֶׁךָ, וְהִדְלִיקוּ נֵרוֹת בְּחַצְרוֹת קָדְשֶׁךָ, וְקָבְע
שְׁמוֹנַת יְמֵי חֲנֻכָּה אֵלּוּ, בְּהַלֵּל וּבְהוֹדָאָה, וְעָשִׂיתָ עִמָּהֶם נִסִּים וְנִפְלָאוֹת
וְנוֹדֶה לְשִׁמְךָ הַגָּדוֹל, סֶלָה.

וְעַל כֻּלָּם
יִתְבָּרַךְ וְיִתְרוֹמַם וְיִתְנַשֵּׂא תָּמִיד שִׁמְךָ מַלְכֵּנוּ לְעוֹלָם וָ
וְכָל הַחַיִּים יוֹדוּךָ סֶּלָה

Between Rosh HaShana and Yom Kippur add these words:

וּכְתֹב לְחַיִּים טוֹבִים כָּל בְּנֵי בְרִיתֶךָ.

וִיהַלְלוּ וִיבָרְכוּ אֶת שִׁמְךָ הַגָּדוֹל בֶּאֱמֶת לְעוֹלָם כִּי טוֹב
הָאֵל יְשׁוּעָתֵנוּ וְעֶזְרָתֵנוּ סֶלָה, הָאֵל הַטּוֹב.
בָּרוּךְ אַתָּה יְהֹוָה
הַטּוֹב שִׁמְךָ וּלְךָ נָאֶה לְהוֹדוֹת.

שִׂים שָׁלוֹם טוֹבָה וּבְרָכָה

חַיִּים חֵן וָחֶסֶד, צְדָקָה וְרַחֲמִים עָלֵינוּ וְעַל כָּל יִשְׂרָאֵל עַמֶּךָ.

וּבָרְכֵנוּ אָבִינוּ כֻּלָּנוּ כְּאֶחָד בְּאוֹר פָּנֶיךָ

כִּי בְאוֹר פָּנֶיךָ נָתַתָּ לָּנוּ יְהֹוָה אֱלֹהֵינוּ תּוֹרָה וְחַיִּים

אַהֲבָה וָחֶסֶד, צְדָקָה וְרַחֲמִים, בְּרָכָה וְשָׁלוֹם.

וְטוֹב בְּעֵינֶיךָ לְבָרְכֵנוּ וּלְבָרֵךְ אֶת כָּל עַמְּךָ יִשְׂרָאֵל

בְּרֹב עֹז וְשָׁלוֹם.

Between Rosh HaShana and Yom Kippur add these words:

בְּסֵפֶר חַיִּים, בְּרָכָה וְשָׁלוֹם, וּפַרְנָסָה טוֹבָה, וִישׁוּעָה וְנֶחָמָה, וּגְזֵרוֹת טוֹבוֹת נִזָּכֵר וְנִכָּתֵב לְפָנֶיךָ, אֲנַחְנוּ וְכָל עַמְּךָ יִשְׂרָאֵל, לְחַיִּים טוֹבִים וּלְשָׁלוֹם.

בָּרוּךְ אַתָּה יְהֹוָה

הַמְבָרֵךְ אֶת עַמּוֹ

יִשְׂרָאֵל בַּשָּׁלוֹם.

אָמֵן.

Between Rosh HaShana and Yom Kippur change the ending of this בְּרָכָה *to these words:*

בָּרוּךְ אַתָּה יְהֹוָה עוֹשֵׂה הַשָּׁלוֹם.

יִהְיוּ לְרָצוֹן אִמְרֵי־פִי וְהֶגְיוֹן לִבִּי לְפָנֶיךָ, יְהֹוָה צוּרִי וְגֹאֲלִי:

Give peace, goodness, and blessing, life, grace, kindness and care to us and all Your people of Israel. Bless us as one

Hashem, You are the Source of all blessing, who blesses His people with peace.

אֱלֹהַי

נְצֹר לְשׁוֹנִי מֵרָע וּשְׂפָתַי מִדַּבֵּר מִרְמָה
וְלִמְקַלְלַי נַפְשִׁי תִדֹּם, וְנַפְשִׁי כֶּעָפָר לַכֹּל תִּהְיֶה.
פְּתַח לִבִּי בְּתוֹרָתֶךָ, וְאַחֲרֵי מִצְוֹתֶיךָ תִּרְדֹּף נַפְשִׁי.
וְכָל הַקָּמִים עָלַי לְרָעָה
מְהֵרָה הָפֵר עֲצָתָם וְקַלְקֵל מַחְשְׁבוֹתָם.
יִהְיוּ כְּמֹץ לִפְנֵי־רוּחַ וּמַלְאַךְ יְהוָה דּוֹחֶה:
עֲשֵׂה לְמַעַן שְׁמֶךָ, עֲשֵׂה לְמַעַן יְמִינֶךָ
עֲשֵׂה לְמַעַן תּוֹרָתֶךָ, עֲשֵׂה לְמַעַן קְדֻשָּׁתֶךָ.
לְמַעַן יֵחָלְצוּן יְדִידֶיךָ, הוֹשִׁיעָה יְמִינְךָ וַעֲנֵנִי:
יִהְיוּ לְרָצוֹן אִמְרֵי־פִי וְהֶגְיוֹן לִבִּי לְפָנֶיךָ, יְהוָה צוּרִי וְגֹאֲלִי:

As you finish the עֲמִידָה you should stop and think that you have just had the opportunity and honor to stand before Hashem. To be respectful, bow as you take three steps back. Then bow to the left, right and center as the pictures show.

Between Rosh HaShana and Yom Kippur say הַשָּׁלוֹם instead of שָׁלוֹם.

עֹשֶׂה שָׁלוֹם | הַשָּׁלוֹם בִּמְרוֹמָיו

הוּא בְּרַחֲמָיו יַעֲשֶׂה שָׁלוֹם

עָלֵינוּ וְעַל כָּל עַמּוֹ יִשְׂרָאֵל
וְאִמְרוּ אָמֵן.

1 אֵין כֵּאלֹהֵינוּ, אֵין כַּאדוֹנֵינוּ

2 אֵין כְּמַלְכֵּנוּ, אֵין כְּמוֹשִׁיעֵנוּ.

3 מִי כֵאלֹהֵינוּ, מִי כַאדוֹנֵינוּ

4 מִי כְמַלְכֵּנוּ, מִי כְמוֹשִׁיעֵנוּ.

5 נוֹדֶה לֵאלֹהֵינוּ, נוֹדֶה לַאדוֹנֵינוּ

6 נוֹדֶה לְמַלְכֵּנוּ, נוֹדֶה לְמוֹשִׁיעֵנוּ.

7 בָּרוּךְ אֱלֹהֵינוּ, בָּרוּךְ אֲדוֹנֵינוּ

8 בָּרוּךְ מַלְכֵּנוּ, בָּרוּךְ מוֹשִׁיעֵנוּ.

9 אַתָּה הוּא אֱלֹהֵינוּ, אַתָּה הוּא אֲדוֹנֵינוּ

10 אַתָּה הוּא מַלְכֵּנוּ, אַתָּה הוּא מוֹשִׁיעֵנוּ.

11 אַתָּה תוֹשִׁיעֵנוּ

12 אַתָּה תָקוּם תְּרַחֵם צִיּוֹן, כִּי־עֵת לְחֶנְנָהּ כִּי־בָא מוֹעֵד:

"Shabbat brings peace. Peace between man and man, peace between man and nature, and peace between man and himself."

How do you think Shabbat can bring peace in these ways?

How will you try and bring peace in this way this coming Shabbat?

We stand when we say עָלֵינוּ.

עָלֵינוּ לְשַׁבֵּחַ לַאֲדוֹן הַכֹּל, לָתֵת גְּדֻלָּה לְיוֹצֵר בְּרֵאשִׁית
שֶׁלֹּא עָשָׂנוּ כְּגוֹיֵי הָאֲרָצוֹת, וְלֹא שָׂמָנוּ כְּמִשְׁפְּחוֹת הָאֲדָמָה
שֶׁלֹּא שָׂם חֶלְקֵנוּ כָּהֶם וְגוֹרָלֵנוּ כְּכָל הֲמוֹנָם.
שֶׁהֵם מִשְׁתַּחֲוִים לְהֶבֶל וָרִיק וּמִתְפַּלְלִים אֶל־אֵל לֹא יוֹשִׁיעַ
וַאֲנַחְנוּ מִשְׁתַּחֲוִים
לִפְנֵי מֶלֶךְ מַלְכֵי הַמְּלָכִים, הַקָּדוֹשׁ בָּרוּךְ הוּא
שֶׁהוּא נוֹטֶה שָׁמַיִם וְיוֹסֵד אָרֶץ, וּמוֹשַׁב יְקָרוֹ בַּשָּׁמַיִם מִמַּעַל
וּשְׁכִינַת עֻזּוֹ בְּגָבְהֵי מְרוֹמִים.
הוּא אֱלֹהֵינוּ, וְאֵין עוֹד אַחֵר
אֱמֶת מַלְכֵּנוּ, וְאֶפֶס זוּלָתוֹ
כַּכָּתוּב בְּתוֹרָתוֹ
וְיָדַעְתָּ הַיּוֹם וַהֲשֵׁבֹתָ אֶל־לְבָבֶךָ
כִּי יְהֹוָה הוּא הָאֱלֹהִים בַּשָּׁמַיִם מִמַּעַל
וְעַל־הָאָרֶץ מִתָּחַת, אֵין עוֹד:

Where can you see in your world that Hashem is King?

עַל כֵּן נְקַוֶּה לְּךָ יְהֹוָה אֱלֹהֵינוּ
לִרְאוֹת מְהֵרָה בְּתִפְאֶרֶת עֻזֶּךָ
לְהַעֲבִיר גִּלּוּלִים מִן הָאָרֶץ, וְהָאֱלִילִים כָּרוֹת יִכָּרֵתוּן
לְתַקֵּן עוֹלָם בְּמַלְכוּת שַׁדַּי.
וְכָל בְּנֵי בָשָׂר יִקְרְאוּ בִשְׁמֶךָ
לְהַפְנוֹת אֵלֶיךָ כָּל רִשְׁעֵי אָרֶץ.
יַכִּירוּ וְיֵדְעוּ כָּל יוֹשְׁבֵי תֵבֵל
כִּי לְךָ תִּכְרַע כָּל בֶּרֶךְ, תִּשָּׁבַע כָּל לָשׁוֹן.
לְפָנֶיךָ יְהֹוָה אֱלֹהֵינוּ יִכְרְעוּ וְיִפֹּלוּ
וְלִכְבוֹד שִׁמְךָ יְקָר יִתֵּנוּ
וִיקַבְּלוּ כֻלָּם אֶת עֹל מַלְכוּתֶךָ
וְתִמְלֹךְ עֲלֵיהֶם מְהֵרָה לְעוֹלָם וָעֶד.
כִּי הַמַּלְכוּת שֶׁלְּךָ הִיא, וּלְעוֹלְמֵי עַד תִּמְלֹךְ בְּכָבוֹד
כַּכָּתוּב בְּתוֹרָתֶךָ, יְהֹוָה יִמְלֹךְ לְעֹלָם וָעֶד:
וְנֶאֱמַר, וְהָיָה יְהֹוָה לְמֶלֶךְ עַל-כָּל-הָאָרֶץ
בַּיּוֹם הַהוּא יִהְיֶה יְהֹוָה אֶחָד וּשְׁמוֹ אֶחָד:

It is good for us to thank Hashem and to sing about Your holy name, and to describe Your kindness in the morning and Your trustworthiness at night.

Each day the Levi'im would sing a different song from סֵפֶר תְּהִלִּים *in the* בֵּית הַמִּקְדָּשׁ. *This is the song for Shabbat.*

מִזְמוֹר שִׁיר לְיוֹם הַשַּׁבָּת: טוֹב לְהֹדוֹת לַיהוָה, וּלְזַמֵּר לְשִׁמְךָ עֶלְיוֹן: לְהַגִּיד בַּבֹּקֶר חַסְדֶּךָ, וֶאֱמוּנָתְךָ בַּלֵּילוֹת: עֲלֵי־עָשׂוֹר וַעֲלֵי־נָבֶל, עֲלֵי הִגָּיוֹן בְּכִנּוֹר: כִּי שִׂמַּחְתַּנִי יְהוָה בְּפָעֳלֶךָ, בְּמַעֲשֵׂי יָדֶיךָ אֲרַנֵּן: מַה־גָּדְלוּ מַעֲשֶׂיךָ יְהוָה, מְאֹד עָמְקוּ מַחְשְׁבֹתֶיךָ: אִישׁ־בַּעַר לֹא יֵדָע, וּכְסִיל לֹא־יָבִין אֶת־זֹאת: בִּפְרֹחַ רְשָׁעִים כְּמוֹ־עֵשֶׂב, וַיָּצִיצוּ כָּל־פֹּעֲלֵי אָוֶן, לְהִשָּׁמְדָם עֲדֵי־עַד: וְאַתָּה מָרוֹם לְעֹלָם יְהוָה: כִּי הִנֵּה אֹיְבֶיךָ יְהוָה, כִּי־הִנֵּה אֹיְבֶיךָ יֹאבֵדוּ, יִתְפָּרְדוּ כָּל־פֹּעֲלֵי אָוֶן: וַתָּרֶם כִּרְאֵים קַרְנִי, בַּלֹּתִי בְּשֶׁמֶן רַעֲנָן: וַתַּבֵּט עֵינִי בְּשׁוּרָי, בַּקָּמִים עָלַי מְרֵעִים תִּשְׁמַעְנָה אָזְנָי: צַדִּיק כַּתָּמָר יִפְרָח, כְּאֶרֶז בַּלְּבָנוֹן יִשְׂגֶּה: שְׁתוּלִים בְּבֵית יְהוָה, בְּחַצְרוֹת אֱלֹהֵינוּ יַפְרִיחוּ: עוֹד יְנוּבוּן בְּשֵׂיבָה, דְּשֵׁנִים וְרַעֲנַנִּים יִהְיוּ: לְהַגִּיד כִּי־יָשָׁר יְהוָה, צוּרִי, וְלֹא־עַוְלָתָה בּוֹ:

אֲדוֹן עוֹלָם

אֲשֶׁר מָלַךְ בְּטֶרֶם כָּל־יְצִיר נִבְרָא.
לְעֵת נַעֲשָׂה בְחֶפְצוֹ כֹּל אֲזַי מֶלֶךְ שְׁמוֹ נִקְרָא.
וְאַחֲרֵי כִּכְלוֹת הַכֹּל לְבַדּוֹ יִמְלֹךְ נוֹרָא.
וְהוּא הָיָה וְהוּא הֹוֶה וְהוּא יִהְיֶה בְּתִפְאָרָה.
וְהוּא אֶחָד וְאֵין שֵׁנִי לְהַמְשִׁיל לוֹ לְהַחְבִּירָה.
בְּלִי רֵאשִׁית בְּלִי תַכְלִית וְלוֹ הָעֹז וְהַמִּשְׂרָה.
בְּלִי עֵרֶךְ, בְּלִי דִמְיוֹן, בְּלִי שִׁנּוּי וּתְמוּרָה.
בְּלִי חִבּוּר, בְּלִי פֵרוּד, גְּדָל כֹּחַ וּגְבוּרָה.
וְהוּא אֵלִי וְחַי גּוֹאֲלִי וְצוּר חֶבְלִי בְּעֵת צָרָה.
וְהוּא נִסִּי וּמָנוּסִי, מְנָת כּוֹסִי בְּיוֹם אֶקְרָא.
בְּיָדוֹ אַפְקִיד רוּחִי בְּעֵת אִישַׁן וְאָעִירָה.
וְעִם רוּחִי גְּוִיָּתִי, יְהֹוָה לִי וְלֹא אִירָא.

What is your favorite Shabbat song?

The Shabbat meal during the day begins with קִדּוּשׁ*, announcing that Shabbat is holy.*

אִם־תָּשִׁיב מִשַּׁבָּת רַגְלֶךָ עֲשׂוֹת חֲפָצֶךָ בְּיוֹם קָדְשִׁי, וְקָרָאתָ לַשַּׁבָּת עֹנֶג לִקְדוֹשׁ יְהֹוָה מְכֻבָּד, וְכִבַּדְתּוֹ מֵעֲשׂוֹת דְּרָכֶיךָ מִמְּצוֹא חֶפְצְךָ וְדַבֵּר דָּבָר: אָז תִּתְעַנַּג עַל־יְהֹוָה, וְהִרְכַּבְתִּיךָ עַל־בָּמֳתֵי אָרֶץ, וְהַאֲכַלְתִּיךָ נַחֲלַת יַעֲקֹב אָבִיךָ, כִּי פִּי יְהֹוָה דִּבֵּר:

וְשָׁמְרוּ בְנֵי־יִשְׂרָאֵל אֶת־הַשַּׁבָּת, לַעֲשׂוֹת אֶת־הַשַּׁבָּת לְדֹרֹתָם בְּרִית עוֹלָם: בֵּינִי וּבֵין בְּנֵי יִשְׂרָאֵל אוֹת הִוא לְעֹלָם, כִּי־שֵׁשֶׁת יָמִים עָשָׂה יְהֹוָה אֶת־הַשָּׁמַיִם וְאֶת־הָאָרֶץ וּבַיּוֹם הַשְּׁבִיעִי שָׁבַת וַיִּנָּפַשׁ:

עַל־כֵּן בֵּרַךְ יְהֹוָה אֶת־יוֹם הַשַּׁבָּת, וַיְקַדְּשֵׁהוּ:

סַבְרִי מָרָנָן

Everyone says:

לְחַיִּים

בָּרוּךְ אַתָּה יְהֹוָה, אֱלֹהֵינוּ מֶלֶךְ הָעוֹלָם

בּוֹרֵא פְּרִי הַגָּפֶן.

Many people like to sing special Shabbat songs (זְמִירוֹת) at their Shabbat meals. There are some here on pages 231–233 and others on pages 176–179.

יוֹם שַׁבָּתוֹן אֵין לִשְׁכֹּחַ, זִכְרוֹ כְּרֵיחַ הַנִּיחֹחַ
יוֹנָה מָצְאָה בוֹ מָנוֹחַ וְשָׁם יָנוּחוּ יְגִיעֵי כֹחַ.

הַיּוֹם נִכְבָּד לִבְנֵי אֱמוּנִים, זְהִירִים לְשָׁמְרוֹ אָבוֹת וּבָנִים
חָקוּק בִּשְׁנֵי לוּחוֹת אֲבָנִים, מֵרֹב אוֹנִים וְאַמִּיץ כֹּחַ.
יוֹנָה מָצְאָה בוֹ מָנוֹחַ וְשָׁם יָנוּחוּ יְגִיעֵי כֹחַ.

וּבָאוּ כֻלָּם בִּבְרִית יַחַד, נַעֲשֶׂה וְנִשְׁמַע אָמְרוּ כְּאֶחָד
וּפָתְחוּ וְעָנוּ יְהֹוָה אֶחָד, בָּרוּךְ נֹתֵן לַיָּעֵף כֹּחַ.
יוֹנָה מָצְאָה בוֹ מָנוֹחַ וְשָׁם יָנוּחוּ יְגִיעֵי כֹחַ.

דִּבֶּר בְּקָדְשׁוֹ בְּהַר הַמֹּר, יוֹם הַשְּׁבִיעִי זָכוֹר וְשָׁמוֹר
וְכָל פִּקּוּדָיו יַחַד לִגְמֹר, חַזֵּק מָתְנַיִם וְאַמֵּץ כֹּחַ.
יוֹנָה מָצְאָה בוֹ מָנוֹחַ וְשָׁם יָנוּחוּ יְגִיעֵי כֹחַ.

הָעָם אֲשֶׁר נָע, כַּצֹּאן תָּעָה, יִזְכֹּר לְפָקְדוֹ בְּרִית וּשְׁבוּעָה
לְבַל יַעֲבָר בָּם מִקְרֵה רָעָה, כַּאֲשֶׁר נִשְׁבַּעְתָּ עַל מֵי נֹחַ.
יוֹנָה מָצְאָה בוֹ מָנוֹחַ וְשָׁם יָנוּחוּ יְגִיעֵי כֹחַ.

יוֹם זֶה מְכֻבָּד מִכָּל יָמִים, כִּי בוֹ שָׁבַת צוּר עוֹלָמִים.

שֵׁשֶׁת יָמִים תַּעֲשֶׂה מְלַאכְתֶּךָ
וְיוֹם הַשְּׁבִיעִי לֵאלֹהֶיךָ
שַׁבָּת לֹא תַעֲשֶׂה בוֹ מְלָאכָה
כִּי כֹל עָשָׂה שֵׁשֶׁת יָמִים.
יוֹם זֶה מְכֻבָּד מִכָּל יָמִים, כִּי בוֹ שָׁבַת צוּר עוֹלָמִים.

רִאשׁוֹן הוּא לְמִקְרָאֵי קֹדֶשׁ
יוֹם שַׁבָּתוֹן יוֹם שַׁבַּת קֹדֶשׁ
עַל כֵּן כָּל אִישׁ בְּיֵינוֹ יְקַדֵּשׁ
עַל שְׁתֵּי לֶחֶם יִבְצְעוּ תְמִימִים.
יוֹם זֶה מְכֻבָּד מִכָּל יָמִים, כִּי בוֹ שָׁבַת צוּר עוֹלָמִים.

There is a legend that the melody of the Maggid of Koznitz that he left behind when he died was learnt from the lips of angels who sang it in honor of Hashem. But one of his Hasidim disagreed with this, and rather believed that the angels learnt it from the Maggid's lips!

אֱכֹל מַשְׁמַנִּים, שְׁתֵה מַמְתַּקִּים
כִּי אֵל יִתֵּן לְכֹל בּוֹ דְבֵקִים
בֶּגֶד לִלְבֹּשׁ, לֶחֶם חֻקִּים
בָּשָׂר וְדָגִים וְכָל מַטְעַמִּים.
יוֹם זֶה מְכֻבָּד מִכָּל יָמִים, כִּי בוֹ שָׁבַת צוּר עוֹלָמִים.

לֹא תֶחְסַר כֹּל בּוֹ, וְאָכַלְתָּ
וְשָׂבָעְתָּ וּבֵרַכְתָּ
אֶת יְהֹוָה אֱלֹהֶיךָ אֲשֶׁר אָהַבְתָּ
כִּי בֵרַכְךָ מִכָּל הָעַמִּים.
יוֹם זֶה מְכֻבָּד מִכָּל יָמִים, כִּי בוֹ שָׁבַת צוּר עוֹלָמִים.

הַשָּׁמַיִם מְסַפְּרִים כְּבוֹדוֹ
וְגַם הָאָרֶץ מָלְאָה חַסְדּוֹ
רְאוּ כָּל אֵלֶּה עָשְׂתָה יָדוֹ
כִּי הוּא הַצּוּר פָּעֳלוֹ תָמִים.
יוֹם זֶה מְכֻבָּד מִכָּל יָמִים, כִּי בוֹ שָׁבַת צוּר עוֹלָמִים.

After the meal we say בִּרְכַּת הַמָּזוֹן *on page 266, thanking Hashem for the meal.*

on page 266

"There are rooms in heaven that only open to the sound of song."
What else can song open?

הַבְדָּלָה helps us say goodbye to Shabbat, and describes the differences between the holiness of Shabbat and the regular weekday. We hold a cup of wine or grape juice, a candle with more than one wick, and nice-smelling spices.

1 רִאשׁוֹן לְצִיּוֹן הִנֵּה הִנָּם וְלִירוּשָׁלַיִם מְבַשֵּׂר אֶתֵּן:

2 אַל־תִּשְׂמְחִי אֹיַבְתִּי לִי כִּי נָפַלְתִּי קָמְתִּי

3 כִּי־אֵשֵׁב בַּחֹשֶׁךְ יְהֹוָה אוֹר לִי:

4 וְנֹחַ מָצָא חֵן בְּעֵינֵי יְהֹוָה:

5 כֵּן נִמְצָא חֵן וְשֵׂכֶל טוֹב בְּעֵינֵי אֱלֹהִים וְאָדָם.

6 קוּמִי אוֹרִי כִּי בָא אוֹרֵךְ, וּכְבוֹד יְהֹוָה עָלַיִךְ זָרָח:

7 כִּי־הִנֵּה הַחֹשֶׁךְ יְכַסֶּה־אֶרֶץ וַעֲרָפֶל לְאֻמִּים

8 וְעָלַיִךְ יִזְרַח יְהֹוָה וּכְבוֹדוֹ עָלַיִךְ יֵרָאֶה:

9 כּוֹס־יְשׁוּעוֹת אֶשָּׂא וּבְשֵׁם יְהֹוָה אֶקְרָא:

10 סַבְרִי מָרָנָן

Everyone says:

11 לְחַיִּים

12 בָּרוּךְ אַתָּה יְהֹוָה, אֱלֹהֵינוּ מֶלֶךְ הָעוֹלָם

13 **בּוֹרֵא פְּרִי הַגָּפֶן.**

When saying this בְּרָכָה, hold the spices and then immediately smell them.

14 בָּרוּךְ אַתָּה יְהֹוָה, אֱלֹהֵינוּ מֶלֶךְ הָעוֹלָם

15 **בּוֹרֵא מִינֵי בְשָׂמִים.**

16 *When saying this בְּרָכָה, lift your hands toward the flame and look at the light shining on your nails and the shadows made by the fire and your hands.*

17 בָּרוּךְ אַתָּה יְהֹוָה, אֱלֹהֵינוּ מֶלֶךְ הָעוֹלָם

18 **בּוֹרֵא מְאוֹרֵי הָאֵשׁ.**

Pick up the cup again and say this בְּרָכָה and then drink the wine or grape juice.

בָּרוּךְ אַתָּה יְהוָה, אֱלֹהֵינוּ מֶלֶךְ הָעוֹלָם, הַמַּבְדִּיל בֵּין קֹדֶשׁ לְחוֹל, בֵּין אוֹר לְחֹשֶׁךְ, בֵּין יִשְׂרָאֵל לָעַמִּים, בֵּין יוֹם הַשְּׁבִיעִי לְשֵׁשֶׁת יְמֵי הַמַּעֲשֶׂה. בָּרוּךְ אַתָּה יְהוָה הַמַּבְדִּיל בֵּין קֹדֶשׁ לְחוֹל.

There once was a wealthy man who had three sons. He wanted to give all of his wealth to the cleverest of his sons, and so set them a task to prove their intelligence. He showed them a barn on his estate, and challenged his sons to fill the barn to the fullest. Whoever best succeeded in this task would win the entire inheritance. The eldest son worked hard gathering rocks and pebbles of all shapes and sizes and filled the barn from the floor to the roof. His father was impressed with his effort, but he found many spaces in between the rocks and stones.

The second son used straw, and packed the barn from floor to roof with the straw that was compact and fit tightly. However, his father still found spaces and pockets of air between the straw. When the turn of the younger son came he took his father by the hand and led him into an empty barn. His father became upset, that he had not taken the challenge seriously, but at that moment, the son took a small candle from his pocket and lit it. Instantly, the barn became filled, from the floor to the roof, in every nook and cranny, with light.

חַגִּים

HOLIDAYS

Holidays		**חַגִּים**
Hallel	238	הַלֵּל
Musaf for Rosh Ḥodesh	248	מוּסָף לְרֹאשׁ הַחֹדֶשׁ
Sefirat HaOmer	258	סְפִירַת הָעֹמֶר
Ḥanukka	260	חֲנֻכָּה
Sukkot	263	סֻכּוֹת

When the Jews left Egypt on their way to Eretz Yisrael, many amazing things happened. The sea took one look and ran away, the River Jordan turned and flowed the other way, and the mountains and hills danced.

"All sorts of miracles happened when the people fulfilled the mitzva of Aliya LaRegel and traveled to the Beit HaMikdash on the festivals. Once, when a man left for Yerushalayim, he forgot to lock his door. When he returned after the festival, he found a snake entwined around the handle to his door, protecting it from intruders. Another time, a man left for Yerushalayim and forgot to bring his chickens into the house to protect them from wild animals. When he returned, the chickens were safe but there were wild cats torn to pieces lying in front of the chicken coop. On another occasion, a man forgot to bring his harvested wheat into the house. When he returned, he found lions standing guard."

לַכֹּל זְמָן וְעֵת לְכָל־חֵפֶץ תַּחַת הַשָּׁמָיִם. (Kohelet 3:1)

How does nature help us tell time? Why do you think it is important to keep track of time?

הַלֵּל is said on Rosh Ḥodesh and holidays. It is made up of chapters from סֵפֶר תְּהִלִּים in which we praise and thank Hashem.

הַלְלוּיָהּ, הַלְלוּ עַבְדֵי יְהֹוָה, הַלְלוּ אֶת־שֵׁם יְהֹוָה: יְהִי שֵׁם יְהֹוָה מְבֹרָךְ, מֵעַתָּה וְעַד־עוֹלָם: מִמִּזְרַח־שֶׁמֶשׁ עַד־מְבוֹאוֹ, מְהֻלָּל שֵׁם יְהֹוָה: רָם עַל־כָּל־גּוֹיִם יְהֹוָה, עַל הַשָּׁמַיִם כְּבוֹדוֹ: מִי כַּיהוָה אֱלֹהֵינוּ, הַמַּגְבִּיהִי לָשָׁבֶת: הַמַּשְׁפִּילִי לִרְאוֹת, בַּשָּׁמַיִם וּבָאָרֶץ: מְקִימִי מֵעָפָר דָּל, מֵאַשְׁפֹּת יָרִים אֶבְיוֹן: לְהוֹשִׁיבִי עִם־נְדִיבִים, עִם נְדִיבֵי עַמּוֹ: מוֹשִׁיבִי עֲקֶרֶת הַבַּיִת, אֵם־הַבָּנִים שְׂמֵחָה, הַלְלוּיָהּ:

בְּצֵאת יִשְׂרָאֵל מִמִּצְרָיִם, בֵּית יַעֲקֹב מֵעַם לֹעֵז: הָיְתָה יְהוּדָה לְקָדְשׁוֹ, יִשְׂרָאֵל מַמְשְׁלוֹתָיו: הַיָּם רָאָה וַיָּנֹס, הַיַּרְדֵּן יִסֹּב לְאָחוֹר: הֶהָרִים רָקְדוּ כְאֵילִים, גְּבָעוֹת כִּבְנֵי־צֹאן: מַה־לְּךָ הַיָּם כִּי תָנוּס, הַיַּרְדֵּן תִּסֹּב לְאָחוֹר: הֶהָרִים תִּרְקְדוּ כְאֵילִים, גְּבָעוֹת כִּבְנֵי־צֹאן: מִלִּפְנֵי אָדוֹן חוּלִי אָרֶץ, מִלִּפְנֵי אֱלוֹהַּ יַעֲקֹב: הַהֹפְכִי הַצּוּר אֲגַם־מָיִם, חַלָּמִישׁ לְמַעְיְנוֹ־מָיִם:

Hashem remembers us and will bless us. The heavens are Hashem's but He gave the earth to humans. We will bless Hashem, now and forever. Halleluya!

Once a small mouse accidently woke a mighty lion who was dozing in the sunshine. Just as the lion was about to eat him the mouse pleaded, "Please don't! One day I might be of help to you." The lion laughed until he almost cried. "What could you possibly help me with?" he sniggered. But he admired the mouse's bravery and let him go. Not long afterwards, the lion became caught in a hunters trap. He struggled to free himself but the ropes were too strong. As he roared loudly in frustration the mouse came running and called out, "Don't worry, I can set you free!" He gnawed through the ropes and the lion went free. As the lion thanked him he said to him, "Who would have thought that someone as tiny as a mouse could save a mighty lion!"

"Hashem said to Adam: 'Look at My beautiful world. Everything I have created I have created for you. But be careful not to spoil and destroy My world. If you do, no one will fix it.'"

How can we care for the world that Hashem created for us?

What will you do today to care for your world?

יהוה זְכָרָנוּ יְבָרֵךְ, יְבָרֵךְ אֶת־בֵּית יִשְׂרָאֵל, יְבָרֵךְ אֶת־בֵּית אַהֲרֹן: יְבָרֵךְ יִרְאֵי יְהוָה, הַקְּטַנִּים עִם־הַגְּדֹלִים: יֹסֵף יְהוָה עֲלֵיכֶם, עֲלֵיכֶם וְעַל־בְּנֵיכֶם: בְּרוּכִים אַתֶּם לַיהוָה, עֹשֵׂה שָׁמַיִם וָאָרֶץ: הַשָּׁמַיִם שָׁמַיִם לַיהוָה, וְהָאָרֶץ נָתַן לִבְנֵי־אָדָם: לֹא הַמֵּתִים יְהַלְלוּ־יָהּ, וְלֹא כָּל יֹרְדֵי דוּמָה: וַאֲנַחְנוּ נְבָרֵךְ יָהּ, מֵעַתָּה וְעַד־עוֹלָם, הַלְלוּיָהּ:

מָה־אָשִׁיב לַיהוָה, כָּל־תַּגְמוּלוֹהִי עָלָי: כּוֹס יְשׁוּעוֹת אֶשָּׂא, וּבְשֵׁם יְהוָה אֶקְרָא: נְדָרַי לַיהוָה אֲשַׁלֵּם, נֶגְדָה־נָּא לְכָל־עַמּוֹ: יָקָר בְּעֵינֵי יְהוָה, הַמָּוְתָה לַחֲסִידָיו: אָנָּה יְהוָה כִּי־אֲנִי עַבְדֶּךָ, אֲנִי־עַבְדְּךָ בֶּן־אֲמָתֶךָ, פִּתַּחְתָּ לְמוֹסֵרָי: לְךָ־אֶזְבַּח זֶבַח תּוֹדָה, וּבְשֵׁם יְהוָה אֶקְרָא: נְדָרַי לַיהוָה אֲשַׁלֵּם, נֶגְדָה־נָּא לְכָל־עַמּוֹ: בְּחַצְרוֹת בֵּית יְהוָה, בְּתוֹכֵכִי יְרוּשָׁלָיִם, הַלְלוּיָהּ:

הַלְלוּ אֶת־יְהוָה כָּל־גּוֹיִם, שַׁבְּחוּהוּ כָּל־הָאֻמִּים:
כִּי גָבַר עָלֵינוּ חַסְדּוֹ, וֶאֱמֶת־יְהוָה לְעוֹלָם
הַלְלוּיָהּ:

Thank Hashem because He is good — His kindness will last forever.
Let the Jewish People say — His kindness will last forever.
Let the house of Aharon say — His kindness will last forever.
Let all people who fear Hashem say — His kindness will last forever.

The Jews are a tiny part of the human race. They are like a single grain of sand on a beach. The world should not have heard of the Jews, but everyone has. The Jewish people have made such a large impact on the world, much larger than you would expect considering how small in number they are. This is even more remarkable because so many powerful nations have tried to destroy them. The Egyptians, the Babylonians, the Persians, the Greeks and the Romans were all the most powerful nations on the planet. Each tried to destroy the Jewish people. And each have now disappeared from history. But the tiny Jewish People still live and breathe, create and build. It seems like all things die and disappear eventually except the Jewish People. What is their secret?

How has Hashem been kind to you?

How will you be kind to others today?

הוֹדוּ לַיהֹוָה כִּי־טוֹב כִּי לְעוֹלָם חַסְדּוֹ:
יֹאמַר־נָא יִשְׂרָאֵל כִּי לְעוֹלָם חַסְדּוֹ:
יֹאמְרוּ־נָא בֵית־אַהֲרֹן כִּי לְעוֹלָם חַסְדּוֹ:
יֹאמְרוּ־נָא יִרְאֵי יְהֹוָה כִּי לְעוֹלָם חַסְדּוֹ:

מִן־הַמֵּצַר קָרָאתִי יָּהּ, עָנָנִי בַמֶּרְחָב יָהּ: יְהֹוָה לִי לֹא אִירָא, מַה־יַּעֲשֶׂה לִי אָדָם: יְהֹוָה לִי בְּעֹזְרָי, וַאֲנִי אֶרְאֶה בְשֹׂנְאָי: טוֹב לַחֲסוֹת בַּיהֹוָה, מִבְּטֹחַ בָּאָדָם: טוֹב לַחֲסוֹת בַּיהֹוָה, מִבְּטֹחַ בִּנְדִיבִים: כָּל־גּוֹיִם סְבָבוּנִי, בְּשֵׁם יְהֹוָה כִּי אֲמִילַם: סַבּוּנִי גַם־סְבָבוּנִי, בְּשֵׁם יְהֹוָה כִּי אֲמִילַם: סַבּוּנִי כִדְבֹרִים, דֹּעֲכוּ כְּאֵשׁ קוֹצִים, בְּשֵׁם יְהֹוָה כִּי אֲמִילַם: דָּחֹה דְחִיתַנִי לִנְפֹּל, וַיהֹוָה עֲזָרָנִי: עָזִּי וְזִמְרָת יָהּ, וַיְהִי־לִי לִישׁוּעָה: קוֹל רִנָּה וִישׁוּעָה בְּאָהֳלֵי צַדִּיקִים, יְמִין יְהֹוָה עֹשָׂה חָיִל: יְמִין יְהֹוָה רוֹמֵמָה, יְמִין יְהֹוָה עֹשָׂה חָיִל: לֹא־אָמוּת כִּי־אֶחְיֶה, וַאֲסַפֵּר מַעֲשֵׂי יָהּ: יַסֹּר יִסְּרַנִּי יָּהּ, וְלַמָּוֶת לֹא נְתָנָנִי: פִּתְחוּ־לִי שַׁעֲרֵי־צֶדֶק, אָבֹא־בָם אוֹדֶה יָהּ: זֶה־הַשַּׁעַר לַיהֹוָה, צַדִּיקִים יָבֹאוּ בוֹ:

Hashem please save us!
Hashem help us succeed!

Hashem please save us!
Hashem help us succeed!

In 1878, before there was a State of Israel, 18 young yeshiva students left Tzefat to build a farming community where they could work the land and study Torah. Although they were inexperienced farmers, they made up for that with their enthusiasm and love of Eretz Yisrael. They bought a small piece of land in the north of Israel that would later be named Rosh Pina and began to build and farm. Their first year there, they planted potatoes in the spring, but were disappointed to see that the potatoes had not grown. So they turned the soil to choose a different crop only to find the potatoes hiding beneath the soil! Many of the original settlers left because life was so hard, but with the help of new waves of Aliya, Rosh Pina grew and today almost 3,000 people live there. The name means "cornerstone." The verse says the stone that was rejected has become the cornerstone. After years of neglect, Rosh Pina was one of the first Zionist settlements and became one of the cornerstones on which the future State of Israel was built.

1 אוֹדְךָ כִּי עֲנִיתָנִי, וַתְּהִי־לִי לִישׁוּעָה:

2 אוֹדְךָ כִּי עֲנִיתָנִי, וַתְּהִי־לִי לִישׁוּעָה:

3 אֶבֶן מָאֲסוּ הַבּוֹנִים, הָיְתָה לְרֹאשׁ פִּנָּה:

4 אֶבֶן מָאֲסוּ הַבּוֹנִים, הָיְתָה לְרֹאשׁ פִּנָּה:

5 מֵאֵת יְהֹוָה הָיְתָה זֹּאת, הִיא נִפְלָאת בְּעֵינֵינוּ:

6 מֵאֵת יְהֹוָה הָיְתָה זֹּאת, הִיא נִפְלָאת בְּעֵינֵינוּ:

7 זֶה־הַיּוֹם עָשָׂה יְהֹוָה, נָגִילָה וְנִשְׂמְחָה בוֹ:

8 זֶה־הַיּוֹם עָשָׂה יְהֹוָה, נָגִילָה וְנִשְׂמְחָה בוֹ:

9 אָנָּא יְהֹוָה הוֹשִׁיעָה נָּא:

10 אָנָּא יְהֹוָה הוֹשִׁיעָה נָּא:

11 אָנָּא יְהֹוָה הַצְלִיחָה נָא:

12 אָנָּא יְהֹוָה הַצְלִיחָה נָא:

You are my God and I will thank You. You are my God and I will say how wonderful You are.

Thank Hashem because He is good, His kindness will last forever.

"It is not for you to complete the work, but you are also not free to give up on it!" (Pirkei Avot 2:21)

Close your eyes and think about Hashem and all that He has done for you, your family, your friends and all people.

Do you think you will ever be able to find the words you need to praise and thank Hashem?
If not, why do we still try?

1 בָּרוּךְ הַבָּא בְּשֵׁם יְהֹוָה, בֵּרַכְנוּכֶם מִבֵּית יְהֹוָה:

2 בָּרוּךְ הַבָּא בְּשֵׁם יְהֹוָה, בֵּרַכְנוּכֶם מִבֵּית יְהֹוָה:

3 אֵל יְהֹוָה וַיָּאֶר לָנוּ

4 אִסְרוּ־חַג בַּעֲבֹתִים עַד־קַרְנוֹת הַמִּזְבֵּחַ:

5 אֵל יְהֹוָה וַיָּאֶר לָנוּ

6 אִסְרוּ־חַג בַּעֲבֹתִים עַד־קַרְנוֹת הַמִּזְבֵּחַ:

7 אֵלִי אַתָּה וְאוֹדֶךָּ, אֱלֹהַי אֲרוֹמְמֶךָּ:

8 אֵלִי אַתָּה וְאוֹדֶךָּ, אֱלֹהַי אֲרוֹמְמֶךָּ:

9 הוֹדוּ לַיהֹוָה כִּי־טוֹב, כִּי לְעוֹלָם חַסְדּוֹ:

10 הוֹדוּ לַיהֹוָה כִּי־טוֹב, כִּי לְעוֹלָם חַסְדּוֹ:

וְהִנֵּה־בֹעַז בָּא מִבֵּית לֶחֶם וַיֹּאמֶר לַקּוֹצְרִים, יְהֹוָה עִמָּכֶם
וַיֹּאמְרוּ לוֹ, יְבָרֶכְךָ יְהֹוָה. (Rut 2:4)

How many words can you think of that can be used to say hello to someone?

Do any of them say anything more than just hello?

Why would you want to use the name of Hashem to say hello?

תְּפִלַּת מוּסָף is said on special days such as Shabbat and Rosh Ḥodesh, in place of the קָרְבַּן מוּסָף in the בֵּית הַמִּקְדָּשׁ. This עֲמִידָה is for Rosh Ḥodesh. Just as in all other עֲמִידוֹת, you should mouth the words of the עֲמִידָה but without a sound. We learn this from the prayer of Ḥanna when she prayed to have a child. Take three steps forward and begin saying the עֲמִידָה while standing with your feet together.

אֲדֹנָי, שְׂפָתַי תִּפְתָּח, וּפִי יַגִּיד תְּהִלָּתֶךָ:

בָּרוּךְ אַתָּה יְהֹוָה

אֱלֹהֵינוּ וֵאלֹהֵי אֲבוֹתֵינוּ

אֱלֹהֵי אַבְרָהָם, אֱלֹהֵי יִצְחָק, וֵאלֹהֵי יַעֲקֹב

הָאֵל הַגָּדוֹל הַגִּבּוֹר וְהַנּוֹרָא, אֵל עֶלְיוֹן

גּוֹמֵל חֲסָדִים טוֹבִים, וְקֹנֵה הַכֹּל

וְזוֹכֵר חַסְדֵי אָבוֹת

וּמֵבִיא גוֹאֵל לִבְנֵי בְנֵיהֶם, לְמַעַן שְׁמוֹ בְּאַהֲבָה.

מֶלֶךְ עוֹזֵר וּמוֹשִׁיעַ וּמָגֵן.

בָּרוּךְ אַתָּה יְהֹוָה

מָגֵן אַבְרָהָם.

1 אַתָּה גִּבּוֹר לְעוֹלָם, אֲדֹנָי

2 מְחַיֵּה מֵתִים אַתָּה, רַב לְהוֹשִׁיעַ

Between Simḥat Torah and Pesaḥ add these words:

3 מַשִּׁיב הָרוּחַ וּמוֹרִיד הַגֶּשֶׁם

Between Pesaḥ and Shemini Atzeret add these words:

מוֹרִיד הַטָּל

4 מְכַלְכֵּל חַיִּים בְּחֶסֶד, מְחַיֵּה מֵתִים בְּרַחֲמִים רַבִּים

5 סוֹמֵךְ נוֹפְלִים, וְרוֹפֵא חוֹלִים, וּמַתִּיר אֲסוּרִים

6 וּמְקַיֵּם אֱמוּנָתוֹ לִישֵׁנֵי עָפָר.

7 מִי כָמוֹךָ, בַּעַל גְּבוּרוֹת

8 וּמִי דּוֹמֶה לָּךְ, מֶלֶךְ מֵמִית וּמְחַיֶּה וּמַצְמִיחַ יְשׁוּעָה.

9 וְנֶאֱמָן אַתָּה לְהַחֲיוֹת מֵתִים. בָּרוּךְ אַתָּה יְהֹוָה

10 מְחַיֵּה הַמֵּתִים.

You are so holy, and Your name is so holy, and those people that are also holy praise You every day! **Hashem, You are the Source of all blessing, the holy God.**

11 אַתָּה קָדוֹשׁ וְשִׁמְךָ קָדוֹשׁ

12 וּקְדוֹשִׁים בְּכָל יוֹם יְהַלְלוּךָ סֶּלָה.

13 בָּרוּךְ אַתָּה יְהֹוָה

14 הָאֵל הַקָּדוֹשׁ.

רָאשֵׁי חֳדָשִׁים לְעַמְּךָ נָתַתָּ
זְמַן כַּפָּרָה לְכָל תּוֹלְדוֹתָם
בִּהְיוֹתָם מַקְרִיבִים לְפָנֶיךָ זִבְחֵי רָצוֹן
שְׂעִירֵי חַטָּאת לְכַפֵּר בַּעֲדָם.
זִכָּרוֹן לְכֻלָּם יִהְיֶה, תְּשׁוּעַת נַפְשָׁם מִיַּד שׂוֹנֵא.
מִזְבֵּחַ חָדָשׁ בְּצִיּוֹן תָּכִין
וְעוֹלַת רֹאשׁ חֹדֶשׁ נַעֲלֶה עָלָיו
וּשְׂעִירֵי עִזִּים נַעֲשֶׂה בְרָצוֹן
וּבַעֲבוֹדַת בֵּית הַמִּקְדָּשׁ נִשְׂמַח כֻּלָּנוּ
וּבְשִׁירֵי דָוִד עַבְדְּךָ נִשְׁמַע בְּעִירֶךָ
הָאֲמוּרִים לִפְנֵי מִזְבְּחֶךָ.
אַהֲבַת עוֹלָם תָּבִיא לָהֶם
וּבְרִית אָבוֹת לַבָּנִים תִּזְכֹּר.

יְהִי רָצוֹן מִלְּפָנֶיךָ, יְהוָֹה אֱלֹהֵינוּ וֵאלֹהֵי אֲבוֹתֵינוּ
שֶׁתַּעֲלֵנוּ בְשִׂמְחָה לְאַרְצֵנוּ, וְתִטָּעֵנוּ בִּגְבוּלֵנוּ
וְשָׁם נַעֲשֶׂה לְפָנֶיךָ אֶת קָרְבְּנוֹת חוֹבוֹתֵינוּ
תְּמִידִים כְּסִדְרָם וּמוּסָפִים כְּהִלְכָתָם.

אֶת מוּסַף יוֹם רֹאשׁ הַחֹדֶשׁ הַזֶּה
נַעֲשֶׂה וְנַקְרִיב לְפָנֶיךָ בְּאַהֲבָה כְּמִצְוַת רְצוֹנֶךָ
כְּמוֹ שֶׁכָּתַבְתָּ עָלֵינוּ בְּתוֹרָתֶךָ
עַל יְדֵי מֹשֶׁה עַבְדֶּךָ מִפִּי כְבוֹדֶךָ
כָּאָמוּר

וּבְרָאשֵׁי חָדְשֵׁיכֶם תַּקְרִיבוּ עֹלָה לַיהוָֹה
פָּרִים בְּנֵי־בָקָר שְׁנַיִם וְאַיִל אֶחָד
כְּבָשִׂים בְּנֵי־שָׁנָה שִׁבְעָה, תְּמִימִם:

"When witnesses came to the court to say they had spotted the new moon, the judges had to let the Jewish communities outside of Israel know it was Rosh Ḥodesh. They lit a torch on top of the Mount of Olives in Jerusalem, and waved the torch until the Jews on the next mountain did the same, and then the Jews on a third mountain would do the same, and so on, until it looked as if the whole diaspora was one large bonfire!"

וּמִנְחָתָם וְנִסְכֵּיהֶם כִּמְדֻבָּר
שְׁלֹשָׁה עֶשְׂרֹנִים לַפָּר, וּשְׁנֵי עֶשְׂרֹנִים לָאָיִל
וְעִשָּׂרוֹן לַכֶּבֶשׂ, וְיַיִן כְּנִסְכּוֹ, וְשָׂעִיר לְכַפֵּר
וּשְׁנֵי תְמִידִים כְּהִלְכָתָם.

אֱלֹהֵינוּ וֵאלֹהֵי אֲבוֹתֵינוּ
חַדֵּשׁ עָלֵינוּ אֶת הַחֹדֶשׁ הַזֶּה לְטוֹבָה וְלִבְרָכָה
לְשָׂשׂוֹן וּלְשִׂמְחָה, לִישׁוּעָה וּלְנֶחָמָה
לְפַרְנָסָה וּלְכַלְכָּלָה, לְחַיִּים טוֹבִים וּלְשָׁלוֹם
לִמְחִילַת חֵטְא וְלִסְלִיחַת עָוֹן

During a leap year between the months of מַרְחֶשְׁוָן *and* אֲדָר שֵׁנִי
Some add this phrase:

וּלְכַפָּרַת פָּשַׁע

וִיהִיֶה רֹאשׁ הַחֹדֶשׁ הַזֶּה סוֹף וָקֵץ לְכָל צָרוֹתֵינוּ
תְּחִלָּה וָרֹאשׁ לְפִדְיוֹן נַפְשֵׁנוּ
כִּי בְעַמְּךָ יִשְׂרָאֵל מִכָּל הָאֻמּוֹת בָּחַרְתָּ
וְחֻקֵּי רָאשֵׁי חֳדָשִׁים לָהֶם קָבָעְתָּ.
בָּרוּךְ אַתָּה יְהֹוָה
מְקַדֵּשׁ יִשְׂרָאֵל וְרָאשֵׁי חֳדָשִׁים.

רְצֵה יְהֹוָה אֱלֹהֵינוּ בְּעַמְּךָ יִשְׂרָאֵל וְלִתְפִלָּתָם שְׁעֵה
וְהָשֵׁב הָעֲבוֹדָה לִדְבִיר בֵּיתֶךָ
וְאִשֵּׁי יִשְׂרָאֵל וּתְפִלָּתָם מְהֵרָה בְּאַהֲבָה תְקַבֵּל בְּרָצוֹן
וּתְהִי לְרָצוֹן תָּמִיד עֲבוֹדַת יִשְׂרָאֵל עַמֶּךָ.

וְאַתָּה בְּרַחֲמֶיךָ הָרַבִּים תַּחְפֹּץ בָּנוּ וְתִרְצֵנוּ
וְתֶחֱזֶינָה עֵינֵינוּ בְּשׁוּבְךָ לְצִיּוֹן בְּרַחֲמִים.
בָּרוּךְ אַתָּה יְהֹוָה

הַמַּחֲזִיר שְׁכִינָתוֹ לְצִיּוֹן.

מוֹדִים אֲנַחְנוּ לָךְ.

שָׁאַתָּה הוּא יְהֹוָה אֱלֹהֵינוּ
וֵאלֹהֵי אֲבוֹתֵינוּ לְעוֹלָם וָעֶד.
צוּרֵנוּ, צוּר חַיֵּינוּ וּמָגֵן יִשְׁעֵנוּ
אַתָּה הוּא לְדוֹר וָדוֹר.
נוֹדֶה לְּךָ וּנְסַפֵּר תְּהִלָּתֶךָ
עַל חַיֵּינוּ הַמְּסוּרִים בְּיָדֶךָ
וְעַל נִשְׁמוֹתֵינוּ הַפְּקוּדוֹת לָךְ.
וְעַל נִסֶּיךָ שֶׁבְּכָל יוֹם עִמָּנוּ
וְעַל נִפְלְאוֹתֶיךָ וְטוֹבוֹתֶיךָ
שֶׁבְּכָל עֵת, עֶרֶב וָבֹקֶר וְצָהֳרָיִם.
הַטּוֹב, כִּי לֹא כָלוּ רַחֲמֶיךָ
הַמְרַחֵם, כִּי לֹא תַמּוּ חֲסָדֶיךָ
כִּי מֵעוֹלָם קִוִּינוּ לָךְ.

מִזְמוֹר לְתוֹדָה: הָרִיעוּ לַיהוה, כָּל־הָאָרֶץ. עִבְדוּ אֶת־
יהוה בְּשִׂמְחָה; בֹּאוּ לְפָנָיו, בִּרְנָנָה. (Tehillim 100:1–2)

Does saying "thank you" make you happy? Why?

During Ḥanukka say עַל הַנִּסִּים.

עַל הַנִּסִּים וְעַל הַפֻּרְקָן וְעַל הַגְּבוּרוֹת וְעַל הַתְּשׁוּעוֹת וְעַל הַנִּפְלָאוֹת
וְעַל הַנֶּחָמוֹת שֶׁעָשִׂיתָ לַאֲבוֹתֵינוּ בַּיָּמִים הָהֵם בַּזְּמַן הַזֶּה.

בִּימֵי מַתִּתְיָה בֶּן יוֹחָנָן כֹּהֵן גָּדוֹל חַשְׁמוֹנַאי וּבָנָיו, כְּשֶׁעָמְדָה מַלְכוּת
יָוָן הָרְשָׁעָה עַל עַמְּךָ יִשְׂרָאֵל לְשַׁכְּחָם תּוֹרָתֶךָ וּלְהַעֲבִירָם מֵחֻקֵּי רְצוֹנֶךָ,
וְאַתָּה בְּרַחֲמֶיךָ הָרַבִּים עָמַדְתָּ לָהֶם בְּעֵת צָרָתָם, רַבְתָּ אֶת רִיבָם,
דַּנְתָּ אֶת דִּינָם, נָקַמְתָּ אֶת נִקְמָתָם, מָסַרְתָּ גִבּוֹרִים בְּיַד חַלָּשִׁים, וְרַבִּים
בְּיַד מְעַטִּים, וּרְשָׁעִים בְּיַד צַדִּיקִים, וּטְמֵאִים בְּיַד טְהוֹרִים, וְזֵדִים
בְּיַד עוֹסְקֵי תוֹרָתֶךָ. לְךָ עָשִׂיתָ שֵׁם גָּדוֹל וְקָדוֹשׁ בְּעוֹלָמֶךָ, וּלְעַמְּךָ
יִשְׂרָאֵל עָשִׂיתָ תְּשׁוּעָה גְדוֹלָה וּפֻרְקָן כְּהַיּוֹם הַזֶּה. וְאַחַר כָּךְ בָּאוּ בָנֶיךָ
לִדְבִיר בֵּיתֶךָ, וּפִנּוּ אֶת הֵיכָלֶךָ, וְטִהֲרוּ אֶת מִקְדָּשֶׁךָ, וְהִדְלִיקוּ נֵרוֹת
בְּחַצְרוֹת קָדְשֶׁךָ, וְקָבְעוּ שְׁמוֹנַת יְמֵי חֲנֻכָּה אֵלּוּ, בְּהַלֵּל וּבְהוֹדָאָה,
וְעָשִׂיתָ עִמָּהֶם נִסִּים וְנִפְלָאוֹת, וְנוֹדֶה לְשִׁמְךָ הַגָּדוֹל, סֶלָה.

וְעַל כֻּלָּם
יִתְבָּרַךְ וְיִתְרוֹמַם וְיִתְנַשֵּׂא תָּמִיד שִׁמְךָ מַלְכֵּנוּ לְעוֹלָם וָעֶד
וְכָל הַחַיִּים יוֹדוּךָ סֶּלָה
וִיהַלְלוּ וִיבָרְכוּ אֶת שִׁמְךָ הַגָּדוֹל בֶּאֱמֶת לְעוֹלָם כִּי טוֹב
הָאֵל יְשׁוּעָתֵנוּ וְעֶזְרָתֵנוּ סֶלָה, הָאֵל הַטּוֹב.
בָּרוּךְ אַתָּה יְהוָה
הַטּוֹב שִׁמְךָ וּלְךָ נָאֶה לְהוֹדוֹת.

שִׂים שָׁלוֹם טוֹבָה וּבְרָכָה
חַיִּים חֵן וָחֶסֶד, צְדָקָה וְרַחֲמִים
עָלֵינוּ וְעַל כָּל יִשְׂרָאֵל עַמֶּךָ.
וּבָרְכֵנוּ אָבִינוּ כֻּלָּנוּ כְּאֶחָד בְּאוֹר פָּנֶיךָ
כִּי בְאוֹר פָּנֶיךָ נָתַתָּ לָּנוּ יְהוָה אֱלֹהֵינוּ תּוֹרָה וְחַיִּים
אַהֲבָה וָחֶסֶד, צְדָקָה וְרַחֲמִים, בְּרָכָה וְשָׁלוֹם
וְטוֹב בְּעֵינֶיךָ לְבָרְכֵנוּ וּלְבָרֵךְ אֶת כָּל עַמְּךָ יִשְׂרָאֵל
בְּרֹב עֹז וְשָׁלוֹם.
בָּרוּךְ אַתָּה יְהוָה
הַמְבָרֵךְ אֶת עַמּוֹ יִשְׂרָאֵל בַּשָּׁלוֹם.
אָמֵן.

יִהְיוּ לְרָצוֹן אִמְרֵי־פִי וְהֶגְיוֹן לִבִּי לְפָנֶיךָ, יְהֹוָה צוּרִי וְגֹאֲלִי:

אֱלֹהַי

נְצֹר לְשׁוֹנִי מֵרָע וּשְׂפָתַי מִדַּבֵּר מִרְמָה
וְלִמְקַלְלַי נַפְשִׁי תִדֹּם, וְנַפְשִׁי כֶּעָפָר לַכֹּל תִּהְיֶה.
פְּתַח לִבִּי בְּתוֹרָתֶךָ, וְאַחֲרֵי מִצְוֹתֶיךָ תִּרְדֹּף נַפְשִׁי.
וְכָל הַקָּמִים עָלַי לְרָעָה
מְהֵרָה הָפֵר עֲצָתָם וְקַלְקֵל מַחְשְׁבוֹתָם.
יִהְיוּ כְּמֹץ לִפְנֵי־רוּחַ וּמַלְאַךְ יְהֹוָה דּוֹחֶה:
עֲשֵׂה לְמַעַן שְׁמֶךָ, עֲשֵׂה לְמַעַן יְמִינֶךָ
עֲשֵׂה לְמַעַן תּוֹרָתֶךָ, עֲשֵׂה לְמַעַן קְדֻשָּׁתֶךָ.
לְמַעַן יֵחָלְצוּן יְדִידֶיךָ, הוֹשִׁיעָה יְמִינְךָ וַעֲנֵנִי:
יִהְיוּ לְרָצוֹן אִמְרֵי־פִי וְהֶגְיוֹן לִבִּי לְפָנֶיךָ, יְהֹוָה צוּרִי וְגֹאֲלִי:

As you finish the עֲמִידָה you should stop and think that you have just had the opportunity and honor to stand before Hashem.
To be respectful, bow as you take three steps back.
Then bow to the left, right and center as the pictures show.

עֹשֶׂה שָׁלוֹם בִּמְרוֹמָיו
הוּא בְּרַחֲמָיו יַעֲשֶׂה שָׁלוֹם עָלֵינוּ
וְעַל כָּל עַמּוֹ יִשְׂרָאֵל
וְאִמְרוּ אָמֵן.

There is a mitzva to count the Omer each night from the second night of Pesaḥ until the night before Shavuot. Some people prepare for this mitzva by saying lines 1–4 before saying the בְּרָכָה.

1 הִנֵּה אֲנַחְנוּ בָּאִים לְקַיֵּם מִצְוַת סְפִירַת הָעֹמֶר
2 כְּדִכְתִיב, וּסְפַרְתֶּם לָכֶם מִמָּחֳרַת הַשַּׁבָּת
3 מִיּוֹם הֲבִיאֲכֶם אֶת־עֹמֶר הַתְּנוּפָה
4 שֶׁבַע שַׁבָּתוֹת תְּמִימֹת תִּהְיֶינָה:

5 בָּרוּךְ אַתָּה יְהוָה, אֱלֹהֵינוּ מֶלֶךְ הָעוֹלָם
6 אֲשֶׁר קִדְּשָׁנוּ בְּמִצְוֹתָיו וְצִוָּנוּ עַל סְפִירַת הָעֹמֶר.

1	הַיּוֹם יוֹם אֶחָד לָעֹמֶר.
2	הַיּוֹם שְׁנֵי יָמִים לָעֹמֶר.
3	הַיּוֹם שְׁלֹשָׁה יָמִים לָעֹמֶר.
4	הַיּוֹם אַרְבָּעָה יָמִים לָעֹמֶר.
5	הַיּוֹם חֲמִשָּׁה יָמִים לָעֹמֶר.
6	הַיּוֹם שִׁשָּׁה יָמִים לָעֹמֶר.
7	הַיּוֹם שִׁבְעָה יָמִים לָעֹמֶר שֶׁהֵם שָׁבוּעַ אֶחָד.
8	הַיּוֹם שְׁמוֹנָה יָמִים לָעֹמֶר שֶׁהֵם שָׁבוּעַ אֶחָד וְיוֹם אֶחָד.
9	הַיּוֹם תִּשְׁעָה יָמִים לָעֹמֶר שֶׁהֵם שָׁבוּעַ אֶחָד וּשְׁנֵי יָמִים.
10	הַיּוֹם עֲשָׂרָה יָמִים לָעֹמֶר שֶׁהֵם שָׁבוּעַ אֶחָד וּשְׁלֹשָׁה יָמִים.
11	הַיּוֹם אַחַד עָשָׂר יוֹם לָעֹמֶר שֶׁהֵם שָׁבוּעַ אֶחָד וְאַרְבָּעָה יָמִים.
12	הַיּוֹם שְׁנֵים עָשָׂר יוֹם לָעֹמֶר שֶׁהֵם שָׁבוּעַ אֶחָד וַחֲמִשָּׁה יָמִים.
13	הַיּוֹם שְׁלֹשָׁה עָשָׂר יוֹם לָעֹמֶר שֶׁהֵם שָׁבוּעַ אֶחָד וְשִׁשָּׁה יָמִים.
14	הַיּוֹם אַרְבָּעָה עָשָׂר יוֹם לָעֹמֶר שֶׁהֵם שְׁנֵי שָׁבוּעוֹת.
15	הַיּוֹם חֲמִשָּׁה עָשָׂר יוֹם לָעֹמֶר שֶׁהֵם שְׁנֵי שָׁבוּעוֹת וְיוֹם אֶחָד.
16	הַיּוֹם שִׁשָּׁה עָשָׂר יוֹם לָעֹמֶר שֶׁהֵם שְׁנֵי שָׁבוּעוֹת וּשְׁנֵי יָמִים.
17	הַיּוֹם שִׁבְעָה עָשָׂר יוֹם לָעֹמֶר שֶׁהֵם שְׁנֵי שָׁבוּעוֹת וּשְׁלֹשָׁה יָמִים.
18	הַיּוֹם שְׁמוֹנָה עָשָׂר יוֹם לָעֹמֶר שֶׁהֵם שְׁנֵי שָׁבוּעוֹת וְאַרְבָּעָה יָמִים.
19	הַיּוֹם תִּשְׁעָה עָשָׂר יוֹם לָעֹמֶר שֶׁהֵם שְׁנֵי שָׁבוּעוֹת וַחֲמִשָּׁה יָמִים.

20 יוֹם עֶשְׂרִים יוֹם לָעֹמֶר שֶׁהֵם שְׁנֵי שָׁבוּעוֹת וְשִׁשָּׁה יָמִים.

21 הַיּוֹם אֶחָד וְעֶשְׂרִים יוֹם לָעֹמֶר שֶׁהֵם שְׁלֹשָׁה שָׁבוּעוֹת.

22 הַיּוֹם שְׁנַיִם וְעֶשְׂרִים יוֹם לָעֹמֶר שֶׁהֵם שְׁלֹשָׁה שָׁבוּעוֹת וְיוֹם אֶחָד.

23 הַיּוֹם שְׁלֹשָׁה וְעֶשְׂרִים יוֹם לָעֹמֶר שֶׁהֵם שְׁלֹשָׁה שָׁבוּעוֹת וּשְׁנֵי יָמִים.

24 הַיּוֹם אַרְבָּעָה וְעֶשְׂרִים יוֹם לָעֹמֶר שֶׁהֵם שְׁלֹשָׁה שָׁבוּעוֹת וּשְׁלֹשָׁה יָמִים.

25 הַיּוֹם חֲמִשָּׁה וְעֶשְׂרִים יוֹם לָעֹמֶר שֶׁהֵם שְׁלֹשָׁה שָׁבוּעוֹת וְאַרְבָּעָה יָמִים.

26 הַיּוֹם שִׁשָּׁה וְעֶשְׂרִים יוֹם לָעֹמֶר שֶׁהֵם שְׁלֹשָׁה שָׁבוּעוֹת וַחֲמִשָּׁה יָמִים.

27 הַיּוֹם שִׁבְעָה וְעֶשְׂרִים יוֹם לָעֹמֶר שֶׁהֵם שְׁלֹשָׁה שָׁבוּעוֹת וְשִׁשָּׁה יָמִים.

28 הַיּוֹם שְׁמוֹנָה וְעֶשְׂרִים יוֹם לָעֹמֶר שֶׁהֵם אַרְבָּעָה שָׁבוּעוֹת.

29 הַיּוֹם תִּשְׁעָה וְעֶשְׂרִים יוֹם לָעֹמֶר שֶׁהֵם אַרְבָּעָה שָׁבוּעוֹת וְיוֹם אֶחָד.

30 הַיּוֹם שְׁלֹשִׁים יוֹם לָעֹמֶר שֶׁהֵם אַרְבָּעָה שָׁבוּעוֹת וּשְׁנֵי יָמִים.

31 הַיּוֹם אֶחָד וּשְׁלֹשִׁים יוֹם לָעֹמֶר שֶׁהֵם אַרְבָּעָה שָׁבוּעוֹת וּשְׁלֹשָׁה יָמִים.

32 הַיּוֹם שְׁנַיִם וּשְׁלֹשִׁים יוֹם לָעֹמֶר שֶׁהֵם אַרְבָּעָה שָׁבוּעוֹת וְאַרְבָּעָה יָמִים.

33 הַיּוֹם שְׁלֹשָׁה וּשְׁלֹשִׁים יוֹם לָעֹמֶר שֶׁהֵם אַרְבָּעָה שָׁבוּעוֹת וַחֲמִשָּׁה יָמִים.

34 הַיּוֹם אַרְבָּעָה וּשְׁלֹשִׁים יוֹם לָעֹמֶר שֶׁהֵם אַרְבָּעָה שָׁבוּעוֹת וְשִׁשָּׁה יָמִים.

35 הַיּוֹם חֲמִשָּׁה וּשְׁלֹשִׁים יוֹם לָעֹמֶר שֶׁהֵם חֲמִשָּׁה שָׁבוּעוֹת.

36 הַיּוֹם שִׁשָּׁה וּשְׁלֹשִׁים יוֹם לָעֹמֶר שֶׁהֵם חֲמִשָּׁה שָׁבוּעוֹת וְיוֹם אֶחָד.

37 הַיּוֹם שִׁבְעָה וּשְׁלֹשִׁים יוֹם לָעֹמֶר שֶׁהֵם חֲמִשָּׁה שָׁבוּעוֹת וּשְׁנֵי יָמִים.

38 הַיּוֹם שְׁמוֹנָה וּשְׁלֹשִׁים יוֹם לָעֹמֶר שֶׁהֵם חֲמִשָּׁה שָׁבוּעוֹת וּשְׁלֹשָׁה יָמִים.

39 הַיּוֹם תִּשְׁעָה וּשְׁלֹשִׁים יוֹם לָעֹמֶר שֶׁהֵם חֲמִשָּׁה שָׁבוּעוֹת וְאַרְבָּעָה יָמִים.

40 הַיּוֹם אַרְבָּעִים יוֹם לָעֹמֶר שֶׁהֵם חֲמִשָּׁה שָׁבוּעוֹת וַחֲמִשָּׁה יָמִים.

41 הַיּוֹם אֶחָד וְאַרְבָּעִים יוֹם לָעֹמֶר שֶׁהֵם חֲמִשָּׁה שָׁבוּעוֹת וְשִׁשָּׁה יָמִים.

42 הַיּוֹם שְׁנַיִם וְאַרְבָּעִים יוֹם לָעֹמֶר שֶׁהֵם שִׁשָּׁה שָׁבוּעוֹת.

43 הַיּוֹם שְׁלֹשָׁה וְאַרְבָּעִים יוֹם לָעֹמֶר שֶׁהֵם שִׁשָּׁה שָׁבוּעוֹת וְיוֹם אֶחָד.

44 הַיּוֹם אַרְבָּעָה וְאַרְבָּעִים יוֹם לָעֹמֶר שֶׁהֵם שִׁשָּׁה שָׁבוּעוֹת וּשְׁנֵי יָמִים.

45 הַיּוֹם חֲמִשָּׁה וְאַרְבָּעִים יוֹם לָעֹמֶר שֶׁהֵם שִׁשָּׁה שָׁבוּעוֹת וּשְׁלֹשָׁה יָמִים.

46 הַיּוֹם שִׁשָּׁה וְאַרְבָּעִים יוֹם לָעֹמֶר שֶׁהֵם שִׁשָּׁה שָׁבוּעוֹת וְאַרְבָּעָה יָמִים.

47 הַיּוֹם שִׁבְעָה וְאַרְבָּעִים יוֹם לָעֹמֶר שֶׁהֵם שִׁשָּׁה שָׁבוּעוֹת וַחֲמִשָּׁה יָמִים.

48 הַיּוֹם שְׁמוֹנָה וְאַרְבָּעִים יוֹם לָעֹמֶר שֶׁהֵם שִׁשָּׁה שָׁבוּעוֹת וְשִׁשָּׁה יָמִים.

49 הַיּוֹם תִּשְׁעָה וְאַרְבָּעִים יוֹם לָעֹמֶר שֶׁהֵם שִׁבְעָה שָׁבוּעוֹת.

On each of the eight nights of Ḥanukka, the lights of the מְנוֹרָה are lit: one on the first night, two on the second, and so on. On each night, the new light is added on the left and lit first.

בָּרוּךְ אַתָּה יְהֹוָה, אֱלֹהֵינוּ מֶלֶךְ הָעוֹלָם 1
אֲשֶׁר קִדְּשָׁנוּ בְּמִצְוֹתָיו וְצִוָּנוּ לְהַדְלִיק נֵר חֲנֻכָּה. 2

בָּרוּךְ אַתָּה יְהֹוָה, אֱלֹהֵינוּ מֶלֶךְ הָעוֹלָם 3
שֶׁעָשָׂה נִסִּים לַאֲבוֹתֵינוּ בַּיָּמִים הָהֵם בַּזְּמַן הַזֶּה. 4

Add this בְּרָכָה on the first night of Ḥanukka.

בָּרוּךְ אַתָּה יְהֹוָה, אֱלֹהֵינוּ מֶלֶךְ הָעוֹלָם 5
שֶׁהֶחֱיָנוּ וְקִיְּמָנוּ וְהִגִּיעָנוּ לַזְּמַן הַזֶּה. 6

We sing this song after lighting the first light.

הַנֵּרוֹת הַלָּלוּ אֲנַחְנוּ מַדְלִיקִין 7
עַל הַנִּסִּים וְעַל הַפֻּרְקָן וְעַל הַגְּבוּרוֹת 8
וְעַל הַתְּשׁוּעוֹת וְעַל הַנִּפְלָאוֹת וְעַל הַנֶּחָמוֹת 9
שֶׁעָשִׂיתָ לַאֲבוֹתֵינוּ בַּיָּמִים הָהֵם בַּזְּמַן הַזֶּה 10
עַל יְדֵי כֹּהֲנֶיךָ הַקְּדוֹשִׁים. 11
וְכָל שְׁמוֹנַת יְמֵי חֲנֻכָּה הַנֵּרוֹת הַלָּלוּ קֹדֶשׁ הֵם 12
וְאֵין לָנוּ רְשׁוּת לְהִשְׁתַּמֵּשׁ בָּהֶם 13
אֶלָּא לִרְאוֹתָם בִּלְבָד 14
כְּדֵי לְהוֹדוֹת לִשְׁמֶךָ 15
עַל נִסֶּיךָ וְעַל נִפְלְאוֹתֶיךָ וְעַל יְשׁוּעוֹתֶיךָ. 16

We light these lights because of the miracles and wonders, rescue and victory, that You, Hashem, did for us, in those days at this time.

We sing this song after all the lights are lit.

מָעוֹז צוּר יְשׁוּעָתִי — לְךָ נָאֶה לְשַׁבֵּחַ
תִּכּוֹן בֵּית תְּפִלָּתִי — וְשָׁם תּוֹדָה נְזַבֵּחַ
לְעֵת תָּכִין מַטְבֵּחַ — מִצָּר הַמְנַבֵּחַ
אָז אֶגְמֹר בְּשִׁיר מִזְמוֹר — חֲנֻכַּת הַמִּזְבֵּחַ.

רָעוֹת שָׂבְעָה נַפְשִׁי — בְּיָגוֹן כֹּחִי כָּלָה
חַיַּי מֵרְרוּ בְּקֹשִׁי — בְּשִׁעְבּוּד מַלְכוּת עֶגְלָה
וּבְיָדוֹ הַגְּדוֹלָה — הוֹצִיא אֶת הַסְּגֻלָּה
חֵיל פַּרְעֹה וְכָל זַרְעוֹ — יָרְדוּ כְּאֶבֶן מְצוּלָה.

דְּבִיר קָדְשׁוֹ הֱבִיאַנִי — וְגַם שָׁם לֹא שָׁקַטְתִּי
וּבָא נוֹגֵשׂ וְהִגְלַנִי — כִּי זָרִים עָבַדְתִּי
וְיֵין רַעַל מָסַכְתִּי — כִּמְעַט שֶׁעָבַרְתִּי
קֵץ בָּבֶל זְרֻבָּבֶל — לְקֵץ שִׁבְעִים נוֹשַׁעְתִּי.

כְּרֹת קוֹמַת בְּרוֹשׁ בִּקֵּשׁ — אֲגָגִי בֶּן הַמְּדָתָא
וְנִהְיְתָה לוֹ לְפַח וּלְמוֹקֵשׁ — וְגַאֲוָתוֹ נִשְׁבָּתָה
רֹאשׁ יְמִינִי נִשֵּׂאתָ — וְאוֹיֵב שְׁמוֹ מָחִיתָ
רֹב בָּנָיו וְקִנְיָנָיו — עַל הָעֵץ תָּלִיתָ.

יְוָנִים נִקְבְּצוּ עָלַי — אֲזַי בִּימֵי חַשְׁמַנִּים
וּפָרְצוּ חוֹמוֹת מִגְדָּלַי — וְטִמְּאוּ כָּל הַשְּׁמָנִים
וּמִנּוֹתַר קַנְקַנִּים — נַעֲשָׂה נֵס לַשּׁוֹשַׁנִּים
בְּנֵי בִינָה יְמֵי שְׁמוֹנָה — קָבְעוּ שִׁיר וּרְנָנִים.

חֲשׂוֹף זְרוֹעַ קָדְשֶׁךָ — וְקָרֵב קֵץ הַיְשׁוּעָה
נְקֹם נִקְמַת עֲבָדֶיךָ — מֵאֻמָּה הָרְשָׁעָה
כִּי אָרְכָה לָנוּ הַשָּׁעָה — וְאֵין קֵץ לִימֵי הָרָעָה
דְּחֵה אַדְמוֹן בְּצֵל צַלְמוֹן — הָקֵם לָנוּ רוֹעִים שִׁבְעָה.

It was the first day of Sukkot and Reb Elimelekh of Lizhensk was standing before the community with his lulav and etrog, about to begin singing Hallel, when he stopped dead, and started to sniff the air. "I can smell Gan Eden," he said, as he began to walk around the shul from person to person, sniffing at every etrog he could see. Finally he stopped in front of a poor, modest-looking man at the back of the shul. "Tell me, Reb Yid, from where did you get your etrog?" the rebbe asked. "Well, that is some story," the man replied. "The mitzva of lulav and etrog is particularly dear to me, and I save half my earnings every year just so I can buy the best etrog available. But this year, on my way to buy it, I came across a poor wagon-driver who barely earned enough money to feed his wife and children. He was weeping and so I asked him what the matter was. He explained that his horse had suddenly died, and he was desperate and didn't know what to do. So I used almost all my money to buy this poor fellow a horse, only leaving me a few rubles to buy this very plain etrog." "This is no plain etrog," Reb Elimelekh exclaimed. "With those few rubles you bought an etrog from the Garden of Eden itself."

On Sukkot there is a mitzva to take the אַרְבָּעָה מִינִים. On days other than Shabbat, hold the לוּלָב with the הֲדַסִּים and the עֲרָבוֹת in your right hand. Hold the אֶתְרוֹג upside down in your left hand, while you say the בְּרָכָה. Then turn the אֶתְרוֹג the right way up and shake the אַרְבָּעָה מִינִים.

1 בָּרוּךְ אַתָּה יְהֹוָה, אֱלֹהֵינוּ מֶלֶךְ הָעוֹלָם

2 אֲשֶׁר קִדְּשָׁנוּ בְּמִצְוֹתָיו, וְצִוָּנוּ עַל נְטִילַת לוּלָב.

Say this בְּרָכָה before shaking the אַרְבָּעָה מִינִים the first time you do this mitzva this year.

3 בָּרוּךְ אַתָּה יְהֹוָה, אֱלֹהֵינוּ מֶלֶךְ הָעוֹלָם

4 שֶׁהֶחֱיָנוּ וְקִיְּמָנוּ וְהִגִּיעָנוּ לַזְּמַן הַזֶּה.

Say this בְּרָכָה on Sukkot before you sit in the sukka for a meal.

5 בָּרוּךְ אַתָּה יְהֹוָה, אֱלֹהֵינוּ מֶלֶךְ הָעוֹלָם

6 אֲשֶׁר קִדְּשָׁנוּ בְּמִצְוֹתָיו, וְצִוָּנוּ לֵישֵׁב בַּסֻּכָּה.

בְּרָכוֹת

Giving Thanks

Birkat HaMazon — בִּרְכַּת הַמָּזוֹן

Shema before Sleep at Night — קְרִיאַת שְׁמַע עַל הַמִּטָּה

לַמְנַצֵּחַ בִּנְגִינֹת, מִזְמוֹר שִׁיר: אֱלֹהִים יְחָנֵּנוּ וִיבָרְכֵנוּ, יָאֵר פָּנָיו אִתָּנוּ סֶלָה: לָדַעַת בָּאָרֶץ דַּרְכֶּךָ, בְּכָל־גּוֹיִם יְשׁוּעָתֶךָ: יוֹדוּךָ עַמִּים אֱלֹהִים, יוֹדוּךָ עַמִּים כֻּלָּם: יִשְׂמְחוּ וִירַנְּנוּ לְאֻמִּים, כִּי־תִשְׁפֹּט עַמִּים מִישֹׁר, וּלְאֻמִּים בָּאָרֶץ תַּנְחֵם סֶלָה: יוֹדוּךָ עַמִּים אֱלֹהִים, יוֹדוּךָ עַמִּים כֻּלָּם: אֶרֶץ נָתְנָה יְבוּלָהּ, יְבָרְכֵנוּ אֱלֹהִים אֱלֹהֵינוּ: יְבָרְכֵנוּ אֱלֹהִים, וְיִירְאוּ אוֹתוֹ כָּל־אַפְסֵי־אָרֶץ:

אֲבָרְכָה אֶת־יְהוָֹה בְּכָל־עֵת, תָּמִיד תְּהִלָּתוֹ בְּפִי: סוֹף דָּבָר הַכֹּל נִשְׁמָע, אֶת־הָאֱלֹהִים יְרָא וְאֶת־מִצְוֹתָיו שְׁמוֹר, כִּי־זֶה כָּל־הָאָדָם: תְּהִלַּת יְהוָֹה יְדַבֶּר פִּי, וִיבָרֵךְ כָּל־בָּשָׂר שֵׁם קָדְשׁוֹ, לְעוֹלָם וָעֶד: וַאֲנַחְנוּ נְבָרֵךְ יָהּ, מֵעַתָּה וְעַד־עוֹלָם, הַלְלוּיָהּ: וַיְדַבֵּר אֵלַי, זֶה הַשֻּׁלְחָן, אֲשֶׁר לִפְנֵי יְהוָֹה:

1 בָּרוּךְ אַתָּה יְהוָה אֱלֹהֵינוּ מֶלֶךְ הָעוֹלָם
2 הָאֵל הַזָּן אוֹתָנוּ וְאֶת הָעוֹלָם כֻּלּוֹ בְּטוּבוֹ
3 בְּחֵן בְּחֶסֶד בְּרֵוַח וּבְרַחֲמִים רַבִּים
4 נֹתֵן לֶחֶם לְכָל־בָּשָׂר כִּי לְעוֹלָם חַסְדּוֹ:
5 וּבְטוּבוֹ הַגָּדוֹל, תָּמִיד לֹא חָסַר לָנוּ
6 וְאַל יֶחְסַר לָנוּ מָזוֹן תָּמִיד לְעוֹלָם וָעֶד
7 כִּי הוּא אֵל זָן וּמְפַרְנֵס לַכֹּל, וְשֻׁלְחָנוֹ עָרוּךְ לַכֹּל
8 וְהִתְקִין מִחְיָה וּמָזוֹן לְכָל בְּרִיּוֹתָיו אֲשֶׁר בָּרָא
9 בְּרַחֲמָיו וּבְרֹב חֲסָדָיו
10 כָּאָמוּר: פּוֹתֵחַ אֶת־יָדֶךָ וּמַשְׂבִּיעַ לְכָל־חַי רָצוֹן:
11 בָּרוּךְ אַתָּה יְהוָה, הַזָּן אֶת הַכֹּל.

12 נוֹדֶה לְךָ, יְהוָה אֱלֹהֵינוּ
13 עַל שֶׁהִנְחַלְתָּ לַאֲבוֹתֵינוּ אֶרֶץ חֶמְדָּה טוֹבָה וּרְחָבָה
14 בְּרִית וְתוֹרָה, חַיִּים וּמָזוֹן
15 עַל שֶׁהוֹצֵאתָנוּ מֵאֶרֶץ מִצְרַיִם וּפְדִיתָנוּ מִבֵּית עֲבָדִים
16 וְעַל בְּרִיתְךָ שֶׁחָתַמְתָּ בִּבְשָׂרֵנוּ
17 וְעַל תּוֹרָתְךָ שֶׁלִּמַּדְתָּנוּ וְעַל חֻקֵּי רְצוֹנְךָ שֶׁהוֹדַעְתָּנוּ
18 וְעַל חַיִּים וּמָזוֹן שָׁאַתָּה זָן וּמְפַרְנֵס אוֹתָנוּ.

During Ḥanukka and Purim say עַל הַנִּסִּים.

עַל הַנִּסִּים וְעַל הַפֻּרְקָן וְעַל הַגְּבוּרוֹת וְעַל הַתְּשׁוּעוֹת וְעַל הַנִּפְלָאוֹת וְעַל הַנֶּחָמוֹת שֶׁעָשִׂיתָ לַאֲבוֹתֵינוּ בַּיָּמִים הָהֵם בַּזְּמַן הַזֶּה.

Ḥanukka

בִּימֵי מַתִּתְיָה בֶּן יוֹחָנָן כֹּהֵן גָּדוֹל חַשְׁמוֹנָאִי וּבָנָיו, כְּשֶׁעָמְדָה מַלְכוּת יָוָן הָרְשָׁעָה עַל עַמְּךָ יִשְׂרָאֵל לְשַׁכְּחָם תּוֹרָתֶךָ וּלְהַעֲבִירָם מֵחֻקֵּי רְצוֹנֶךָ, וְאַתָּה בְּרַחֲמֶיךָ הָרַבִּים עָמַדְתָּ לָהֶם בְּעֵת צָרָתָם, רַבְתָּ אֶת רִיבָם, דַּנְתָּ אֶת דִּינָם, נָקַמְתָּ אֶת נִקְמָתָם, מָסַרְתָּ גִבּוֹרִים בְּיַד חַלָּשִׁים, וְרַבִּים בְּיַד מְעַטִּים, וּרְשָׁעִים בְּיַד צַדִּיקִים, וּטְמֵאִים בְּיַד טְהוֹרִים, וְזֵדִים בְּיַד עוֹסְקֵי תוֹרָתֶךָ. לְךָ עָשִׂיתָ שֵׁם גָּדוֹל וְקָדוֹשׁ בְּעוֹלָמֶךָ, וּלְעַמְּךָ יִשְׂרָאֵל עָשִׂיתָ תְּשׁוּעָה גְדוֹלָה וּפֻרְקָן כְּהַיּוֹם הַזֶּה. וְאַחַר כָּךְ בָּאוּ בָנֶיךָ לִדְבִיר בֵּיתֶךָ, וּפִנּוּ אֶת הֵיכָלֶךָ, וְטִהֲרוּ אֶת מִקְדָּשֶׁךָ, וְהִדְלִיקוּ נֵרוֹת בְּחַצְרוֹת קָדְשֶׁךָ, וְקָבְעוּ שְׁמוֹנַת יְמֵי חֲנֻכָּה אֵלּוּ, בְּהַלֵּל וּבְהוֹדָאָה, וְעָשִׂיתָ עִמָּהֶם נִסִּים וְנִפְלָאוֹת, וְנוֹדֶה לְשִׁמְךָ הַגָּדוֹל, סֶלָה.

Purim

בִּימֵי מָרְדְּכַי וְאֶסְתֵּר בְּשׁוּשַׁן הַבִּירָה, כְּשֶׁעָמַד עֲלֵיהֶם הָמָן הָרָשָׁע, בִּקֵּשׁ לְהַשְׁמִיד לַהֲרֹג וּלְאַבֵּד אֶת־כָּל־הַיְּהוּדִים מִנַּעַר וְעַד־זָקֵן טַף וְנָשִׁים בְּיוֹם אֶחָד, בִּשְׁלוֹשָׁה עָשָׂר לְחֹדֶשׁ שְׁנֵים־עָשָׂר, הוּא חֹדֶשׁ אֲדָר, וּשְׁלָלָם לָבוֹז: וְאַתָּה בְּרַחֲמֶיךָ הָרַבִּים הֵפַרְתָּ אֶת עֲצָתוֹ, וְקִלְקַלְתָּ אֶת מַחֲשַׁבְתּוֹ, וַהֲשֵׁבוֹתָ לּוֹ גְּמוּלוֹ בְּרֹאשׁוֹ, וְתָלוּ אוֹתוֹ וְאֶת בָּנָיו עַל הָעֵץ, וְעָשִׂיתָ עִמָּהֶם נִסִּים וְנִפְלָאוֹת, וְנוֹדֶה לְשִׁמְךָ הַגָּדוֹל, סֶלָה.

(וְ)עַל הַכֹּל, יְהֹוָה אֱלֹהֵינוּ
אֲנַחְנוּ מוֹדִים לָךְ וּמְבָרְכִים אֶת שְׁמָךְ.
כָּאָמוּר: וְאָכַלְתָּ וְשָׂבָעְתָּ
וּבֵרַכְתָּ אֶת־יְהֹוָה אֱלֹהֶיךָ
עַל־הָאָרֶץ הַטֹּבָה אֲשֶׁר נָתַן־לָךְ:
בָּרוּךְ אַתָּה יְהֹוָה, **עַל הָאָרֶץ וְעַל הַמָּזוֹן.**

רַחֵם יְהֹוָה אֱלֹהֵינוּ עָלֵינוּ וְעַל יִשְׂרָאֵל עַמָּךְ
וְעַל יְרוּשָׁלַיִם עִירָךְ וְעַל הַר צִיּוֹן מִשְׁכַּן כְּבוֹדָךְ
וְעַל הֵיכָלָךְ וְעַל מְעוֹנָךְ וְעַל דְּבִירָךְ
וְעַל הַבַּיִת הַגָּדוֹל וְהַקָּדוֹשׁ שֶׁנִּקְרָא שִׁמְךָ עָלָיו
אָבִינוּ, רְעֵנוּ, זוּנֵנוּ, פַּרְנְסֵנוּ, כַּלְכְּלֵנוּ
הַרְוִיחֵנוּ, הַרְוַח לָנוּ מְהֵרָה מִכָּל צָרוֹתֵינוּ
וְאַל תַּצְרִיכֵנוּ, יְהֹוָה אֱלֹהֵינוּ לִידֵי מַתְּנוֹת בָּשָׂר וָדָם
וְלֹא לִידֵי הַלְוָאָתָם, שֶׁמַּתְּנָתָם מְעוּטָה וְחֶרְפָּתָם מְרֻבָּה
אֶלָּא לְיָדְךָ הַמְּלֵאָה וְהָרְחָבָה, הָעֲשִׁירָה וְהַפְּתוּחָה.
יְהִי רָצוֹן שֶׁלֹּא נֵבוֹשׁ בָּעוֹלָם הַזֶּה
וְלֹא נִכָּלֵם לָעוֹלָם הַבָּא
וּמַלְכוּת בֵּית דָּוִד מְשִׁיחָךְ
תַּחֲזִירֶנָּה לִמְקוֹמָהּ בִּמְהֵרָה בְיָמֵינוּ.

On Shabbat add this paragraph.

רְצֵה וְהַחֲלִיצֵנוּ, יְהוָה אֱלֹהֵינוּ, בְּמִצְוֹתֶיךָ
וּבְמִצְוַת יוֹם הַשְּׁבִיעִי, הַשַּׁבָּת הַגָּדוֹל וְהַקָּדוֹשׁ הַזֶּה
כִּי יוֹם זֶה גָּדוֹל וְקָדוֹשׁ הוּא לְפָנֶיךָ
לִשְׁבָּת בּוֹ, וְלָנוּחַ בּוֹ בְּאַהֲבָה כְּמִצְוַת רְצוֹנֶךָ
וּבִרְצוֹנְךָ הָנִיחַ לָנוּ, יְהוָה אֱלֹהֵינוּ
שֶׁלֹּא תְהֵא צָרָה וְיָגוֹן וַאֲנָחָה בְּיוֹם מְנוּחָתֵנוּ
וְהַרְאֵנוּ, יְהוָה אֱלֹהֵינוּ, בְּנֶחָמַת צִיּוֹן עִירֶךָ
וּבְבִנְיַן יְרוּשָׁלַיִם עִיר קָדְשֶׁךָ
כִּי אַתָּה הוּא בַּעַל הַיְשׁוּעוֹת וּבַעַל הַנֶּחָמוֹת.

On Rosh Ḥodesh and Ḥol HaMo'ed add יַעֲלֶה וְיָבוֹא:

אֱלֹהֵינוּ וֵאלֹהֵי אֲבוֹתֵינוּ, יַעֲלֶה וְיָבוֹא, יַגִּיעַ, יֵרָאֶה וְיֵרָצֶה, יִשָּׁמַע, יִפָּקֵד וְיִזָּכֵר זִכְרוֹנֵנוּ וְזִכְרוֹן אֲבוֹתֵינוּ, זִכְרוֹן יְרוּשָׁלַיִם עִירֶךָ, וְזִכְרוֹן מָשִׁיחַ בֶּן דָּוִד עַבְדֶּךָ, וְזִכְרוֹן כָּל עַמְּךָ בֵּית יִשְׂרָאֵל, לְפָנֶיךָ, לִפְלֵטָה לְטוֹבָה לְחֵן, לְחֶסֶד וּלְרַחֲמִים לְחַיִּים טוֹבִים וּלְשָׁלוֹם, בְּיוֹם

Rosh Ḥodesh	Pesaḥ	Sukkot
רֹאשׁ הַחֹדֶשׁ הַזֶּה	חַג הַמַּצּוֹת הַזֶּה	חַג הַסֻּכּוֹת הַזֶּה
	בְּיוֹם מִקְרָא קֹדֶשׁ הַזֶּה	בְּיוֹם מִקְרָא קֹדֶשׁ הַזֶּה

לְרַחֵם בּוֹ עָלֵינוּ וּלְהוֹשִׁיעֵנוּ. זָכְרֵנוּ יְהוָה אֱלֹהֵינוּ בּוֹ לְטוֹבָה, וּפָקְדֵנוּ בוֹ לִבְרָכָה, וְהוֹשִׁיעֵנוּ בוֹ לְחַיִּים טוֹבִים. בִּדְבַר יְשׁוּעָה וְרַחֲמִים חוּס וְחָנֵּנוּ וַחֲמֹל וְרַחֵם עָלֵינוּ וְהוֹשִׁיעֵנוּ, כִּי אֵלֶיךָ עֵינֵינוּ, כִּי אֵל מֶלֶךְ חַנּוּן וְרַחוּם אָתָּה.

וְתִבְנֶה יְרוּשָׁלַיִם עִירְךָ בִּמְהֵרָה בְיָמֵינוּ.

בָּרוּךְ אַתָּה יְהוָה, בּוֹנֵה יְרוּשָׁלָיִם, אָמֵן.

בָּרוּךְ אַתָּה יְהוָה, אֱלֹהֵינוּ מֶלֶךְ הָעוֹלָם לָעַד
הָאֵל אָבִינוּ, מַלְכֵּנוּ, אַדִּירֵנוּ
בּוֹרְאֵנוּ, גּוֹאֲלֵנוּ, קְדוֹשֵׁנוּ, קְדוֹשׁ יַעֲקֹב
רוֹעֵנוּ, רוֹעֵה יִשְׂרָאֵל, הַמֶּלֶךְ הַטּוֹב וְהַמֵּטִיב לַכֹּל
שֶׁבְּכָל יוֹם וָיוֹם
הוּא הֵיטִיב, הוּא מֵטִיב, הוּא יֵיטִיב לָנוּ
הוּא גְמָלָנוּ, הוּא גוֹמְלֵנוּ, הוּא יִגְמְלֵנוּ לָעַד
חֵן וָחֶסֶד וְרַחֲמִים, וְרֶוַח וְהַצָּלָה וְכָל טוֹב.

הָרַחֲמָן הוּא יִשְׁתַּבַּח עַל כִּסֵּא כְבוֹדוֹ.
הָרַחֲמָן הוּא יִשְׁתַּבַּח בַּשָּׁמַיִם וּבָאָרֶץ.
הָרַחֲמָן הוּא יִשְׁתַּבַּח בָּנוּ לְדוֹר דּוֹרִים
הָרַחֲמָן הוּא קֶרֶן לְעַמּוֹ יָרִים.
הָרַחֲמָן הוּא יִתְפָּאַר בָּנוּ לְנֵצַח נְצָחִים.
הָרַחֲמָן הוּא יְפַרְנְסֵנוּ בְּכָבוֹד.
וְלֹא בְּבִזּוּי בְּהֶתֵּר וְלֹא בְאִסּוּר
בְּנַחַת וְלֹא בְצַעַר.
הָרַחֲמָן הוּא יִתֵּן שָׁלוֹם בֵּינֵינוּ.
הָרַחֲמָן הוּא יִשְׁלַח בְּרָכָה רְוָחָה וְהַצְלָחָה
בְּכָל מַעֲשֵׂה יָדֵינוּ.

1 הָרַחֲמָן הוּא יַצְלִיחַ אֶת דְּרָכֵינוּ.

2 הָרַחֲמָן הוּא יִשְׁבֹּר עֹל הַגּוֹיִם מְהֵרָה מֵעַל צַוָּארֵנוּ.

3 הָרַחֲמָן הוּא יְרַפְּאֵנוּ רְפוּאָה שְׁלֵמָה

4 רְפוּאַת הַנֶּפֶשׁ וּרְפוּאַת הַגּוּף.

5 הָרַחֲמָן הוּא יִפְתַּח לָנוּ אֶת יָדוֹ הָרְחָבָה.

6 הָרַחֲמָן הוּא יְבָרֵךְ אֶת מְדִינַת יִשְׂרָאֵל, רֵאשִׁית צְמִיחַת גְּאֻלָּתֵנוּ.

7 הָרַחֲמָן הוּא יְבָרֵךְ אֶת חַיָּלֵי צְבָא הַהֲגָנָה לְיִשְׂרָאֵל הָעוֹמְדִים עַל
מִשְׁמַר אַרְצֵנוּ.

8 הָרַחֲמָן הוּא יְבָרֵךְ כָּל אֶחָד וְאֶחָד מִמֶּנּוּ בִּשְׁמוֹ הַגָּדוֹל

9 כְּמוֹ שֶׁנִּתְבָּרְכוּ אֲבוֹתֵינוּ

10 אַבְרָהָם יִצְחָק וְיַעֲקֹב, בַּכֹּל, מִכֹּל, כֹּל

11 כֵּן יְבָרֵךְ אוֹתָנוּ יַחַד בְּרָכָה שְׁלֵמָה

12 וְכֵן יְהִי רָצוֹן וְנֹאמַר אָמֵן.

13 הָרַחֲמָן הוּא יִפְרֹשׂ עָלֵינוּ סֻכַּת שְׁלוֹמוֹ.

On Shabbat add this line:

14 הָרַחֲמָן הוּא יַנְחִילֵנוּ עוֹלָם שֶׁכֻּלּוֹ שַׁבָּת וּמְנוּחָה לְחַיֵּי הָעוֹלָמִים.

On Rosh Ḥodesh add this line:

15 הָרַחֲמָן הוּא יְחַדֵּשׁ עָלֵינוּ אֶת הַחֹדֶשׁ הַזֶּה לְטוֹבָה וְלִבְרָכָה.

On Sukkot add this line:

16 הָרַחֲמָן הוּא יָקִים לָנוּ אֶת סֻכַּת דָּוִד הַנּוֹפֶלֶת.

17 הָרַחֲמָן הוּא יִטַּע תּוֹרָתוֹ וְאַהֲבָתוֹ בְּלִבֵּנוּ

18 וְתִהְיֶה יִרְאָתוֹ עַל פָּנֵינוּ לְבִלְתִּי נֶחֱטָא

19 וִיהִיוּ כָל מַעֲשֵׂינוּ לְשֵׁם שָׁמָיִם.

הָרַחֲמָן הוּא יְחַיֵּינוּ וִיזַכֵּנוּ וִיקָרְבֵנוּ לִימוֹת הַמָּשִׁיחַ
וּלְבִנְיַן בֵּית הַמִּקְדָּשׁ וּלְחַיֵּי הָעוֹלָם הַבָּא.

On Shabbat, Holidays, and Rosh Ḥodesh say this word instead:

מַגְדִּל | מִגְדּוֹל

יְשׁוּעוֹת מַלְכּוֹ
וְעֹשֶׂה־חֶסֶד לִמְשִׁיחוֹ, לְדָוִד וּלְזַרְעוֹ עַד־עוֹלָם:
כְּפִירִים רָשׁוּ וְרָעֵבוּ, וְדֹרְשֵׁי יְהוָֹה לֹא־יַחְסְרוּ כָל־טוֹב:
נַעַר הָיִיתִי גַּם־זָקַנְתִּי
וְלֹא־רָאִיתִי צַדִּיק נֶעֱזָב וְזַרְעוֹ מְבַקֶּשׁ־לָחֶם:
כָּל־הַיּוֹם חוֹנֵן וּמַלְוֶה, וְזַרְעוֹ לִבְרָכָה:
מַה שֶּׁאָכַלְנוּ יִהְיֶה לְשָׂבְעָה
וּמַה שֶּׁשָּׁתִינוּ יִהְיֶה לִרְפוּאָה
וּמַה שֶּׁהוֹתַרְנוּ יִהְיֶה לִבְרָכָה
כִּדְכְתִיב:
וַיִּתֵּן לִפְנֵיהֶם וַיֹּאכְלוּ וַיּוֹתִרוּ כִּדְבַר יְהוָֹה:
בְּרוּכִים אַתֶּם לַיהוָֹה, עֹשֵׂה שָׁמַיִם וָאָרֶץ:
בָּרוּךְ הַגֶּבֶר אֲשֶׁר יִבְטַח בַּיהוָֹה, וְהָיָה יְהוָֹה מִבְטַחוֹ:
יְהוָֹה עֹז לְעַמּוֹ יִתֵּן, יְהוָֹה יְבָרֵךְ אֶת־עַמּוֹ בַשָּׁלוֹם:
עוֹשֶׂה שָׁלוֹם בִּמְרוֹמָיו, הוּא בְּרַחֲמָיו יַעֲשֶׂה שָׁלוֹם עָלֵינוּ
וְעַל כָּל עַמּוֹ יִשְׂרָאֵל, וְאִמְרוּ אָמֵן.

This special בְּרָכָה and the first paragraph of the שְׁמַע are said before you fall asleep at night.

בָּרוּךְ אַתָּה יְהֹוָה, אֱלֹהֵינוּ מֶלֶךְ הָעוֹלָם, הַמַּפִּיל חֶבְלֵי שֵׁנָה עַל עֵינַי וּתְנוּמָה עַל עַפְעַפָּי, וּמֵאִיר לְאִישׁוֹן בַּת עָיִן. יְהִי רָצוֹן מִלְּפָנֶיךָ, יְהֹוָה אֱלֹהַי וֵאלֹהֵי אֲבוֹתַי, שֶׁתַּשְׁכִּיבֵנִי לְשָׁלוֹם וְתַעֲמִידֵנִי לְחַיִּים טוֹבִים וּלְשָׁלוֹם, וְתֵן חֶלְקִי בְּתוֹרָתֶךָ, וְתַרְגִּילֵנִי לִדְבַר מִצְוָה, וְאַל תַּרְגִּילֵנִי לִדְבַר עֲבֵרָה, וְאַל תְּבִיאֵנִי לִידֵי חֵטְא, וְלֹא לִידֵי נִסָּיוֹן וְלֹא לִידֵי בִזָּיוֹן, וְיִשְׁלֹט בִּי יֵצֶר הַטּוֹב וְאַל יִשְׁלֹט בִּי יֵצֶר הָרָע, וְתַצִּילֵנִי מִיֵּצֶר הָרָע וּמֵחֳלָאִים רָעִים, וְאַל יַבְהִילוּנִי חֲלוֹמוֹת רָעִים וְהִרְהוּרִים רָעִים, וּתְהֵא מִטָּתִי שְׁלֵמָה לְפָנֶיךָ, וְהָאֵר עֵינַי פֶּן אִישַׁן הַמָּוֶת. בָּרוּךְ אַתָּה יְהֹוָה, הַמֵּאִיר לָעוֹלָם כֻּלּוֹ בִּכְבוֹדוֹ.

1 הַמַּלְאָךְ הַגֹּאֵל אֹתִי מִכָּל־רָע יְבָרֵךְ אֶת־הַנְּעָרִים
2 וְיִקָּרֵא בָהֶם שְׁמִי וְשֵׁם אֲבֹתַי אַבְרָהָם וְיִצְחָק
3 וְיִדְגּוּ לָרֹב בְּקֶרֶב הָאָרֶץ:

Say the first first verse (line 5) aloud while covering your eyes with your right hand. Say line 6 quietly to yourself.

4 אֵל מֶלֶךְ נֶאֱמָן

5 שְׁמַע יִשְׂרָאֵל, יְהוָה אֱלֹהֵינוּ, יְהוָה ׀ אֶחָד:

6 בָּרוּךְ שֵׁם כְּבוֹד מַלְכוּתוֹ לְעוֹלָם וָעֶד.

7 וְאָהַבְתָּ אֵת יְהוָה אֱלֹהֶיךָ, בְּכָל־לְבָבְךָ וּבְכָל־נַפְשְׁךָ וּבְכָל־
8 מְאֹדֶךָ: וְהָיוּ הַדְּבָרִים הָאֵלֶּה, אֲשֶׁר אָנֹכִי מְצַוְּךָ הַיּוֹם, עַל־
9 לְבָבֶךָ: וְשִׁנַּנְתָּם לְבָנֶיךָ וְדִבַּרְתָּ בָּם, בְּשִׁבְתְּךָ בְּבֵיתֶךָ וּבְלֶכְתְּךָ
10 בַדֶּרֶךְ, וּבְשָׁכְבְּךָ וּבְקוּמֶךָ: וּקְשַׁרְתָּם לְאוֹת עַל־יָדֶךָ וְהָיוּ
11 לְטֹטָפֹת בֵּין עֵינֶיךָ: וּכְתַבְתָּם עַל־מְזֻזוֹת בֵּיתֶךָ וּבִשְׁעָרֶיךָ:

Hashem, You are the Source of all blessing, please help me to fall asleep peacefully, and to wake up peacefully. Make sure I have sweet dreams, and bring light to my eyes.

KOREN PUBLISHERS JERUSALEM